D1521305

THE

CENTENARY EDITION

OF THE WORKS OF

NATHANIEL HAWTHORNE

Volume XX

THE CONSULAR LETTERS,

1856–1857

EDITORS

General Editors

WILLIAM CHARVAT, 1905–1966

ROY HARVEY PEARCE

CLAUDE M. SIMPSON, 1910–1976

THOMAS WOODSON

FREDSON BOWERS, *General Textual Editor*

BILL ELLIS, *Associate Textual Editor*

JAMES A. RUBINO, *Associate Textual Editor*

A PUBLICATION OF

THE OHIO STATE UNIVERSITY CENTER

FOR TEXTUAL STUDIES

NATHANIEL HAWTHORNE

THE CONSULAR LETTERS,
1856–1857

Edited by

Bill Ellis

Ohio State University Press

Library of Congress Cataloging-in-Publication Data

Hawthorne, Nathaniel, 1804–1864.
   [Correspondence. Selections]
   The consular letters, 1856–1857 / Nathaniel Hawthorne;
edited by Bill Ellis.
       p. cm.—(The Centenary edition of the works of Nathaniel
Hawthorne; v. 20)
       "A publication of the Ohio State University Center for Textual
Studies"—P.
       "Comprehensive index to volumes xv–xx"—CIP galley, table of
contents.
   ISBN 0–8142–0462–7
   1. Hawthorne, Nathaniel, 1804–1864—Correspondence.
2. Novelists, American—19th century—Correspondence.
3. Consuls—United States—Correspondence.   4. Consuls—
Great Britain—Correspondence.
I. Ellis, Bill, 1950–   . II. Ohio State Center for Textual
Studies.   III. Title.   IV. Series: Hawthorne, Nathaniel,
1804–1864.
Works.   1962; v.20.
PS1850.F63 vol. 20
[PS1881.A4]
813'.3 s—dc19
[813'.3]
[B]   88–5299 CIP

CONTENTS

ABBREVIATIONS AND SHORT TITLES

References to Hawthorne works are to the Centenary Edition (Columbus: Ohio State University Press, 1962–) with the exception of EN: *The English Notebooks*, which is individually identified. References to Hawthorne letters use the numbers assigned to them in the Centenary Edition: numbers 1–1311 refer to the personal letters in Volumes XV–XVIII; numbers C1–C147 refer to the consular correspondence in Volume XIX; numbers C147A–C245 refer to the consular correspondence in Volume XX. In the editorial matter, library locations of manuscripts indicate that their texts have been quoted or cited.

ACM	*The American Claimant Manuscripts*
AL	*American Literature*
Berg	The Henry W. and Albert Berg Collection of the New York Public Library
Boase	Frederic Boase, *Modern English Biography* (Truro:Netherton and Worth, 1892–1921)
Buchanan	*The Works of James Buchanan*, ed. John Bassett Moore (Philadelphia: J. B. Lippincott, 1909)
Byers	John R. Byers, Jr., "Consular Despatches of Nathaniel Hawthorne," *EIHC*, 113 (1977): 237–322.
CO	Correspondence Outward, C10.8, Liverpool Consular Records, Record Group 84, NA

Cortissoz	Paul C. Cortissoz, "The Political Life of Nathaniel Hawthorne," Ph.D. dissertation, New York University, 1955
DAB	*Dictionary of American Biography*, ed. Allen Johnson and Dumas Malone (New York: Scribner, 1943)
Despatches	Consular Despatches, Liverpool, Record Group 84, NA
DNB	*Dictionary of National Biography*, ed. Leslie Stephen and Sidney Lee (London: Smith, Elder & Co., 1885–1901; Supplement, 1901; Second supplement, 1912–13)
EIHC	*Essex Institute Historical Collections*
EN	*The English Notebooks*, ed. Randall Stewart (New York: Modern Language Association, 1941)
Essex	Essex Institute, Salem, Mass.
FIN	*The French and Italian Notebooks*
F.O.	Foreign Office Records, PRO
Hall	Lawrence Sargent Hall, *Hawthorne: Critic of Society* (New Haven: Yale University Press, 1944)
Herringshaw	Thomas William Herringshaw, *Herringshaw's National Library of American Biography* (Chicago: American Publishers' Association, 1909–14)
H.O.	Home Office Records, PRO
HW	Henry J. Wilding, NH's secretary
Instructions	Instructions from State and Treasury, Liverpool Consular Records, Record Group 84, NA
Mays	James O'Donald Mays, *Mr. Hawthorne Goes to England* (Ringwood, Hampshire New Forest Leaves, 1983)
Memories	Rose Hawthorne Lathrop, *Memories of Hawthorne*, 2nd ed. (Boston: Houghton Mifflin, 1923)
MOM	*Mosses from an Old Manse*
Moran	*The Journal of Benjamin Moran, 1857–1865*, ed. Sarah Agnes Wallace and

ABBREVIATIONS AND SHORT TITLES

	Frances Elma Gillespie (Chicago: University of Chicago Press, 1948)
Morgan	Pierpont Morgan Library, New York
NA	National Archives, Washington, D.C.
Name Index	Name Index to the Appointment of United States Diplomatic and Consular Officers 1776–1933, Record Group 59, NA
NH	Nathaniel Hawthorne
NHHW	Julian Hawthorne, *Nathaniel Hawthorne and His Wife: A Biography* (Boston: James R. Osgood, 1884)
OOH	*Our Old Home*
PRO	Public Record Office, London, England
SAR	*Studies in the American Renaissance*
SH	Sophia Hawthorne
SL	*The Scarlet Letter*
Sweeney	Mark Francis Sweeney, "An Annotated Edition of Nathaniel Hawthorne's Official Dispatches to the State Department, 1853–1857," Ph.D. dissertation, Bowling Green University, 1975.
Virginia	Alderman Library, University of Virginia

THE CONSULAR LETTERS,

1856–1857

C 147A. TO H. J. REDFIELD, NEW YORK

[Consulate, U.S.A.
Liverpool, Jan. 2, 1856]

[On Consulate business]¹

1. Known only as a catalogue reference; see Textual Note.

United States Consulate
Liverpool 4th January 1856

Sir,

A penalty is supposed to have been incurred by J Michaels of Philadelphia Master of the Ship Burlington of that place for a violation of the fourth section of the Act of 28th February 1803 (Statutes at Large p.   ) for refusing to take on board a destitute seaman on being so required to do by me, and for which he is liable to be prosecuted in my name, as Consul of the United States for this port.[1]

You, or the proper law officer of the United States, are authorised, at their proper costs and charges, to institute in my name a suit to recover the same for their use and benefit, and the same to control, and to discharge, according to law, in such court having jurisdiction thereof, as you or he shall deem proper.

Witness my hand and Consular Seal

US Consul[2]

Hon W^m L Marcy
Secretary of State

1. The act in question (*Statutes at Large*, II, 204) requires masters of American ships to transport destitute seamen to the United States when required to do so by a consul, under threat of a $100 penalty. It adds, "the certificate of any such consul . . . given under his hand and official seal, shall be *prima facie* evidence of such refusal in any court of law. . . . "

2. The letter evidently was forwarded to the U.S. District Attorney in Philadelphia, as it was not bound with the other despatches in Washington.

Consulate of the United States
Liverpool 8 Jan[y] 1856

Dear Sir,

For the ends of Justice it is desirable that I should send in your Vessel, a Prisoner now in Custody here, charged with assault with intent to commit murder, together with a Witness in the case, and I will thank you to inform me whether you can take them, & when it will be convenient for you to receive them on board.

Resp[y]
Your Obed[t] Serv[t],

Capt Comstock
SS Baltic

1. Captain J. J. Comstock had been captain of the Collins Line steamer *Baltic* since 1852. Moran recalls him as "a burly English looking fellow of about 10 feet girth" (I, 236).

Consulate USA
Liverpool 8 Jany 1856

In reply to your Letter I beg to inform you that I am endeavouring to procure you a passage in the Steamer sailing on Saturday next for New York.[1] That if you cannot go in her you will be sent in the Cultivator which sails on the 14th Inst.

Your Ob^t Servt,

H N Johnson

––––––––

1. Johnson's letter is unrecovered. On December 29, 1855, Buchanan wrote NH that Johnson had complained to him "that he has been waiting five months in prison in Liverpool to be sent to New York for trial." Buchanan cautioned, "It is against the humane policy of our laws, not to grant the accused 'a speedy trial.'" NH's response is also unrecovered, but he noted on Buchanan's letter, "Answered the within—the man, by his own tricks, had been the cause of whatever delay had occurred, and had no mind to be sent home or brought to trial at all" (MS, 732/71 John Rylands University Library).

Consulate of the United States
Liverpool 9 Jany 1856

Sir,

I beg to inform you that I have made arrangements to send Henry Norris Johnson, a prisoner in your custody, to New York in the Ship Cultivator, which is intended to sail on the 14 Inst. It may possibly be a day or two later, but the 14th is the day at present fixed upon.

In the mean time I should be obliged by your having sent to me a Doctor's Certificate that Johnson is fit to go.

Respectfully
I am Your Ob^t Servt
Nathl Hawthorne.

Wm Jameson
Governor Boro
Gaol

Liverpool 11 January 1856

Sir,

Referring to my Letter of the 30 Nov I beg to inform you that I have sent a Seaman named John Brown in the steamer "Baltic," by which this is also sent, who was a seaman on board the Assyria at the time of the illtreatment of Andrew Ritchie, which resulted in his death, & was a witness of it.[1] I have given him a note addressed to you, & he will likely apply to you—he belongs to Mason Hilsboro Co N H.

I am
your obed Servant
Nath¹ Hawthorne.

The District Attorney
New York

1. On April 24, William Wilson was tried and convicted in New York; he was sentenced to ten days' imprisonment and fined twenty-five dollars. John Hansom was tried the next day and acquitted (New York *Daily Tribune*, April 25, 1856, 7:5; April 26, 5:6; May 20, 8:3).

C153. TO H. J. REDFIELD, NEW YORK

Consulate of the United States
Liverpool 11 January 1856

Dr Sir,

   I enclose herewith the papers, consisting of Register, List of Crew and Dup articles, of the ship "Escort" Captain D Lynch,[1] which sailed for New York on Monday last, the Capt forgetting his papers.

I am Resp^y
Your obed Servant

To the Collector of Customs
Port of New York

---

  1. The Consulate's Copies of Ships' Registers records Dominick Lynch as master of the *Escort.*

Consulate of the United States
Liverpool 15 January 1856

Dear Sir,

You will please receive from officers Carlysle & Cousins, the Prisoner Henry N Johnson for conveyance to New York. For your information, as to his accommodation and treatment, I annex you copy of a statement made by the surgeon of the Liverpool Borough Gaol, and request that the recommendations therein contained be complied with.

I am Respectfully
your obed^t Servant

Capt Austin
Ship Cultivator

Consulate of the United States
Liverpool 24 Jany 1856.

Sir,

    During the passage of the ship "Driver" from New York to Liverpool, one of the seamen under strong provocation stabbed another, & the injured man on the Ship's arrival here being placed in the Hospital, died there yesterday.[1]
    An Inquest on the Body today resulted in a verdict of Manslaughter, & the accused has been committed by the coroner to gaol.[2] The Coroner made some remarks to me relative to the jurisdiction in the case;[3] of course I could not assent to the jurisdiction of an English Court over offences committed under the American flag on the high seas (tho' the particular case is not one in which to resist that jurisdiction if they are determined to exercise it) and observed that if the accused were given up to me I could send him to the United States for trial, & the Coroner expressing an opinion that he could be so given up (notwithstanding that the offence with which he is charged is not included in the Treaty) I have addressed a Letter to him and send you a copy, thinking it proper you should be timely informed of the case.

I am very Respectfully
Your obed^t Servant
Nathl Hawthorne

His Excellency
James Buchanan
&^c. &^c. &^c

1. According to testimony taken at the Coroner's inquest, the *Driver* was off the southern coast of Ireland when the third mate ordered Peter Connolly, a seventeen-year-old ship's boy from Liverpool, to loose the jib. He was slow about it, so the mate sent an older hand, William Henry Barnes (an American), to do it. According to one witness, Barnes then turned to Connolly and said "'for two pins he would Knock his teeth down his throat.' [Connolly] said in reply 'Try it.' [Barnes] then struck [Connolly] with his shut fist who backed. [Barnes] then followed [Connolly] and struck him a severe blow and knocked his head against the water cask. [Barnes] then knocked [Connolly] down and when he was down kicked him on the face with all his might. He had either a boot or a shoe on when he kicked [Connolly]. [Connolly's] face was covered with blood." A second witness added that at this point Barnes "commenced choking [Connolly] with his hands to his neck and [Connolly] told him to let go of him. He did not let go right away. [Connolly] then hauled off and struck at [Barnes] with a knife in the right bosom. [Connolly] then said take that. [Barnes] clapped his two hands to his bosom and hallo'd out that he was stabbed and would die. I heard the third mate say that it would have been good for him if the boy had ripped his guts out." Barnes lived long enough to make a dying deposition, incriminating Connolly, who, at the inquest, claimed that he acted in self defense: "I did not know but that he was going to kill me as he had threatened before" (MSS, H.O. 45/6330, PRO).

2. NH's Pocket Diary entry for January 24 reads "Attended Coroner's inquest on stabbed seaman" (MS, Morgan).

3. See C133, C157. Later, NH indicated that Curry had felt that if the seaman died in Liverpool, British authorities could claim jurisdiction (C208).

Consulate of the United States
Liverpool 24 Jany 1856

Dear Sir,

Referring to the proceedings in your court this morning which resulted in a verdict of manslaughter against Peter Connolly for stabbing W^m H Barnes on board the American Ship "Driver" on her passage from New York hither, and to the opinion you then expressed relative to the accused being given up to me to be sent to the United States for trial, the offence having been committed within the jurisdiction of the United States, I beg to inform you of my readiness to receive him & send him to the United States for Trial, and request that he may be given up to me to be put on board the Ship "Driver," on board of which the offence was committed, when she is ready to sail on her outward voyage.[1]

Respectfully
I am Dear Sir
Your obed^t Servant
Nathl Hawthorne.

P. F. Curry Esqr
Coroner
Liverpool

1. On January 26, Curry replied to NH, "I have had an interview with the Mayor and Town Clerk on the subject of Peter Connolly. ¶ The Mayor is advised that he has not the power to comply with your request to give up the prisoner to you. . . . ¶ I have not the power to do so. ¶ The Mayor will send the depositions to the Secretary of State on Monday, to whom I must now refer you." Two days later, John Stewart, Mayor of Liverpool, forwarded NH's letter and the depositions from the Coroner's inquest to Home Secretary Sir George Grey, adding, "I . . . shall be glad to act upon any instruction which you may be pleased to give on the subject." Undersecretary Horatio Waddington noted on the request, "He cannot be given, as the case is not within the Extradition Treaty—but he ought to be discharged out of Custody as the Prisoner ↓ being an American ↑ cannot be tried here for an offence committed on board an American Ship on the High Seas, & he would be liable to be tried again in America if caught there." Grey initialed this ruling, and Waddington sent a reply to the same effect to Stewart on January 30. On February 4, Curry acknowledged this ruling, but added, "I am informed by the Consul that the Act of treaty between the two Countries England and America does not recognize cases of Manslaughter but only cases of Murder and Assaults with intent to commit Murder on the high seas. Under any circumstances the case is one in which there are many mitigating circumstances and as your Lordship thinks the Prisoner should be released from Gaol, perhaps your Lordship will send the necessary order as the Magistrates have no power in the matter. ¶ I ought to have stated that although the man was Stabbed on the high seas he died within the Borough of Liverpool." To this Waddington noted, "It may certainly be contended that the Prisoner (being as I collect a British Subject) is bound by our Statute against Murder & Manslaughter wherever the Act is committed. I should not like to recommend a Pardon without consulting the Law Officers. If the Prisoner had been an American, there would have been no doubt at all" (MSS, H.O. 45/6330, PRO). Grey accordingly referred the appropriate documents to the Queen's Law Officers, Sir Alexander James Edward Cockburn (1800–73) and Richard Bethnell (1802–80), who, on February 11, ruled: "We are of opinion that Conoley [sic] is liable to be tried in this Country on a charge of Manslaughter. ¶ We think he ought not to be surrendered to the American Consul 1, because the offense which he has committed is within the jurisdiction of our own Courts & ought to be tried by them; 2, because by the 6 & 7 Vic. c. 76, upon which the power to surrender American subjects rests, Manslaughter is not one of the offences in respect of which Extradition can take place" (MS, H.O. 48/44, PRO). Connolly was tried in Liverpool during the Spring Assizes on March 29; he was convicted of manslaughter, but the jury recommended mercy, and the judge imposed the minimum sentence of one month imprisonment at hard labor (Liverpool *Mercury*, March 31, 1856, 2:4; MS, P.L. 26/214, PRO).

C157. TO CAPTAIN JAMES MONTGOMERY, *PIONEER*[1]

Consulate USA
Liverpool 24 Jan[y]
1856

Dear Sir,

It having been officially represented to me[2] that three seamen, named Davis, Nelson & Campbell, belonging to Her Majesty's Ship "Impregnable" have been shipped in and are now on board of your Vessel, I beg to request that you will ascertain whether such be the fact, & if it be, that you will cause them to be immediately sent ashore, should either be American or claim to be so you will immediately communicate the fact to me.

I am
your obed Serv[t],
Nath[l] Hawthorne.

Capt Montgomery
Ship Pioneer

1. The *Pioneer* of New York, Captain James Montgomery, had arrived on December 24 from New Orleans and was to depart for New York on January 26.

2. NH's Pocket Diary entry for January 24 reads, "Captain Bevis, R.N. called" (MS, Morgan).

Consulate of the United States
Liverpool 25 Jany 1856

Sir,

Referring to my Despatch N° 46 and to the copies of depositions accompanying it, I have the honor to inform you that the Prisoner Henry N Johnson, with a Witness Stephen Brogan, were sent to New York in the Ship "Cultivator" Captain Austin which sailed on the 18ᵀᴴ Inst, of which I have informed the District Attorney, & forwarded him copies of the depositions taken by me in the case.

Herewith I send you a copy of the Certificate given to the captain of the Cultivator, by which you will see that I agreed that he should be paid Ten pounds for carrying the Prisoner.

I may also state that I found great difficulty in getting a passage for the Prisoner, having no power of compulsion, & most captains refusing to carry him on *any* terms.

I have the honor to be your
Obedient Servant
Nathˡ Hawthorne

Hon Wᵐ L Marcy
Secretary of State
Washington

Consulate of the United States
Liverpool 26 January 1856

Sir,

    I beg to inform you that I have sent in the ship "Cultivator"
G. B. Austin Master which sailed hence for New York on the
18th Inst, a prisoner named Henry N Johnson, delivered up
pursuant to the tenth article of the Treaty with Great Britain
of 1842, on the charge of assault with intent to commit
murder, within the jurisdiction of the United States. A
witness named Stephen Brogan (a Boy) was sent in the same
vessel. The other Witnesses examined by me absconded
before the committal of the Prisoner. The Witness Chas
Ryan described himself as belonging to the City of New York,
and as far as I have been able to ascertain sailed for that
place. Enclosed are copies of the depositions taken by me in
the case.[1]

    The Prisoner when landed here was in a state of disease,
dropsy, & appeared to be also suffering from improper
confinement & treatment, & was an inmate of the Hospital in
charge of the Police for over three months before the
Magistrates would commit him to Gaol. He was a prisoner in
Gaol for 2 months (& there in the Prison Hospital) before I
could procure a passage for him to New York.[2]

I am Resp^y
Your obed Servant

District Attorney
New York

1. See C99.1.

2. The *Cultivator* arrived in New York on March 22, but no record exists that Johnson was apprehended or prosecuted there. Captain Austin, however, was arrested and tried for mistreating three of his crew, during the passage, and NH evidently sent Marcy a clipping reporting this case, as it was pasted on a separate page in the Despatch volume (NA).

C160. TO JAMES ARROTT,[1] DUBLIN

Consulate of the United States
Liverpool 31 Jany 1856

Dear Sir,

In reply to your commun[n] of the 30 I beg to inform you that the "John Bright"[2] was at the time of striking on the Arklow Bank, and is still, an American Vessel, belonging to Mess[rs] J S Williams Wm H Guion Stephen B Guion & others of New York.[3]

M[r] S. B. Guion is I believe the only partner in "Guion & Co" who is an American Citizen.

I am D[r] Sir
Your obed Servant
Nath[l] Hawthorne.

Jas Arnott Esq[r]
U S Consul
Dublin

———

1. James Arrott, formerly a prominent Philadelphia merchant, had been appointed to the Dublin Consulate in 1855. He held the post until 1858, when he was transferred to Belfast.
2. The *John Bright* of New York, Robert C. Cutting master, outbound from Liverpool, had encountered dense fog in the Irish Channel. On August 24, she grounded on Arklow Bank, but the crew lightened ship and managed to get her free later that day. In the process, one of her boats was swamped in the surf, and the two sailors manning it had to be rescued by members of the Arklow Marine Society.

Leaving these seamen behind, the *John Bright* returned to Liverpool for repairs. Arrott loaned the two sailors fifteen shillings and sent them to Liverpool; he also forwarded a bill from the rescuers for their costs in the rescue, hoping that the owners of the ship would pay it. HW raised the subject with the captain, who contacted the owners, Guion & Co. On September 18, they responded to Arrott, "we are informed by the U.S. Consul here that the expense should be borne by your Consulate, and charged to your Government, who have a Fund, to which the John Bright, in common with all other American ships, contributed, specially applicable to the above purpose" (MS, enclosure, Arrott to Marcy, November 15, 1855, Consular Despatches, Dublin, NA).

3. The *New York City Directory* for 1852–53 lists John S. Williams and Stephen B. Guion as merchants at 40 Fulton, and a William H. Guion, carpet-seller, at 292 Broadway.

C161. TO WILLIAM L. MARCY, WASHINGTON

Consulate of the United States
Liverpool 1 February 1856

Sir,

I have the honor to report the rescue from shipwreck, of the Crew, 15 in number, of the American Bark "Olivia" of New York, George S Span master, by the English Bark "Emperor," Captain   Ferguson, of Liverpool, under circumstances reflecting great credit on the latter.[1]

The "Olivia" sailed from Cardiff 18 Decr, bound for New York with a cargo of Iron, & experiencing very boisterous weather, the Cargo broke adrift and the vessel sprung a leak. On the 9th of January she had seven feet of water in the hold, & the Cargo surged about so that it was dangerous to attempt to secure it, a hard gale blowing with a very high sea, forbade any idea of resorting to the Boats, and the condition of the vessel becoming rapidly worse, the position of the crew was getting critical. In this emergency, they say "An American Ship hove in sight, we hoisted a signal of distress, she passed within three miles of us, hoisted her Ensign and sailed away."[2] About an hour and a half after "A Bark hove in sight standing towards us. She proved to be the Emperor of & for Liverpool, she hove to under our lee and offered us any assistance and to lay by us." She laid by them about four hours, when they abandoned their vessel in their own Life boat & were received on board of her.

She was short of Provisions & her Crew were put on short allowance to provide for the newcomers. On the 15 she put into Crookhaven for Provisions, where the master & mate, to reach Liverpool more speedily overland, left her, as did also eight of the sailors who received the offer of £5 each to work another vessel to Liverpool. The others remained on board and were landed at Liverpool on the 26th Instant. They all speak in the highest terms of the treatment they received. There being no American Consul at Crookhaven they were kindly subsisted on board the vessel while there windbound.

The master of the Emperor is a very old man, & from enquiries I have made, I believe he has been unfortunate, & is very poor, so that I suspect any recognition of his service in this matter, would be most acceptable in money.[3]

I must also report a further statement made by the Crew. That about the same time or soon after the "Emperor" came to their rescue, a Brig, supposed the "Eventua," hove to near them, & laid by them until they were all safely on board the Emperor, when she telegraphed that she was bound to S[t] John N B, and would take any on board that chose to come. It was not deemed prudent to venture into the Boat again however, & the offer was declined, but the circumstance reflects so much credit on the Crew of the Brig whoever they were, that it deserves mention.

Respecting the statement of an American vessel recognising the signal of distress, & disregarding its appeal, I trust there is some mistake. I would not believe that any American could commit the act the statement implies. It sometimes occurs that vessels hoist signals of distress for the mere purpose of speaking another vessel. A case recently came under my notice of a vessel hoisting a signal of distress, & on another vessel going to her assistance, hauling it down, & sailing away without speaking. Such wanton acts tend to weaken the effect of the signal and deserve punishment.

I should be glad to be informed respecting the payment of subsistence money to the owners of the Emperor, if they should apply to me.[4]

> With high respect
> I have the honor to be
> Your Obed[t] Servant
> Nath[l] Hawthorne

To
Hon W[m] L Marcy
Secretary of State

1. Captain James Ferguson. At the time of the award, he was living at 69 Grove Street, Liverpool (MS, F.O. 5/659, PRO).

2. Details of the wreck are quoted and paraphrased (with minor variation of detail) from the Marine Extended Protest given by Captain George S. Spratt before NH on January 16, 1856 (MS, NA).

3. On June 24, Assistant Secretary J. A. Thomas reported that President Pierce had awarded Captain Ferguson a bill of exchange for fifty pounds (MS, Instructions, 2, NA). It was presented to him on April 2, 1856 by the chairman of the Local Marine Board. Ferguson "briefly thanked the committee and retired. His feelings were evidently too strong at the moment to find full utterance in words" (Liverpool *Mercury*, April 4, 1856, 6:5). The following day, in a letter to the Board of Trade, Ferguson acknowledged the gift as a "very handsome and unexpected mark of approbation," adding "I did nothing beyond that, which common humanity would have dictated to any one placed in similar circumstances" (MS, F.O. 5/659, PRO).

4. In acknowledging this letter on February 25, Thomas instructed NH to compensate the owners "in the manner provided by the instructions given to your predecessor" (MS, Instructions, 2, NA). See C4.2.

Consulate of the United States
Liverpool 5th February 1856

Sir,

I have the honor to acknowledge receipt of your despatch of the 18th Jany, & also of the copy of a Despatch of the 23^d November.[1]

As concerning the latter Despatch of 23 Nov I would respectfully observe, that it does appear to me that the change of circumstances that has taken place, since the allowance of £100 per annum was granted to the Liverpool Consulate for receiving & transmitting Despatches,[2] calls rather for an increase in the amount, than for its withdrawal, considering that the consul's remuneration has been reduced much below the remuneration of the Office at that time, that the business has increased to nearly eight times the amount, & that the particular service for which the £100 was paid has increased tenfold—from 2 sailing vessels a month to 2 steamers a week—besides being of a much more onerous character. So far as I am personally concerned or as to any profit from the £100, I should hail with pleasure its withdrawal to pay a Despatch Agent if one were appointed by the Department, but so long as the Consul is required to perform the service, I think he is certainly entitled to the allowance, in addition to regular & certain expenses, to compensate him for expenses of an occasional kind which I should in vain attempt to explain, so that you could understand, & which if presented to any of the Auditors for settlement would doubtless be rejected.[3]

As to the regular & certain expenses attending the arrival

& departure of each steamer.[4] There are alternately each week two inward & one outward & one inward & two outward steamers requiring a man permanently employed, at $6 a week, for day watching, getting packages from & to depôts, Railways, Custom House, out-sailing vessels &c, & an extra man to watch during from one to three nights in one week, and from two to five nights in the other, to whom I pay 6/– or $1.50 per night.

Car Hire for conveyance of Despatches from & to the Steamers, the Consulate & Railways, & porterage, cost, for inward Steamers from 75 cents to $2, according to the number of packages the distance &c being often landed at the steam dock a distance of nearly four miles from the Consulate & five from the London Railway station; for outward steamers from 50 to 75 cents; which has always been charged to & paid by the department.

In reply to the despatch of the 18 of Jany I beg leave to state that the adoption of your suggestion that I should be personally on the alert in order to board the steamers immediately on arrival and convey the despatches ashore, would involve a watch on the pier during from four to five nights of each week, & I question whether such vigils might not somewhat impair my ability to discharge the important & onerous duties which demand my attention during the intervening days.[5] I shall therefore, unless otherwise directed, employ a trustworthy agent.

The delays, to which the despatches are subject, have usually arisen from the difficulty, particularly at night, of seeking out the despatch bearers in the hurry and confusion of the moment, getting his luggage passed, which is usually insisted on before he will part with the despatches, & the Bags from his state Room to the steamer alongside, in the very brief time required to transfer the Mail Bags (which are always in readiness) from the deck of one to the deck of the other vessel.[6] And as it is altogether an act of courtesy in the mail officials to receive our despatch Bags on board their tender, we could not reasonably expect them to wait our convenience.

No method of remedying this difficulty suggests itself to me, other than the abolition of the present system of despatch bearers; in lieu of whom, I would recommend that the despatches should in all cases be confided to the pursers of the Steamers. These Officers are trustworthy men, of established character & permanent responsibility, in which particulars they have greatly the advantage over some of the gentlemen to whom the despatches are confided, under the present loose and casual system. Having no connection with the government (except for this one temporary purpose) & having accepted the trust with a view of passing more easily through the Custom House, the Despatch bearers have generally no feeling of duty & really care very little whether the Despatches come to hand at all, or when, or how.

By employing the pursers of the Steamers we should secure the prompt delivery of the Bags on board the mail tender, & thus the principal cause of past delays would be remedied. In case any bag were missing we should know where to place the responsibility. These Officers would undoubtedly expect remuneration, but the expense would be trifling compared with the advantages gained. Five pounds a voyage would probably be deemed sufficient.[7]

> With high respect I have the honor
> to be, your obedient Servant
> Nath[l] Hawthorne.

Hon J. A. Thomas
Assis[t] Secretary of State

1. Marcy's letter of November 23, asking NH to justify the expense of one hundred pounds for receiving and transmitting despatches, was received at the Consulate on December 11, but NH had failed to answer it. Thomas's reminder of January 18 enclosed a copy of this letter, adding "As no reply to that communication has been received, it is apprehended that the original may have miscarried" (MS, Instructions, 2, NA).

2. Marcy's letter began: "The Consul of the United States at Liverpool has for upwards of twenty years past been allowed one hundred pounds Sterling per annum for his Services and expenses in receiving and forwarding public despatches. From the investigation which I have made of the subject, I am under the impression that the allowance was originally just. The circumstances attending the business have, however, so much changed of late, that doubts may be entertained whether the charge, or the whole of it, should continue to be allowed" (MS, Instructions, 2, NA).

3. Perhaps an allusion to NH's difficulties in getting his printing expenses approved by the Fifth Auditor; see C141.

4. Marcy had requested, at NH's "earliest convenience," a statement of expenses "attending the departure or arrival of every Steamer or other vessel which may carry public despatches."

5. Thomas's letter, complaining of delays in transmitting despatches to London, had concluded by suggesting that the easiest way to assure prompt delivery "would, perhaps, be for you to be on the alert for the arrival of the Steamers, and board them at once, so that the person in whose custody the bag is sent, may experience no difficulty or delay in delivering it to you." He added, however, that this advice was intended "as a suggestion, merely," and that NH was at liberty to make any other arrangement that would accomplish the same end.

6. See C110, C140.

7. On March 1, Thomas announced that NH's allowance of one hundred pounds had been continued. He added that the department did not think that the additional expense of sending despatches by pursers could be warranted. The suggestion, however, was studied, and on April 9 and April 15 NH was informed that the State Department had indeed contracted with the Cunard and Collins steamer lines to have pursers take charge of despatch bags (MSS, Instructions, 2, NA).

Consulate of the United States
Liverpool 13 Febry 1856

Dr Sir,

Your Letter of 7th by the 2nd mate & Crew has been received.

I should have replied yesterday but you gave me no address, & I was in doubt where to write to.

I could better advise you if I knew in what you particularly wanted advice.

Of course as agent, which you are, for all concerned, you are bound to take every possible means of protecting the General interest, & will be liable for any neglect &^c.

As to the disposal of the Cargo you will have communicated with the several consignees.

You should take the opinion of Lloyd's agent & other competent persons within reach, respecting the vessel, but must still bear in mind that their recommendations will not relieve you of responsibility, & you must exercise your own judgement. Be careful not to act in recommendation of any person who has, or may have, any interest in what they recommend. Lastly, remember that it will be only unquestioned necessity that will justify your selling the vessel, & in case of doing so it must be in the most public manner & after duly advertising &^c.

I give this general advice in my ignorance of what you particularly want.

I am Dear Sir
Your obed[t] Servant
Nath[l] Hawthorne.

Capt Emery
Ship Henry Pratt

1. The *Henry Pratt*, Amaziah Emery Captain, had left Mobile on December 18 with a load of cotton. While in the Irish Channel, she encountered dense fog, and, on February 7, she ran aground at Hell's Mouth in Cardigan Bay, North Wales. The ship soon became a total wreck, but part of the cargo was salvaged (Marine Extended Protest, 2/2, NA).

Consulate of the United States
Liverpool 14 February 1856

Dear Sir,

A Survey requiring to be holden on the ship "Ocean Rover" Pickering—master—from Charleston for Liverpool, now lying stranded on Crosby Point[2] I have nominated you to act as one of the surveyors and shall be obliged by your attending at said ship at Crosby Point tomorrow (friday) morning at 10 O'Clock, when you will be joined by Captain Bisset & other persons appointed to act with you.[3]

I am
Your obed Serv[t]
Nath[l] Hawthorne

Capt Howes
of Boston

1. The Liverpool agent to the Boston underwriter; see C187.

2. On February 6, the *Ocean Rover* was driven by heavy gales onto Crosby Point northwest of Liverpool Harbor. At first, the ship settled into the sand and was left dry by low tides, but gradually it disintegrated. In the Marine Extended Protest, made before NH on February 15, Captain Charles F. Pickering said, "the vessel has filled each tide has become badly hogged . . . and we continue to discharge cargo as the tides permit & have stripped her and the survey [to determine extent of loss] has this day been holden upon her" (MS, NA).

3. NH and Captain Howes had already attempted to see the ship once: on February 9 NH noted in his Pocket Diary, "At 4, went in cab to Bootle, with Capt. & Mrs. Howes, to see stranded ship. Broke down, & returned by rail from Crosby" (MS, Morgan).

Consulate of the United States
Liverpool 16 Feby 1856

Sir,

Referring to my letter of the 21st December 1855 I now beg to inform you that I have succeeded in obtaining by correspondence a settlement of the Dixon claim on the Reading Savings Bank.

I have received, being principal & interest
£45.9.0 ——————————————————— £45.9.0
from which I have to deduct Bank
commission——————————————— 2/3
Postages ————————————————— 1/6
my Commission @ 5% —————————— 2.5.3   2.9—
Balance ———————————————————— 43.0.0
with which I have bought a Bill on demand on Brown Brothers New York for $205.42 payable to James Dixon, which I enclose herewith.

I am
Your obed Serv[t]
Nath[l] Hawthorne

A H Lewis Esq
Cincinnati

1. Azahel H. Lewis was an attorney at 148 Main Street (*Williams' Cincinnati Directory*, 1856). His letter is unrecovered.

Consulate of the United States
Liverpool 22 February 1856

Sir,

I have the honor to advise you of the rescue of the Crew of the American Brig Crusader, by the British Bark "Sarah" of Belfast, Captain R. Wilson, from Savannah.[1]

The Crusader belonged to Boston, and was commanded by Captain Joseph B Wooster, her crew consisted of master, two mates, cook & four Seamen. She sailed from Jacksonville, Florida, on the twenty third of December, laden with lumber and Rosin, for Bordeaux in France, sprung a leak on the 6th of January, & was fallen in with in a sinking state by the Sarah, during a Gale on the morning of the 10th. The sea ran so "fearfully high," as they state, that the Crusader's crew, not supposing that any Boat could live in it, asked the Sarah to lie by them. She did so until the afternoon, when four of the Crew volunteered to go in the Boat, which they did, & after pulling several times under the Crusader's lee, the Captain & one man leaped into the Boat, the men then got scared & returned to the Sarah, but encouraged by their Captain three of them ventured to renew the attempt, and finally succeeded in saving the rest. They were landed in this Port on the 8th February.

The names & addresses of the brave fellows who manned the Boat are

Geo W Blanchard (an American) ⎤ care of John J.
                              ⎥ Butcher   300
Geo Finnis (an American)   ⎬ North St
                              ⎦ Boston, Mass

• 33 •

Geo Lee ⎫ Brothers—John Pengeley, Old Quay,
      ⎬ West Teignmouth
Wm Lee ⎭ Devonshire England.

The three first named went in the Boat the second time.

I have also to advise of the rescue of the survivors of the Crew of Am Schooner Mayflower by the British Bark Baticola of Liverpool Captain Joseph Clark.[2]

The Mayflower belonged to New Port RI, was commanded by Captain Dupray, she sailed from Georgetown SC with Lumber for Boston on the 30th of December, was capsised on the 6th of January, when all but the Captain & two others were drowned. These remained on the wreck subsisting on raw pork nuts & water for 12 days, when they were taken off by the Baticola, & landed here on the 9th of February.

I have not been applied to yet for subsistence money in either case, but probably shall, & should be glad to receive your instructions to pay.[3]

> I have the honor to be
> Your Obed^t Servant
> Nathl Hawthorne.

To The Hon W^m L Marcy
Secretary of State

1. The following details are paraphrased from the Marine Extended Protest given by Captain Joseph B. Wooster before NH on February 9 (3, NA). The names and addresses of the sailors who manned the boat, have, however, been added to this account.

2. Details paraphrased from the Marine Extended Protest given by Captain Charles A. Dupray before NH on February 11 (MS, 3, NA).

3. On June 24, J. A. Thomas informed NH that these cases had been shown to President Pierce, who had awarded gold chronometers to Captains Wilson and Clark

and silver medals to the four crewmen who manned the *Crusader*'s lifeboat (MS, Instructions, 2, NA). Captain Robert Wilson received his award in Hull on July 10. Captain Joseph P. Clark received his chronometer from the Liverpool Local Marine Board at a ceremony held July 30. "The chronometer, which was a beautiful piece of workmanship, bore the following inscription: 'Presented to Joseph Clark by the President of the United States, for his humane and gallant conduct in rescuing from shipwreck the master and part of the crew of the schooner Mayflower.' [Clark] was at a loss to find language to express his feelings of gratitude . . . although he was not more delighted than at the moment when he saw those poor men placed in safety on board his own ship" (Liverpool *Mercury*, August 1, 1856, 7:2). In a letter to the Board of Trade acknowledging the award, Clark said, "It shows the feeling that exists between the President and subject of a Mighty Nation—long may that feeling exist and long may that feeling exist in the breast of every British subject to render assistance to any citizen of the United States in distress and vice-versa . . . " (Transcript, F.O. 5 / 661, PRO). No mention of subsistence money appears in following correspondence.

Consulate USA
Liverpool 25 Febry 1856

Sir,

I have this day received a Commission to take your
testimony in the case of the Ballard Vale Co vs George S
Mason & am informed that you would be written to by the
same mail, & would wait for a Communication from me
stating when it would be convenient to attend to the
business.[1] I beg to inform you that Thursday next will be a
convenient day for me. If that does not suit your convenience,
be so good as name[2] another day that will.

You will be called upon to produce a contract made
between Plaintiffs & defendant respecting a certain patent,
or a copy thereof. If in your power to produce either, you will
please bring it with you.[3]

I am your obed Servant,
Nath[l] Hawthorne

M[r] Jno Morland
Larchfield Mills
Leeds

1. The dispute, filed by the Ballard Vale Company in the Court of Chancery,
Chittenden County, Vermont, involved a patent "for certain improvements in the
art of spinning wool and other fibrous substances without the use of oil." A
document dated September 10, 1855, appointed NH a commissioner to take
testimony in this case (MS, General Correspondence Inward, NA).

2. An idiom characteristic of letters drafted by HW; see C61.2

3. Moreland responded on February 28 that he preferred to give his testimony in
person and was leaving at once for the States (MS, General Correspondence Inward,
NA).

Consulate of the United States
Liverpool 26th February 1856

Sir,

Presuming on the kindness I know you to have shown on former occasions to Americans in your custody, I venture to trouble you with a reply to a letter I have this day received from James Carr, a Prisoner, who states that he awaits his trial at the assizes on a charge of Wilful Murder; that he is an American; & requests me to employ Counsel for his defense.[1]

I am unable to comply with his request having no funds at my disposal for such purpose.[2]

I do not think he can do better than place himself in the hands of an English court of assize, which will secure to him a fair & impartial trial, which is all I could desire to obtain for an American Citizen.[3]

By conveying this assurance to the Prisoner

You will oblige Sir
your obed Servant
Nath[l] Hawthorne.

Capt Gibbs
Governor of Kirkdale Gaol

———

1. James Carr and Phillip Wall were American sailors accused of garrotting and stripping a fellow sailor in the red-light district of Liverpool. On April 1 they were tried at the Spring Assizes, convicted, and sentenced to death, the sentence subsequently commuted to transportation for life. See London *Times*, February 22, 1856, 10:6; April 3, 10:1; April 14, 12:2.

2. This was a standard limitation on consuls' authority, but apparently the rule could be bent if the consul desired. On February 3, 1853, Crittenden had written to U.S. Minister Ingersoll, admitting that he had been warned not to use consulate funds for the defense of seamen in British jails; still, he requested permission to hire counsel for a seaman charged with manslaughter, "as I believe the prisoner to be an American, and to be destitute" (Letterpress copy, CO, 12B, 37, NA). Similarly, after NH's resignation, HW proposed to Dallas on March 23, 1859, that an officer charged with assaulting a seaman "should have competent legal assistance to enable him to prove his innocence if he can. As I have no funds for such a purpose, I propose to accept the aid of any Americans who are willing to give or to employ Counsel for his defense" (Letterpress copy, CO, 13B, 29, NA). Benjamin Moran replied on March 24, however, that whereas Dallas saw nothing wrong with *private* efforts to secure counsel, "as no funds for such a purpose are at the disposition of the Consul, & as the case does not appear to be one which calls for it, any *official* intervention, direct or indirect, would be best avoided" (MS, Offical Correspondence Inward, 3, NA).

3. Compare NH's comments on the British trial system, *EN*, pp. 71–72.

Consulate of the United States
Liverpool 11 March 1856

Dear Sir,

On receipt of your Letter of 19 Septr, I employed a Broker to pay the Duty &c on the 3 Boxes addressed to Mr Scharit, and clear them from the Custom House, but while he was doing so, in consequence of his omitting to have them erased from the List, into which they had been already entered, they were sold on account of Duty and charges. The Contents as previously advised were, a Flag and seal press.

I am Dear Sir
Yours Resp^y & Truly

Alfred Fox Esqr
U.S. Consul, Falmouth

1. Alfred Fox, an Englishman, had been Vice Consul at Falmouth under Augustus W. Scharit, but in July 1855 Scharit returned abruptly to the United States, leaving behind allegations that he had "acted in an improper manner" (Transcript, Buchanan to William Downing, July 13, 1855, Miscellaneous Correspondence of the Legation, NA). Fox was first given permission to settle Scharit's correspondence; then, in December, he was appointed to fill his place. At the time Fox was also serving as Consul for Argentina, Belgium, Denmark, Greece, Hanover, and Venezuela. See Moran, II, 1234, 1309.

Consulate of the United States
Liverpool 20 March 1856

Sir,

I beg to acknowledge receipt of your Letter of the 13 Ulto²
& herewith forward duplicate of the account for the quarter
ending 30 September with vouchers, amended as requested,
& trust it will be found satisfactory.³

The 6/– Boat hire for Peter Drury in voucher 43, being
paid by Messrs Henry, is charged in their account only. I have
now entered it on Drury's clothing rect Nº 3.⁴

I wish you would either forward me some more forms
Nº 7, or authorise me to get some printed.⁵

Very Respectfully
I am sir
Your obedt Servant
Nathl Hawthorne.

J M Smith Esqr
Actg 5th Auditor of the Treasury
Washington

1. Chief Clerk to the 5th Auditor since 1855; see C143.3.

2. See C146.1.

3. In his response of April 25, Smith tacitly approved the format of NH's
amended accounts, but added an additional $45 to the balance due the U.S. See
C185.

4. On February 13, Smith had said, "In Voucher No 43 is a charge of 6/– for boat hire for Peter Drury 'voucher 3' but no such charge is in the voucher. Please explain" (MS, Instructions, 2, NA).

5. Another complaint about NH's difficulty in getting printing expenses approved; see C141. In his response, Smith told NH that his most recent charge for printing had been allowed by the State Department, and that his request for more forms had been referred to them. A further letter on May 20 directed NH, "You will not include in your account for seamen, any charge for Stationery or printing, but make out a separate account, and enclose to State Department" (MS, Instructions, 2, NA).

Consulate of the United States
Liverpool 28th March 1856[1]

Sir,

I have the honor to transmit herewith transcript of the Record of Treasury Fees of this Consulate for the quarter ending 30th Sept 1855;[2] together with a debtor & creditor account for the same quarter, shewing a Balance in favor of the United States on 1 Oct° of $2584.21, which at $4.84 to the pound sterling is equal to £533.18.6.

The delay in the transmission of these accounts, is owing to the late period (latter part of November) at which the new forms of Official Records & returns were received, the accumulated work being thrown on the office at a season when the influx of shipwrecked & destitute seamen, & the number of vessels, render the current business very heavy. I have been obliged to employ an extra clerk for the duty & hope to be able to transmit by the steamer of the 5th or that of the 12th prox° the accounts for the succeeding quarter.

With high respect
I have the honor to be
Your obed^t Servant

Hon James Guthrie
Secretary of the Treasury

1. NH had left Liverpool for London on the afternoon of March 20 and was not to return to the Consulate until the morning of April 11. While in London, however, he received letters from HW (*EN*, p. 294), presumably including this letter and the following one for his signature.

2. NH was now obliged to send records of fees collected to the Treasury instead of the State Department (compare C50).

Consulate of the United States
Liverpool 28 March 1856[1]

Sir,

I have the honor to acknowledge receipt of your Letter of the 7th Inst requesting that the London Times of the day of the steamer's sailing may be forwarded to the Department.[2] I will take care that this is done when practicable, which however is not often, the steamers generally sailing in a morning, frequently as early as eight o'Clock, before the Times arrives in Liverpool, & as under the present system of forwarding the Despatches, I am obliged to send them on board with the Passengers an hour or more before the Boat takes the mail off, it is very seldom indeed that the "Times" of the day can be had in time to go with them, but I have always hitherto sent it separately through the agents when it could be had in time. Your Letter inclines me to think you never received it. Hereafter I will *always* send (through the agents for the reasons before mentioned) the Times when it can be had, or the latest Liverpool paper, which generally contains a Telegraph embodying any important Article contained in the Times of the morning.

I have the honor to be
Your obed[t] Servant
Nath[l] Hawthorne

Hon J A Thomas
Ass[t] Secretary of State
Washington

1. See C170.1. Although signed by NH, this despatch must have been drafted by HW and forwarded to London for NH's signature.

2. Thomas's letter of March 7 said, "It is very desirable that we should receive at the department the London Times published the day the Steamer sails from Liverpool, and I have to request of you the favor to forward it to us" (MS, Instructions, 2, NA).

C172. TO MURRAY MCCONNEL AND WILLIAM M. MARCY, WASHINGTON

Consulate of the United States
Liverpool 11th April 1856

Sir,

I have the honor to forward herewith the accounts of this Consulate for the Quarter ending 31st Decr 1855 for

Disbursements for Destitute Seamen ————£77.7.2
or at Exchange 47¾^d per dollar————————$388.81
For Postages Newspapers &^c ————————£28.8.10
or at Exchange as above————————————$142.95
also for the half year ending same date

For expenses incurred in receiving and transmitting Despatches————————————————————$242.00

I enclose also Messrs Brown Shipley & Co's Certificate of Exchange.

Very Respectfully
I am
Your obed^t Servant

The 5th Auditor of the Treasury
Washington

Consulate of the United States
Liverpool 11 April 1856

Sir,

I have the honor to inform you that by the Steamer Arabia,

sailing tomorrow for Boston, I shall forward to the 5th Auditor of the Treasury, the accounts of this Consulate for the quarter ending 31st Decem[r] 1855, as follows,

For disbursements for Destitute Seamen ———£77.7.2
or at Exchange 47¾ pence per dollar ————$388.81
For Postages Newspapers &[c] ————————£28.8.10
or at Exchange as above——————————$142.95

For Expenses in receiving and transmitting Despatches for the 6 months ending same date——————$242.00

I enclose herewith Mess[rs] Brown Shipley & Co's Certificate of Exchange.

With high respect
I have the honor to be
Your obed[t] Servant
Nath[l] Hawthorne.

Hon W[m] L Marcy
Secretary of State
Washington
D.C

Consulate of the United States
Liverpool 26 April 1856

Sir,

I had the honor to forward on the 11th Inst the accounts of this Consulate for the Quarter ending 31 Dec[r] 1855 viz

For Disbursements for Dest Seamen————£77.7.2
or at Exchange 47¾[d] per $ ———————$388.81
For Postages Newspapers &[c] ———————£28.8.10
or at Exchange ———————————————$142.95
and for the half year ending same date

For expenses incurred in receiving and transmitting despatches———————————————————————————$242.00

I beg to inform you that for said amounts I have this day drawn on the Secretary of State at 30 days sight in favor of Wm D. Ticknor[1].

I am very respectfully
Your obed Servant
Nathl Hawthorne

The Fifth Auditor
of the Treasury
Washington

Consulate of the United States
Liverpool 26 April 1856

Sir,

I had the honor on the 11th Inst to forward the accounts of this Consulate for the quarter ending 31 Decr 1855 viz

For disbursements for destitute Seamen ———£77.7.2
or at Exchange 47$^{3/4d}$ per dollar——————————$388.81
For Postages Newspapers &^{c} ———————————£28.8.10
or at Exchange as above————————————————$142.95
and for the Half year ending same date

For expenses incurred in receiving and transmitting Despatches———————————————————————————$242.00

I now have the honor to inform you that I have this day drawn on you at 30 days sight in favor of W^m D Ticknor.

> With high respect
> I have the honor to be
> Your Obed^t Servt
> Nathl Hawthorne.

Hon W^m L Marcy
Secretary of State
Washington

1. See 866, 869.

Consulate USA
Liverpool 17th April
1856

Dear Sir,

This is the *third* note I have addressed to you respecting one of your men named Franklin Strange. I will repeat the statement made to me. It is that having been absent without leave part of Saturday you refuse to allow him on board again, although he presented himself next morning & acknowledged his offence.

Such absence although it incurs certain forfeitures does not constitute the man a deserter, & I request that you receive him on board, & return him to the United States. If such request be not complied with, I shall treat the man as a Seaman illegally forced on shore in a foreign Port & leave you to the action of the Government.

I am

Capt Hayden
Ship Isabella

1. The *Isabella* of Baltimore, Captain J. F. Hayden, had arrived on April 9 from New Orleans and was to clear May 24 for New York (Report of American Vessels, NA).

C174. TO JAMES GUTHRIE, WASHINGTON

Consulate of the United States
Liverpool 18th April 1856

Sir,

On the 28th Ulto I had the honor of writing you with the accounts of Fees of this Consulate for the Quarter ending 30th Sept 1855. I have now the honor to forward the accounts for the Quarter ending 31 Decr 1855.

After deduction of money paid in the matter of persons charged with Crimes against the United States,[1] for which I herewith forward an account with Vouchers, and my salary, there is a Balance on the Quarter of $4190.33 in favor of the United States.

With high respect
I have the honor to be
Your obed Servant
Nathl Hawthorne.

Hon Jas Guthrie
Secretary of the Treasury
Washington

1. The Consulate collected $6169.75 in fees during this quarter. NH deducted his usual salary, plus $104.42, presumably money expended in the care of Henry Norris Johnson while awaiting extradition. See C186, C188.

Consulate of the United States
Liverpool 16th May 1856

Sir,

I have the honor to acknowledge receipt of your Letter of the 18th Ulto, with enclosure.[1]

It is the Custom of shippers of Beer Ale & Porter from Liverpool, to fill the Casks & provide against any possible fermentation during the voyage by the insertion of porous spiles near the Bung.[2]

I am informed by persons largely engaged in the trade that Ale & Porter if more than a year old when shipped undergoes little if any fermentation, & that great care is taken by exporters to have it of such an age.

It has been stated to me by several parties, that they have been lately advised by their correspondents in America not to include in their Invoices of Goods sent from other places to be transshipped from Liverpool, the freight or carriage to Liverpool, it not being the practise under a recent regulation of the Treasury, to include those charges in the cost for duty; so that in the case of Iron purchased at Glasgow & sent thence to Liverpool for shipment to America, the duty is now assessed on the cost at Glasgow, & excluding the cost of conveyance to & shipment at Liverpool. Some shippers go so far as to state that the regulation applies to goods from the interior & sent by land carriage to Liverpool for shipment to the United States.

Having no official information of the subject I could only acknowledge my ignorance of any such regulation, & recommend that all charges to shipboard at Liverpool be included in the Invoices as hitherto. I should be glad to be informed whether there be any such regulation and to what cases it extends.[3]

I am frequently asked whether packages of Bottled Beer Ale or Porter containing six dozen *pints* are legal. The Law prescribes not less than six dozen *bottles*, but does not state whether pints or quarts. What is the practise of the Revenue Officers in this respect?[4]

With high respect I have the
honor to be Your obed[t] Servant
Nath[l] Hawthorne.

Hon James Guthrie
Secretary of The Treasury

1. On April 18, Guthrie had forwarded a letter from Milton S. Rathbone, Collector of Customs in San Francisco, who inquired how many gallons of ale, beer, or porter were actually exported inside 64-gallon casks. Importers in the States, Rathbone observed, were claiming that merchants filled such casks only to sixty gallons to prevent them from bursting through fermentation. Others claimed that the casks were filled to the top, with "spiles" inserted to avoid bursting. As assessing the value per gallon depended on knowing how many gallons were being imported, Rathbone asked what the custom was in Liverpool (MS, Instructions, 2, NA).

2. A spile-hole is a small hole drilled into a cask near the bung-hole, to let air come in when the cask is broached, allowing the liquid to flow out freely. Usually such holes were stopped by solid wood plugs, or spiles; here, the spiles were porous to vent any excess gas caused by fermentation.

3. On June 20, Guthrie replied that in certain cases transportation to the port of shipping was a dutiable charge and enclosed printed instructions for NH's use (MS, Instructions, 2, NA).

4. Guthrie responded that so long as six dozen bottles were shipped in each package, it did not matter whether they were quart or pint bottles.

Consulate of the United States
Liverpool 23 May 1856

Sir,

In a report accompanying my Despatch N° 22, dated 12th July 1854, & made in compliance with a circular from the Department, dated 8th Oct° 1853, I gave the substance of a statement made by two scientific men of Liverpool, (who had been appointed by the English Board of Trade to enquire into the Circumstances attending the loss of an Emigrant vessel in the Irish Channel) to the effect that there were deviations of the Compass in the Irish Channel, on board of both wood & Iron vessels, which could not be accounted for.[1] The subject has continued to excite great interest among scientific & nautical men, & a committee was some time since appointed to investigate it. A Letter from the secretary of that committee[2] has lately been published, & seems to me of sufficient importance to be communicated to you, with a view to its being disseminated, along with the previous statement before mentioned, among American Navigators, & others interested in the navigation of the Irish Channel. Its importance in connection with the stowage of Cargoes can scarcely be overrated.

"The recent loss of a noble vessel" in the letter, refers to the fine American Ship Racer lately wrecked on the Arklow Bank Coast of Ireland.[3]

I have heard it said with reference to the loss of the Racer, that all, or nearly all, of the vessels wrecked on the Arklow & Blackwater Banks are American, & I believe that such is the remarkable fact. The value of American property annually lost on those Banks is enormous, & what is more remarkable still, is that most of the vessels wrecked have been commanded by men of established reputation for prudence & Skill, & experienced in the navigation of the Irish Channel.

With High respect
I have the honor to be
Your obed[t] Serv[t]
Nath[l] Hawthorne.

Hon W[m] L Marcy
Secretary of State

1. See C51, II.21.

2. John Thomas Towson; see C51.55.

3. The American ship *Racer* of New York, Captain Ainsworth, was bound from Liverpool to New York with about 700 emigrants when, on May 6, she grounded on Mizenhead Bank in the vicinity of Arklow. All the passengers and some of the cargo was saved (James Arrott to Marcy, May 9, 1856, Consular Despatches, Dublin, NA).

Consulate of the United States
Liverpool 26th May 1856

Sir,

I beg to enclose Depositions of two persons, by which Charles Stevens is charged with the murder of C E Ross[1] on board the American Ship Mary E Balch, within the jurisdiction of the United States, in order that you may make requisition for the surrender of the accused, in accordance with the 10th Article of the Treaty of 1842, & the Act of Parliament 6 & 7th Vict° Cap 76.

The accused at my request is at present in custody, but as it is illegal without the Warrant of the Secretary of State, I shall be glad to receive such warrant as early as possible.[2]

I am very Resp[y]
Your Obed Servant
Nath[l] Hawthorne.

His Excellency
G M Dallas
&[c]. &[c]. &[c]

1. On May 24 Charles (or Theodore) Stevens, second mate of the *Mary E. Balch*, had been examined before Mansfield at the complaint of a seaman, Charles Alexander, who claimed that, during the passage, he had seen the mate strike an unknown seaman with a marling spike, after which the seaman had not been seen

again. Mansfield, "after ascertaining that it was an American ship, sent to ask Mr. Hawthorne, the American consul, if he wished to make proceedings in the matter. . ." (Liverpool *Mercury*, May 26, 1856, 3:5). NH noted in his Pocket Diary that on May 24 he "examined witness in case of missing boy, supposed to be thrown overboard"; on May 26 he examined another witness (MS, Morgan). See C180.

2. Dallas did not forward the letter to Clarendon until May 28. The warrant was issued by the Home Office on May 30 and forwarded to Dallas May 31. On the same day, however, HW wrote to Dallas, sending a copy of NH's letter and warning that if no reply were forthcoming, Stevens might be released by the Liverpool authorities (MS, F.O. 5 / 656, PRO). This note crossed the letter sending the Warrant, but to make sure of Stevens' detention, Undersecretary Waddington "caused a Telegraphic Message to be sent to the Mayor of Liverpool requesting that the Prisoner . . . may be detained until the arrival of the Secretary of State's Warrant" (Transcript, F.O. 5 / 660, PRO).

Consulate of the United States
Liverpool 28 May 1856

Dear Sir,

Not having received the Warrant from the Secretary of State, nor any communication from the minister, in the case of Chas Stevens charged with the murder of C E Ross on board the American Ship Mary E Balch at Sea, I must again request a remand of the accused.

I am very Resp^y
Your Obed Servt
Nathl Hawthorne.

Jno Smith Mansfield Esqr

C179. TO ANDREW K. BLYTHE, HAVANA[1]

Consulate of the United States
Liverpool 3^d June 1856

Dear Sir,

The bearer of this, Mr William H. Dougherty, has applied to me for a Passport, stating himself to be a naturalized citizen of the U States, but having no sufficient proof of the fact here, I am obliged to refuse his application, & he has concluded to write to Washington, for one to be sent to you, to meet him on his arrival at Havana.

I am Resp^y
Your Obed^t Servant
Nathl Hawthorne,
Consul, &c.

To the Consul of the U S
Havana

————

1. Andrew K. Blythe was U.S. Consul at Havana 1856–58.

Consulate of the United States
Liverpool 5th June 1856

Sir,

Referring to my Letter of the 26 May & your reply with a warrant in the case of Chas Stevens (otherwise Theodore Stevens) charged with murder on board the Mary E Balch, I beg to inform you that after a final examination to-day the prisoner was fully committed, so that it only remains to obtain the warrant of the secretary of state for his surrender according to the Treaty.[1] The Mary E Balch will sail in about ten days & I should be glad to receive the warrant in time for the Prisoner to go in her.[2] I think I had better be named in the warrant to receive the Prisoner.

I am with much respect
your obed Servant
Nathl Hawthorne.

To
His Excellency
Geo M Dallas
&^c &^c &^c

1. Stevens was examined by Magistrates Maxwell and Turner on June 5. At this time Charles Alexander testified that five days after the ship had sailed from New

Orleans, "he observed [Stevens] on the forecastle deck, and a Swedish boy, whose name he did not know, was passing, when [Stevens] said—'Come out of this, you ——, or I'll knock you down,' and struck him on the head with a marlin-spike. The boy was not seen afterwards" (Liverpool *Mercury*, June 6, 1856, 6:7). Later, when Stevens was tried in New York, Alexander expanded his account: ". . . I heard [Stevens] say 'You G—d d—d son of a b—h, I'll knock you down,' and he then struck him on the head with an iron marling spike and knocked him down, and then kicked him; I was standing with one foot in the house and one out; I saw it distinctly; he struck him but once; he fell at once; I heard Ross say nothing, but he squirmed, like, on the deck, and then [Stevens] kicked him in the stomach" (New York *Daily Times*, May 29, 1857, 8:1). At the hearing Alexander was joined by seaman John M. Watts, who was on deck at the wheel at the same time. Watts "said he saw [Stevens] take the boy, who was lying on the deck, by the collar, and put his body on the port rail; he then took him by the legs and tipped him over the side. The captain and mate were then about coming out of the cabin, and [Stevens], after he had thrown the boy over, came past [Watts] looking very pale; [Watts] then turned and looked over the stern, when he saw the body of the boy sinking" (*Mercury*). Alexander and Watts's testimony was contradicted by Augustus Wilson, the ship's carpenter, who remembered seeing Ross after the time of the alleged murder, but the magistrates "considered there was sufficient evidence to warrant them in committing the prisoner" (*Mercury*).

2. The warrant, "directing the Keeper of the Borough Gaol at Liverpool to deliver to Mr Nathaniel Hawthorne United States Consul at Liverpool, Charles Stevens," was issued by the Home Office on June 7 and transmitted to NH on the same day. On June 18, HW sent a copy of the warrant to Captain Jacob T. Woodbury of the *Mary E. Balch*, authorizing him to carry Stevens to the United States. HW directed Woodbury to "appropriate some especial place to the Prisoner's use where he can be safely kept. You will keep Irons on him no more than may be necessary to his safe custody, & allow him to have needful air & exercise on deck, but at times when he can be under strict surveillance, & be prevented [from] holding any intercourse with the Witnesses. ¶ On your arrival at New York you will deliver the Prisoner to the Officers of Justice & report to the District Attorney" (Letterpress copy, CO, 12B, [303], NA).

U.S. Consulate,
Liverpool, June 20th '56.

My dear Sir,

I told the writer of the enclosed note that I had no authority to deal with him in the matter proposed; and he earnestly requested that I would make application on the subject to you.[1] I send his note accordingly.

With great respect,
Sincerely yours,
Nathl Hawthorne

His Excellency,
G. M. Dallas

---

1. James Rae, of 115 Everton Terrace, Liverpool, had written NH on June 20, expressing his willingness "to sell through you to the United States Government the Quadrant that their Servant Paul Jones was in possession off [sic] when he attempted to take Lord Selkirk Prisoner. . ." (MS, William L. Marcy Papers, Vol. 70, No. 48469, Library of Congress). On April 23, 1778, John Paul Jones raided St. Mary's Isle in an unsuccessful attempt to take the fourth Earl of Selkirk hostage. On June 24 Dallas sent the note to Marcy, commenting, "The quadrant . . . ought certainly to be among other revolutionary relics in the Navy Department; and it would give me pleasure to secure it. Should you gentlemen agree with me, let me be duly authorised to purchase [it] at a reasonable price, on proof of it's [sic] identity, and give orders how to pay" (MS, Marcy Papers, Vol. 70, No. 48483, Library of Congress).

C182. TO WILLIAM L. MARCY, WASHINGTON

Consulate of the United States
Liverpool 27th June 1856

Sir,

I have the honor to inform you that I sent in the Ship "Mary E Balch," Jacob T Woodbury Master, which sailed hence on the 20th Inst for New York a prisoner named Charles Stevens charged with the crime of murder committed on board the before mentioned vessel during her voyage from New Orleans to Liverpool, and delivered up pursuant to the Treaty of 1842 between the United States & Great Britain.

Two Witnesses named Charles Alexander and John M Watts were sent with the Prisoner.

Enclosed I forward copies of the Depositions on which I made the application for the Prisoner's extradition. Copies will also be sent by this mail to the District Attorney at New York.

I also enclose you a copy of a certificate given to the Captain of the Mary E Balch, by which you will see, that I agreed on behalf of the Government to pay him $50 for the passage of the Prisoner, & $15 for the Passage of the Witness Chas Alexander.

I also forward a statement of money paid on account of the last named Witness in order that deduction may be made in settling with him on account of his expenses. Being an Englishman with a wife in London, I was obliged to advance him £4 sterling for his wife, & to resort to arbitrary measures (for which I had no legal warrant) to detain him here & induce him to go back to America to give evidence.[1]

> With high respect
> I have the honor to be
> Your Obed[t] Servant
> Nath[l] Hawthorne

Hon W[m] L Marcy
Secretary of State
Washington

---

1. Alexander subsequently spent ten months in the Tombs in New York City, awaiting Stevens's trial. See C183.1

Consulate of the United States
Liverpool 27th June 1856.

Sir,

I beg to inform you that I sent in the Mary E Balch—
Woodbury—Master which sailed from Liverpool for New
York on the 20th Inst, a Prisoner named Charles Stevens,
charged with the crime of murder on board said Ship within
the jurisdiction of the United States, & delivered up pursuant
to the Treaty with Great Britain; together with two Witnesses, Cha[s] Alexander & John M Watts.[1]

Enclosed I forward copies of the Depositions taken by me;
also of an account of money advanced to & for the Witness
Cha[s] Alexander on account of his expenses.

I am Respectfully
Your Obed Servant
Nath[l] Hawthorne

District Attorney
New York

1. The *Mary E. Balch* arrived in New York on August 1; Stevens was arrested and
formally indicted on September 22, while the other two were housed in the Tombs
in protective custody. Steven's trial was postponed to secure the attendance of other
members of the crew as witnesses, and he was not tried until May 28, 1857. After
hearing Alexander, Watts, and Wilson repeat their testimony, the jury acquitted
Stevens. See New York *Daily Times*, May 29, 1857, 8:1.

C184. TO MURRAY MCCONNEL AND WILLIAM L. MARCY, WASHINGTON

Consulate of the United States
Liverpool 18th July 1856

Sir,

With this I shall forward the following accounts of this Consulate for the quarter ending 31 March 1856 viz
For disbursements for destitute Seamen

$1475.07 £298.9.7

Accompanied by an account current
For disbursements for departm^t of state

$162.07 £32.4.11

I also forward an account current for the Quarter ending 31 December 1855, which will serve as a reply to your Letter of the 25th of April, except as to the sum of $1.45 "allowed at the Department of State more than claimed by" me which will be included in my account ending 30 June.[1]

It appears to have escaped the recollection of the Comptroller that the Law requires me to account for Extra wages half yearly only. In entering Randle's extra wages in the September statement it was only to render it strictly true. It will certainly avoid confusion to charge only the one month's wages, and at once include it in the general account, as you suggest, & I shall hereafter do so.[2]

In reply to the second paragraph in your letter of the 20th May, I beg to state, that the $19.16 was not extra wages, but expenses (Hospital & funeral &^c) incurred as credited in the previous account ending 30 June, & repaid by his wife Mary Devow;[3] & in the General account ending same date is included the one month's wages retained. In reply to 3^d

Paragraph of same letter.[4] John & Ellen Wheeler, as stated in account, were discharged at Cardiff, & the 71^{75}/$_{100}$ was remitted to me for them by the Consular Agent there, being the two months wages to which they were entitled.

In reply to paragraph 7 same Letter.[5] The charge for shipping Seamen has appeared in the accounts for the past 6 years. Its payment was authorised by the Secretary of State in a communication dated August 30th 1850, in reply to a Despatch addressed to him by my predecessor dated 22nd March 1850.[6]

It is paid to a shipping master for procuring engagements for seamen who, though destitute, are able to work, mostly for shipwrecked men, & effects a considerable saving in passages & clothing, besides putting the men in a better position.

Respectfully
I am Sir
Your obed^t Servant

5th Auditor Treasury
Washington

Consulate of the United States
Liverpool 18th July 1856

Sir,

I have the honor to inform you that I shall forward by the "Arabia," hence for Boston tomorrow, the accounts of this Consulate for the Quarter ending 31 March viz

For disbursements for Destitute Seamen
————————————————————$1475.07 or £293.9/7

Department of State for Postages Newspapers &^{c}
———————————————————$162.07 or £32.4/11
to the 5th Auditor of the Treasury.

> With high respect
> I have the honor to be
> Your Obed^t Servant
> Nathl Hawthorne

Hon W^m L Marcy
Secretary of State
Washington
D.C

> Consulate of the United States
> Liverpool 15th August 1856^7

Sir

Under date 18th July I forwarded the Accounts of this
Consulate for the quarter ending 31 March 1856—viz—
For disbursements for Dest Seamen
$1475.07 equal to £293.9.7
For disbursements for Dep of State
$162.07 or £32.4.11
I beg to inform you that I have this day drawn on the
Secretary of State @ 30 days sight in favor of W^m D Ticknor
for the sums above named.^{8}

> I am very respectfully
> Your obed Servt

J M Smith Esqr
The Fifth Auditor
of the Treasury
Washington

Consulate of the United States
Liverpool 15th August 1856

Sir,

Under date 18th of July 1856 I had the honor to advise the accounts of this Consulate, for the quarter ending 31 March, forwarded to the 5th Auditor of the Treasury viz—
Disbursements for Seamen ————$1475.07 or £293.9.7
Department of State——————$162.07 or £32.4.11
@ 47¾ pence per dollar; and at the same time to forward Messrs Brown Shipley & Co's Certificate of Exchange.
I have now the honor to inform you that I have this day drawn upon you at 30 days sight in favor of W^m D Ticknor, for the amounts above stated.

With high respect
I have the honor to be
Your obed^t Servt
Nathl Hawthorne

Hon W^m. L. Marcy
Secretary of State
Washington

1. On April 25, T. M. Smith, Acting Auditor, had noted that extra wages due to one George Randley had been entered in the statement but not in NH's general account: "The amount . . . appears to have been overlooked by you" (MS, Instructions, 2, NA).

2. See C141.4.

3. Smith's letter of May 20 asked why NH had claimed $19.16 extra wages for John Devow in his September accounts, then entered $50.00 extra wages refunded him in his December accounts (MS, Instructions, 2, NA).

4. Smith had asked why one month of the Wheeler's extra wages had not been retained as usual. See also C114.

5. Smith had said, "The amounts charged . . . for shipping seamen, are suspended for Explanation; being an unusual charge."

6. Crittenden had written John M. Clayton, then Secretary of State, on March 22, 1850: "The Custom of this Port in Shipping Seamen for vessels is to do so by shipping masters who are paid for so doing by the Seaman & it has I understand been the practice of this office when Seamen who are fit to work are from shipwreck or other cause chargeable to it to pay this charge (generally 5/–) for them thus enabling them to obtain wages & clothe themselves, saving the United States Considerable expense which must otherwise be incurred for their Passages & necessary clothing. Although such a payment is without question the means of saving considerable to the destitute Seaman's fund yet it may not be in strict accordance with the Letter of the Law & I should be glad if you would inform me your opinion as an instruction for my future Government" (MS, 'N° 13', Despatches, 11, Liverpool, NA). Incoming Secretary of State Daniel Webster responded on August 30, "the Department authorizes your paying that fee for shipping seamen, who, though destitute, may be able to earn wages and to work their passage home, as it is manifest that a great saving will, thereby, accrue to the fund for their relief" (MS, Instructions, 2, NA).

7. NH left Liverpool for Blackheath on July 26, returning to the Consulate on August 8, explaining the unusual delay in sending the duplicate accounts.

8. See 901.

Consulate of the United States
Liverpool 18th July 1856

Sir,

I have the honor to forward herewith, transcript of the Record of Treasury Fees of this Consulate, for the Quarter ending 31 March 1856,[1] also an account between me & the United States for the same period, shewing a Balance due the United States on the Quarter of $3810.32, after deducting my salary, & money paid in the case of Henry N. Johnson charged with the crime of attempt at murder within the jurisdiction of the United States.[2]

With high respect
I have the honor to be
Your obed^t Servt

Hon James Guthrie
Secretary of the Treasury
Washington
D.C

1. The Consulate collected $5821.69 in fees during this quarter. NH deducted his usual salary, plus $136.37 on account of Henry N. Johnson (U.S. Treasury Fees, 1, NA).

2. On August 9, McConnel disallowed this expense as "not payable out of Salary" (MS, Instructions, 2, NA). See C188.

C186. TO MURRAY MCCONNEL AND WILLIAM D. MARCY,
WASHINGTON

Consulate of the United States
Liverpool 26 Aug 1856

Sir,

By the Arabia to sail for Boston on Saturday the 30th I shall
forward the accounts of this Consulate for the quarter ending
30 June 1856 viz
For Disbursements for Destitute Seamen
£183.8.3 @ 47³/₄[d] per dollar $921.87
Department of State for Postages &[c]
£29.12.9 @ 47³/₄[d] per dollar $148.96
For the six months ending same date
For expenses incurred in receiving & transmitting Des-
patches ─────────────────────────────────$242.00
I also forward an account current with the account of
Disbursements for Seamen and a Certificate of Exchange.[1]

I am with much respect
Your obed Servant
Nath[l] Hawthorne

M M[c]Connell Esq[r]
5th Auditor of the Treasury

Consulate of the United States
Liverpool 26 Aug 1856

Sir,

I have the honor to inform you that I shall forward to the

5th Auditor of the Treasury by the "Arabia" to sail for Boston on the 30th Inst the Accounts of this Consulate for the Quarter ending 30 June 1856 viz

Disbursements for Destitute Seamen

£183.8.3 @ 47^{3}/$_{4}$^{d} per dollar ———————————$921.87

Department of State for Postages &^{c}

————————————————£29.12.9 $148.96

For the six months ending same date

For Expenses incurred in receiving and transmitting Despatches———————————————————————$242.00

> I have the honor to be
> With high respect
> Your obed^t Servant
> Nathl Hawthorne

Hon W^m L Marcy
Secretary of State

> Consulate of the United States
> Liverpool 25th Septem^r 1856[2]

Sir,

By the Steamer "Arabia" on the 26th Aug ulto I forwarded the accounts of this Consulate for the Quarter ending 30 June 1856 viz—

Disbursements for Destitute Seamen

£183.8.3 equal to $921.87 @ 47^{3}/$_{4}$^{d} per dollar

Department of State for Postages Newspapers &^{c}

£29.12.9 equal to $148.96 @ 47^{3}/$_{4}$^{d} per dollar

and for the half year ending same date

For expenses incurred in receiving & transmitting Despatches—————————————————————$242.00

I have now the honor to inform you, that I have this day drawn on the Secretary of State at 30 days sight in favor of W^m D Ticknor, for the several sums above stated.[3]

Very respectfully
I am
Your obed^t Servant

Murray McConnell Esq
5th Auditor of the Treasury

Consulate of the United States
Liverpool 25th Sept 1856

Sir,

Under date 26th August ulto, I had the honor to advise forwarding, to the Fifth Auditor of the Treasury, the accounts of this Consulate for the Quarter ending 30 June 1856 viz

For disbursements for destitute Seamen,

$£183.8.3$ equal to $921.87 @ $47^{3/4}$^d p dollar

Department of State for Postages Newspapers &^c,

$£29.12.9$ equal to $148.96 @ $47^{3/4}$^d p dollar

and for the half year ending same date,

For expenses incurred in receiving & transmitting Despatches—————————————————————$242.00

I have now the honor to inform you, that I have this day drawn on you in favor of M^r W^m D Ticknor, at 30 days sight, for the several sums above stated, in dollars, & enclose herewith Messrs Brown Shipley & Co's Certificate of Exchange.

> With high respect I have
> the honor to be
> Your obedient Servant
> Nathl Hawthorne.

Hon W^m L Marcy
Secretary of State
Washington

1. On January 31, 1857, McConnel acknowledged receipt of these accounts and notified NH that, by a decision of the First Comptroller, his account had been credited with the sum of $81.07, apparently the total of the various disputed charges mentioned in previous letters to the Treasury (MS, Instructions, 2, NA).

2. Again, the duplicate accounts were delayed due to NH's absence from the Consulate. He left Liverpool for Blackheath on August 26 and returned September 8.

3. See 914.

Consulate of the United States
Liverpool 18 Aug 1856

Sir,

As suggested in your note of the 16th to Captain Sawyer of
the Cuba, I appointed Mr Eben Howes agent at this place to
the Boston underwriter to state the Deck load which said
vessel could have safely carried from Jamaica to this place, &
herewith enclose you his report.[1] The charge of £1.1.0 ought
I think to be equally divided between the charterers & the
vessel.

I am your Ob^t Servt
Nathl Hawthorne.

A. H. Lawrence

1. The brig *Cuba* of Millbridge, Captain Franklin Sawyer, had arrived in
Liverpool August 15 from Jamaica (Report of American Vessels, NA).

Consulate of the United States
Liverpool 19 Septr 1856

Sir,

I have the honor to forward herewith the account of Fees
received at this Consulate during the Quarter ending 30th
June 1856, together with a transcript of the Record of
Treasury Fees, also an account current for the half year
ending same date.[1]

I also forward an account of Expenses, with vouchers,
incurred on account of persons charged with crimes against
the United States, which I am directed to include in the
account of Fees by the 224th & 225th Articles of General
Instructions.

I have also the honor to acknowledge rec^t of your Letter of
27th August Ulto advising me that "as it appears from a
statement furnished by the accounting officers of the Treasury, that the excess (of fees) in your (my) hands on the 31st
of March last amounted to a sum of $10.825.65" you had
drawn on me in favor of the Treasurer of the United States
for £2150.3.5 equal to $10,500 @ 9⅞% Exch.

The draft endorsed payable to Messrs Baring Brothers &
Co was duly presented, and has been paid by me. I herewith
forward Messrs Barings' Certificate of the payment.

The accounting officers have excluded the amount paid by
me on account of persons charged with crimes against the
United States, on the ground that they are not payable out of
Fees, notwithstanding the plain directions contained in
Articles 224 & 225 of General Instructions. These amounts
being brought to my credit, the excess in my hands on 31

March last would be $10584.86 instead of $10825.65, as will appear by the acc^t current before mentioned.

Your direction as to the payment of the excess at the close of each quarter hereafter is duly noted, & on being informed of the correctness of the account now sent I will pay the Balance to Messrs Baring Brothers & Co, unless otherwise instructed in the meantime.[2]

With great respect
I am your obed^t Servant
Nathl Hawthorne

Hon James Guthrie
Secretary of the Treasury
Washington

1. The Consulate collected $6205.21 in fees during this quarter. NH deducted his usual salary, plus $73.61 on account of persons charged with crimes (U.S. Treasury Fees, 1, NA).

2. In his letter of August 27, Guthrie had instructed NH that "Any excess in your hands at the close of any quarter hereafter, you will be pleased to deposit with Messrs Baring Brothers & Co, Bankers of the U. States at London, in Sterling money, to be held subject to the draft or order of the Secretary of the Treasury—and to take duplicate receipts for the same one of which to be sent to this Department" (MS, Instructions, 2, NA).

C189. TO WILLIAM L. MARCY, WASHINGTON

Consulate of the United States
Liverpool 26th September 1856

Sir,

I have the honor to transmit for the information of the Department a report made by a Committee of the House of Commons, lately appointed to enquire into the Local charges on shipping levied in this country.

The Committee grew out of an attempt made by the Government during the last session, to pass a Bill, for placing such charges under the Control of the Board of Trade, with a view to their partial or total abolition. [1]

Although the Corporations interested, of which Liverpool undoubtedly stands first, [2] aided by the fears of some, and the reverence for vested interests, & the rights of property, so deeply rooted in the minds of all the English, resisted the attempt with success this time, it is plain that tolls so contrary to the spirit of the present Commercial legislation of this country, cannot long continue to exist, certainly not in their present form. [3]

Our own large & increasing commerce with England, gives us a deep interest in the matter.

I also transmit, with a view to its publication for the information of mariners &^c, a notice lately issued by the

Dock Committee of Liverpool, respecting changes in the Lighting and Buoying of the approaches to the Port.

With high respect
I have the honor to be
Your Obed^t Servant
Nathl Hawthorne

Hon Wm L. Marcy
Secretary of State
Washington

1. In her speech opening Parliament on January 31, 1856, Queen Victoria had mentioned complaints about "The system under which Merchant Shipping is liable to pay Local Dues and Passing Tolls" (*Parliamentary Debates*, 140 [1856]: 3). On February 4, Robert Lowe (1811–92), Vice President of the Board of Trade, asked the House of Commons to consider a bill abolishing such local taxes. After two rounds of lively debate, the bill was withdrawn, and Prime Minister Palmerston proposed a Select Committee to consider the merits of such changes and propose more specific legislation (*Parliamentary Debates*, 140 [1856]: 152–78, 1314–88, 1412–25). This committee, with Lowe as chairman, met on July 3 to consider its recommendations. Thomas Emerson Headlam (1813–75), M.P. from Newcastle, presented a report favoring Liverpool's local charges, which met with strong opposition from free-trade advocate Richard Cobden (1804–65), who argued that the committee ought not to approve any report at the present stage of its inquiries. Finally the committee voted simply to "report to the House the evidence already taken" and disband (*London Times*, July 4, 1856, 6:2). No further action was taken on local charges that year.

2. On February 4, Robert Lowe had observed that "The whole amount of town dues appropriated to municipal purposes in England, Scotland, and Ireland, in 1852, was 163,000*l*., and of that amount the municipal corporation of Liverpool levied by dues upon shipping no less that £105,250. Out of this they are obliged by law to apply to maritime purposes the magnificent sum of £400 a year. They are, however, better than the law obliges them to be, for in that year they applied to those purposes no less that £3,044, the remainder being expended for the benefit of the ratepayers of the borough. . . . Besides the enormous tax I have mentioned, the docks of Liverpool levy on the shipping £273,284, the whole of which is by no means paid for services conferred" (*Parliamentary Debates*, 140 [1856]: 159).

3. See C51, I.5, III.24.

Consulate of the United States
Liverpool 3 Oct° 1856

Sir,

I have the honor to forward herewith copy of an advertisement appearing in the London Globe, & submit whether it
would not be well to give it publicity in America.[1]

The premiums will no doubt be handsome enough to be
worth competing for, & competition for a building of such
magnitude, cannot fail to have a highly improving effect on
the competitors, & tend to advance the art of Architecture in
America.[2]

Plans &c could readily be obtained through the minister in
London, as could also information, as to the character & style
of the buildings, in the neighborhood of the proposed site.

With high respect
I have the honor to be
Your Obt Servant
Nathl Hawthorne

Hon Wm L. Marcy
Secretary of State
Washington
D.C

1. The advertisement, signed by Alfred Austin (1805–84), Secretary to the Office of Works, requested "Designs from Architects of all countries" for new buildings to house the Foreign Office and the War Office, as well as for an overall scheme "for the concentration of the principal Government Offices" around the two new buildings. The notice also appeared in the London *Times*, September 22, 1856, 7:1.

2. The Government Buildings Competition, as it was later known, became largely a political affair, the ruling Liberals advocating classical designs, the opposition Tories supporting gothic-revival plans harmonizing with the new Houses of Parliament. At the time the government offices were housed in a series of "old barns" on Downing Street, precariously patched together by a network of makeshift beams and girders (Edward Walford, *Old and New London* [London: Cassell Petter & Galpin, 1875], III: 392). In 1855 Parliament authorized money to buy a site for new buildings, and by April Sir Benjamin Hall (1802–67), chief commissioner of works, reported that the government had settled on a block of land on the east side of Whitehall between Downing and Great George Streets. He proposed that, "as the buildings to be erected would be of a national character, the competition for their design should be thrown open to the architects not only of England but of the whole world, in order that we might at last have some public building worthy of the metropolis" (*Parliamentary Debates*, 141 [1856]: 367). Two hundred eighteen designs were submitted, but the judges' decision, awarding the prizes to three different obscure architects, pleased no one, and Palmerston rejected these plans. After the Tories took power in 1858, the commission went to Sir George Gilbert Scott (1811–78), whose gothic tendencies satisfied the conservatives. The block of buildings was completed in 1873. On the "battle of the styles" surrounding this competition, see Roger Dixon and Stefan Muthesius, *Victorian Architecture* (London: Oxford University Press, 1978), pp. 161–62, and John Physick and Michael Darby, *'Marble Halls': Drawings and Models for Victorian Secular Buildings* (London: HMSO, 1973), p. 37.

Consulate of the United States
Liverpool 10th Oct° 1856

Sir,

    I have the honor to acknowledge receipt of your communication of the 15th Sept, & in reply to inform you, that the Despatches alluded to were put into the Post Office in America, not at Liverpool, & were not addressed to my care.[1]
    The Despatches forwarded in charge of the Purser of the Persia, on the voyage alluded to, were not sent to the office of the Cunard Company.[2] The Persia was detained at the bar by the lowness of the water, & her mails sent up by a steam Tender. The Despatches were sent along with them, & received by my messenger on board the Tender on her arrival, about 7 O'Clock. The Ship herself did not arrive for several hours afterwards.
    The Purser must have been misunderstood, or his recollection have failed him.[3]

I am very respectfully
Your obedient Servant
Nathl Hawthorne.

Genl J A Thomas
Assistant Secretary of State
Washington

1. Thomas's letter informed NH that information had been received from John Miller, Despatch Agent at London, "that despatches which were forwarded by the Persia from New York on the 6TH of last month had been placed in the Post Office on the arrival of that Steamer at Liverpool. . ." (MS, Instructions, 2, NA).

2. Thomas said that from inquiries made in New York, "it appears that when the Persia reached Liverpool on the trip adverted to, you and your Agent were absent and the despatches were consequently carried to the office of the Cunard Company, by whose Agent it is presumed they were sent to the Post Office. ¶ Any explanation upon this subject which you can conveniently furnish, would be acceptable."

3. Or perhaps not all the despatch bags were sent by the tender; see C192.

Consulate USA
Liverpool 11 Oct° 1856

Dear Sir,

As a precaution, & an advice of the number of Packages forwarded, I would suggest that you always write on *each* package the number of packages forwarded, which will inform my Messenger the number of Bags &^{c} he ought to receive.

I am
yours truly
Nathl Hawthorne.

Samuel R. Glen Esqr
US Despatch Agent
Boston

————

Consulate of the United States
Liverpool 24th Oct° 1856

Sir,

I have the honor to inform you that I have appointed Mr Alfred Davy to be Consular Agent at Manchester. Mr Davy is Son of Mr Albert Davy Consul of the United States at Leeds.[1] I shall be glad to receive your approval of such appointment.[2]

I have the honor to be
Your Obed^t Servant
Nathl Hawthorne.

Hon W^m L Marcy
Secretary of State
Washington

1. NH's Pocket Diary records that on October 20, "Mr. Davy called" (MS, Morgan). According to Moran, "Davy is a Philadelphian. He has been consul at Leeds for more than 30 years [as of 1857], and being a good officer ought to be retained. The place is not worth much altho' it takes in Hull, New Castle, Sunderland & other small ports on the coast" (I, 7). Later, he noted, "He is a man who looks out for the main chance and never comes here [the London Legation] unless he has something to gain by it' (I, 554). He was removed in 1861 (Moran, II, 866). NH once considered using "the consul of Leeds" as the basis for a character in his English romance (ACM, p. 58).

2. Thomas responded on November 11, "The appointment of Mr Alfred Davy . . . is approved. You will be held responsible for his official acts. ¶ You are reminded that, by the Act approved the 18th of August last, provision has been made for a salaried Consular Officer at Manchester, and in now sanctioning the temporary appointment of a Consular Agent, it must be understood that it is not improbable the President may consider it expedient hereafter to appoint a Consul at that place" (MS, Instructions, 2, NA).

Consulate of the United States
Liverpool 29 Oct° 1856

Dear Sir,

Under date 26 June last, I was advised by the Department
of State, that a Gold Medal had been forwarded to the
Legation at London, for presentation to Captain Langcake of
the British ship "Windermere," & a silver medal for M^r
McRitchie mate of the same vessel.[1] Captain Langcake i's
now in Liverpool, & informs me that he has never received
the medal. Will you have the goodness to inform me what
disposition was made of it? I shall be glad of a reply by return
of Post as Captain L sails again on Monday.[2]

I am very Respectfully
Your obed^t Servant
Nathl Hawthorne.

His Excellency
G. M. Dallas

1. See C134. Captain William Langcake was now in command of the British bark
James Carthy.

2. The medals had previously been transmitted to the Liverpool Local Marine
Board, who presented Langcake with his medal on November 6. According to the
Liverpool *Mercury*, "The medal is of solid gold, weighing about seven or eight
ounces, and valued at nearly £100. On the obverse side is the following inscription:—'The President of the United States to Captain William Langcake, of the

British barque Windemere, for his humanity towards citizens of the United States in 1855.' The inscription is encircled with a wreath, in which the stars and the American eagle are very appropriately introduced. The reverse side bears a representation, in relief, of a drowning man clinging to a broken mast, while in the distance is seen a vessel coming to his assistance. Mr J. Lockett [of the Local Marine Board] . . . was satisfied, though he had seen several medals given by the French and other nations, he had never seen one so magnificent as the one that had been presented to Captain Langcake" (November 7, 1856, 7:2). Langcake acknowledged the medal in a letter to the Board, saying "I shall ever esteem it a very high honor to have been deemed worthy of receiving so valuable a testimonial from so distinguished a person as the President of the United States" (Transcript, F.O. 5 / 663, PRO).

Consulate of the United States
Liverpool 7th November 1856

Sir,

I have the honor to transmit, with a view to its distribution, should you think it of sufficient importance, a small specimen of Sorghé seed.[1] The parcel from which I obtained it was brought from Venice, & was distributed gratis to persons having means of trying its cultivation. Much importance is attached to the experiments that will be made here, but it is all but certain they will fail, the grain requiring similar soil & climate to Indian corn, neither of which it can have in England.

The varied uses it may be applied to, & its great yield, will render it a valuable addition to the crops of our Western States and Territories, & there it would be most likely to flourish.[2]

I annex a description furnished by the person from whom I obtained the specimen.[3]

With high respect
I am
Your obed[t] Servant
Nath[l] Hawthorne.

Hon W[m] L Marcy
Secretary of State
Washington

1. Although broomcorn, a variety of sorghum, had been grown in America since colonial times, sorgo, or sugar-producing sorghum was a novelty. In 1850 the French consul at Shanghai sent back to Paris a sample of sorghum seed, which was increased and sold by the seed firm Vilmorin, Andrieux & Co. Small amounts of this seed had been privately imported into the United States beginning in 1853, and, in January, 1857, the United States Agricultural Society (at this time a division of the Patent Office) resolved "to investigate and experiment upon the *Sorgho sucré*, or Chinese Sugar-cane, with the view of determining its value." A large quantity of seed was imported from France, distributed to ninety locations, and the results published. The committee responsible found that "The soil and geographical range . . . correspond nearly with those of Indian corn" and concluded that "the Sorgho sucré possesses qualities which commend it to the especial attention of the agriculturalists of all parts of the country, as . . . it is well suited to our national economy, and supplies what has been long a great desideratum" (*Report of the Commissioner of Patents for the Year 1857: Agriculture* [House of Representatives, 35th Congress, 1st Session, Ex. Doc. No. 32, 1858], pp. 181–83). The Chino-French variety, later termed Chinese Amber, was subsequently superseded by more productive varieties brought in from South Africa. See Peter Collier, *Sorghum: Its Culture and Manufacture* (Cincinnati: Robert Clark &Co., 1884), pp. 64–69, and H. Doggett, *Sorghum* (London: Longmans, 1970), p. 250.

2. Production of sorghum molasses was first noted in U.S. census figures in 1857 and totalled only 1,645 gallons; two years later production had risen to 6,747,123 gallons. By 1880 cultivation of sugar-producing sorghum was centered in the midwest, particularly in Ohio, Minnesota, Iowa, Illinois, and Kansas, and total production of sorghum molasses averaged eleven million gallons nationwide (Collier, *Sorghum*, xi, 39, 410–11).

3. The description enclosed by NH read: "'Sorghe' or 'sucre' of the French, a valuable grain bearing plant. Its cultivation is attracting much attention in the South of France. It is a native of the north of China, where it is largely cultivated for the manufacture of sugar; it grows to a height of about nine feet, and each plant produces from four to six stalks, and on each of these there is a bunch containing from 2000 to 3000 seeds; it is grown precisely in the same manner as maize or millet, and the same descriptions of Soil are suitable for it. Sugar and alcohol, can be obtained from the stalk, and the Leaf in its green state makes an excellent fodder for Cattle and Horses, and may be dried for winter use; another valuable property of the Sorghé is, that the saccharine principle of the stalk is never so great as at the full maturity of the seed. The seed is greedily eaten by Horses and Pigs, but not so by fowls" (Enclosure, Despatches, 13, 78, NA).

Consulate of the United States
Liverpool 21 Nov 1856

Sir,

I beg to report the loss, near the entrance of this port, on the 12th Inst, of three large American vessels—the Samuel M Fox, Ainsworth, Master—Silas Wright, Freeman Master—& Louisiana, Sullivan, Master, all belonging to New York.[1]

The Silas Wright of 1443 Tons and Samuel M Fox of 1063 Tons, were nearly new vessels & were laden with general cargoes bound for New York. The Louisiana of 758 Tons had on board a Cargo of Salt & Coal for New Orleans.

They left the Mersey, in tow of Steamers & in charge of regularly licensed Pilots, about ten in the morning, & were all wrecked between one & Two in the afternoon, close together on the Burbo Banks at the entrance of Victoria channel the Pilots being on board & steamers with them.

The alledged cause of the disasters, was a strong north (head) wind suddenly increasing to a Gale, with violent squalls, so that the steamers could not make head against it, the vessels became unmanageable and went ashore. They all became total wrecks, but considerable portions of Cargoes & Materials are being saved in a very damaged state.

The fact of three large vessels being wrecked within so short a time of leaving Port, so near together & within the same hour; with steamers towing & Pilots in charge; is very remarkable. The occurrence is I believe unprecedented in the history of this port. An enquiry has been made by the Pilots committee, but no blame is attributed to any one.

The Crews together included over a hundred men, & as they lost their clothing, I have had to incur large expense in providing for them.

With high respect
I have the honor to be
Your Obed[t] Servant
Nath[l] Hawthorne

Hon W[m] L Marcy
Secretary of State
Washington

1. Details in this despatch are drawn from the Marine Extended Protests taken by HW from Captain James Sullivan of the *Louisiana* on November 17, by Captain Thomas F. Freeman of the *Silas Wright* on November 18, and by Captain Allen Cainsworth of the *Samuel M. Fox* on November 21 (NA).

Consulate of the United States
Liverpool 25 Nov 1856

Dear Sir,

Referring to my Letters to Mr Buchanan of the 7 & 14 Nov 1855, & your communication to me of the 19 May 1856,[1] I have the honor to transmit a number of documents which have to-day been handed to me by the Agents for the Ship Ellwood Walter of New York, in support of the claim of the owners of that vessel, for compensation on account of losses sustained by them, in being obliged to reland a quantity of Saltpetre, under the operation of the order in council of 1 Nov 1855.

The claim being of the class acknowledged by Her Majesty's Government as entitled to compensation, I presume no objection will be made to it.[2]

The claimants are American Citizens residing at New York.

I am Resp^y
Your Obed Servant
Nathl Hawthorne

His Excellency
Geo M Dallas
&^{c} &^{c} &^{c}

1. See C133.1.

2. The claim, by Messrs. Jacot, Taylor and Tipper of Liverpool for £1123.3.1, was submitted by Dallas to Clarendon on November 28. As the case was being studied by the Commissioners of Customs, the claimants submitted a second statement of costs on July 22, 1857, which listed the costs of alleged damages that, in the Commissioners' opinion, "differ[ed] so materially from those set forth in the original application as to give rise to the opinion that the original claim was for the most part a fabrication." Finding little evidence for any of the damages claimed and considerable evidence of fraud, the Commissioners concluded on September 5, 1857, "we should not consider ourselves justified in recommending to your Lordships that any payment should be made to the parties under those heads, and We would beg to observe that the present claim is from the Consignees of the vessel, and we are not aware that any application has been made by the Owners of the Saltpetre for the loss which they may have sustained" (Transcript, F.O. 5 / 686, PRO). Clarendon passed on this report to Dallas, who wrote the owners, "unless your right as Consignees to receive whatever sum may be ultimately allowed be proved, I shall not feel myself at liberty . . . to press the claim farther upon the British Government" (Miscellaneous Correspondence of the London Legation, 10, NA). On the same day, Moran noted, "I remember this detention when it occurred: and the opinion I then formed of the claimants was not changed on reading this report. They deserve nothing. Their charges are shameful. . . . It strikes me they are a set of English sharpers, and not being the owners of the saltpetre landed, really have no claim. The Brit. Go't behave well in this case and seem disposed to indemnify the real sufferers on sufficient proof' (I, 165).

Consulate of the United States
Liverpool 26th Nov 1856

Sir,

I beg to enclose the statements, sworn to before me, of three of the men of the ship "Neptune" who charge James Courtney Collins[1] 3[d] mate of that vessel, with the murder of John Smith one of the Crew, during the voyage from New York to this Port.[2] I do not think from the statements at present before me that the charge can be sustained, but it will be better to demand the surrender of the accused on the charge and obtain a Warrant so that he may be properly examined in open court when other evidence may be obtained of a more positive character.

I shall be glad to receive your reply as early as convenient.[3]

I am
Your obed Servant
Nath[l] Hawthorne

His Excellency
G. M. Dallas

---

1. Alias Peter Campbell; see C218.

2. The depositions are unrecovered. According to the Liverpool *Mercury*, Smith had hidden away after being mistreated, and when he later came out, he was lashed to the rigging and beaten with the "cat." The next night, according to seaman

William Thompson, Collins was seen pursuing Smith with "a hard wood stick in his hand, saying 'By —— if I find him I'll make a finish of him.' He went up to the port anchor, and came back again, saying that he had found Smith, who had hung himself, and he cut him down. Thompson says he saw the deceased, who was not the least black in the face, but he had a lump under his right ear, as if he had taken a blow." Before Smith's body was buried at sea, Thompson also testified, "when his shirts were taken off they brought off the skin and flesh with them where he had been previously beaten." The *Mercury* noted that "The American Consul has already taken the requisite steps for a full enquiry in the matter, and the accused are in custody" (December 1, 1856, 4:4).

3. Dallas requested the warrant on November 27, which was granted and forwarded to NH on November 29.

C199. TO GEORGE M. DALLAS, LONDON

Consulate of the United States
Liverpool 3^d Decr 1856

Sir,

I had the honor to receive your Letter of the 29th Nov, enclosing a Warrant in the Case of James C Collins. The accused was finally examined to-day & acquitted, the evidence not being such as would justify his committal for trial had the alledged offence been committed in England.[1]

I am
Your Obed^t Servt,

His Excellency
Geo M Dallas

1. On the following day, Wybergh Garrett informed Sir George Grey that Collins had been "brought before George Grant Esqr, one of H. M. Justices of the Peace for this Borough . . . but there not being sufficient evidence of criminality to justify his committal for trial, he was therefore discharged from custody" (MS, F.O. 5 / 663, PRO).

Consulate of the United States
Liverpool 19th December 1856

Sir,

I have the honor to acknowledge receipt of a newspaper containing the Act of Congress approved August 18, 1856,[1] and also the pamphlet containing the Statutes passed at the first and second sessions of the Thirty-fourth Congress.

With high respect
I have the honor to be
Your obed^t Servt
Nathl Hawthorne

Hon Wm L. Marcy
Secretary of State
Washington

1. This was the Act to regulate the Diplomatic and Consular Systems of the United States (*Statutes at Large*, XI: 52–65). It limited the salary of the Consul at Liverpool to $7500, out of which all services and personal expenses were to be paid. NH's Pocket Diary records that on September 11 he "Called at News Room to read American papers" (MS, Morgan), and on the following day he gave Ticknor his reaction to the new bill (905). Two weeks later NH told Ticknor that he intended to remain in office until the end of his four-year term (914), but he did not respond directly to the Department until he received Marcy's Circular No. 16 of November 8. This called consuls' attention to "A newspaper containing the abovementioned act . . . sent to your address immediately after its passage," and concluded, "In the event of your declining to remain in office under the provisions of the act . . . you will, at your earliest convenience, apprise the Department of that fact. . ." (Instructions, 2, NA). On December 19, NH also wrote Bridge, asking him to inform Buchanan that he intended to resign effective August 31, 1857 (933). See C205.

C201. TO H. J. REDFIELD, NEW YORK

Consulate USA
Liverpool 30 Decr 1856

Dr Sir,

I beg to inform you that by some mistake of this office the Certificate of Registry of the Steamer Ericsson was left behind on her sailing for New York on the 24 Inst. The mistake was not discovered until too late for the steamer of the 27, & the Certificate will be forwarded by the next mail on 3^d January.

I am
Your obed^t Servt
Nathl Hawthorne.

The Collector of Customs
New York

Consulate of the United States
Liverpool 9th Jany 1857

Sir,

Some time in 1854 Wm Hathaway an American citizen, whose relatives reside in Gardiner Maine, died on board the Brig (English) "Magician," & the proceeds of his effects & wages (£13) were paid by the Master into the Sailor's Home at Liverpool. A Mr Israel S Jordan, on behalf of the parents, subsequently applied for the money, & was furnished with forms to be filled up in America. These forms he returned with about 6 weeks ago, filled up & attested by the British Consul, presented them, but up to this time has not been able to get an answer. Being about to leave for home again he applied to me, & on yesterday applying to the Master of the Sailor's home² I am referred to "The Secretary Marine Department Board of Trade London."

I am informed that the relatives are very poor, & am desirous of procuring an answer to the application in time for Mr Jordan, who sails on Monday next, to take home with him. Being forbidden to communicate directly with the authorities I presume to trouble you and am

Yours very Respectfully
Nathl Hawthorne

---

1. This letter lacks an interior address in the letterpress copy; the recipient has been supplied from the copybook's index.

2. Richard Ainley; see C51.38.

C202. TO CAPTAIN G. M. POLLAND, *PARLIAMENT*[1]

Consulate USA
Liverpool 12 Febry 1857

Dr Sir,

Jullian Dominic & Jno Bias complain that they have been sent to a Tailor to receive their wages, & have been offered in payment, part money, & part clothes, the latter being reckoned much above their value.[2] I beg to call your attention to the matter, & to inform you that no discharge is legal unless with my consent.

I am
Yours truly
Nathl Hawthorne.

Capt Pollard
Ship Parliament

---

1. The Consulate's Copies of Ships' Registers lists George M. Polland of Boston as master of the *Parliament.*

2. This was evidently a common way of cheating discharged seamen; three letters signed by HW warn captains to put an end to this practice: "it is a very reprehensible proceeding and calculated to bring the American service into disrepute" (HW to Captain Sawyer, March 4, 1856, [Letterpress copy, CO, 12A, 302, NA]). See "Consular Letters Not Printed."

C203. TO JAMES BUCHANAN, WASHINGTON

Consulate of the United States,
Liverpool, Feb^r 13th 1857

Sir,

I beg permission to resign my office as Consul of the
United States at this Port, from and after the date of August
thirty-first, 1857.[1]

Very Respectfully,
Your obedient Serv't,
Nath[l] Hawthorne.

To
The President of the United States.

1. In letters of December 19 (933) and January 15 (939), NH had already
informed Bridge that he planned to resign as soon as Buchanan was inaugurated, but
intended to remain in office until August 31, the date Crittenden had left office in
1853. The resignation itself was forwarded to Bridge, along with a letter dated the
same day (946). NH instructed Bridge to forward the resignation to Buchanan "as
soon as you think proper after the inauguration," adding, "If he wants the office
sooner, he is welcome to remove me; but I should suppose (as it could not be done
without some slight odium) that he would prefer my offered resignation." On March
13, NH wrote Ticknor that Bridge had delivered the resignation to Buchanan and
had reported, "the old fellow was very gracious and complimentary towards me, and
said that I might take my own time" (957). The resignation was not officially
accepted until September 24, when NH's successor, N. Beverley Tucker,
(1820–90),had been approved and dispatched to Liverpool; see C223.8.

Consulate of the United States
Liverpool 13th Feby 1857

Sir,

I have to inform you of the total loss on the 23 Ulto, near the entrance of this port, of the Ship "Confederation" Asa A Corning master of New York, attended with the loss of the master, mate Jas Bonewell & Boy W^m J Holcom.

The vessel sailed from Philadelphia on the 22nd Decr, received a Liverpool Pilot on the 22 Jan^y, & was proceeding under his directions through one of the channels leading into this port, the wind blowing a Gale with a heavy sea: when about nine a m next morning she struck on the edge of a sandbank. Steamers and Life Boats went to her assistance, she was got off, but having lost her Rudder, was again driven on by the Gale. The Life Boats then advised the Crew to escape, & all left (with the Captain's wife) except the Captain mates steward one seaman & a Boy who refused to leave.

The Life Boats & all but one steamer then left. Subsequently the 2nd & 3^d mates steward & man left in one of the ship's Boats & got on board the Steamer. The approach of night, the Gale and Sea, & the ebbing tide obliged the Steamer to leave. As soon as the tide permitted another Steamer went down but the vessel had disappeared & the before mentioned persons perished.

Little of the Cargo or Materials have been saved, the Bank being very exposed & several miles from the main.

Shipmasters generally attributed the wreck to the carelessness of the Pilot, & Capt Corning had been heard to express himself to the same effect. Accordingly the matter was investigated by Liverpool Pilots Committee, but their decision has not yet been made public. I also procured an enquiry to be made, before the Liverpool Dock Committee, into the conduct of the crew of the Life Boat, but, although they used no exertion entitling them to praise, they did not seem to have neglected their ordinary duty.[1]

> With high respect
> I have the honor to be
> Your Obed[t] Servant
> Nath[l] Hawthorne

Hon W[m] L Marcy
Secretary of State

1. The testimony of the surviving crew members of the *Confederation* was taken before NH on January 26. According to this, the ship had been proceeding up the channel under the pilot's direction, when Captain Corning asked the pilot, "Isn't there more water nearer the Light Ship? you are too far from it." Shortly thereafter the ship suddenly struck bottom and immediately began breaking up. After futile attempts to tow the *Confederation*, the pilot and captain of the Life Boat told the crew to look out for their lives, and all entered the boat except for the captain, three mates, and four others. It soon became certain that the ship would disintegrate, and two of the mates and two others shipped the *Confederation*'s lifeboat, expecting the others to follow, but had to pull clear of the ship to keep the boat from being crushed. They asked the crew of the steamer *Sea King* to help them return and rescue the captain and others, but "They refused and said they had waited to the last minute with the steamer at the risk of their lives as there was scarcely water left to float her then and they could not remain any longer." As they departed, they could see the vessel going to pieces and "the Mate waving his hands for the steamer to come back but the Captain of her refused" (MS, Marine Extended Protest, NA).

Consulate of the United States

Liverpool 13th February 1857

Sir,

I have the honor to forward herewith a special report of a Society established in Liverpool, for the relief of Foreigners in distress.[1] The Society is composed of the most influential, & intelligent Foreigners residing in Liverpool, & their opinions are entitled to great consideration.

I also enclose a copy of Resolutions adopted at a meeting of American Shipmasters, lately held in Liverpool.[2]

I have on several previous occasions, called your attention to the system of shipping seamen for our merchant service, and the evils resulting;[3] & am constrained to do so again, by the enclosed papers having been forwarded to me—the first mentioned having been also published in the London Times,[4] & the Local newspapers—& by the frequent occurrence of late, of cases of gross cruelty occurring on board our vessels, during the voyage from the United States.[5] Scarcely a vessel arrives from New York, or any of the Southern ports of the US, the Crew of which does not almost entirely consist of persons totally ignorant of the duties for which they shipped—or rather were shipped—mere landsmen. And these persons are subjected to the most revolting treatment at the hands of the officers, and, in very many cases, at the hands of their irritated shipmates. They arrive here almost naked, & in a state of great debility, the result of exposure & illtreatment combined.

Latterly I have been almost daily called upon to investigate complaints made by such persons, of assaults committed upon them by the inferior officers or their shipmates, or of their being plundered of the little clothing they brought on board. A Despatch which accompanies this, will inform you of a recent case of a man (by trade a grocer, never before at sea but once as passenger to America) dying in the Liverpool Hospital, from the effect of ill usage from the 2nd & 3rd mates & Boatswain of his vessel. And unless this fatal result occurs, & in Liverpool, the perpetrators go unpunished, the authorities having no jurisdiction; & the Treaty giving me none, unless I can make out a case of murder, assault with intent to commit murder, or Robbery.

It is not easy to remedy the evil of inefficient manning of our vessels, of which all the other evils are but branches—& when I speak of inefficient manning I include the entire [6] for I am sorry to say the officers need improvement, almost as much as seamen, & are becoming rapidly worse; but if what I have before suggested were done—a competent commission of enquiry instituted—I am sure a remedy would be found. The abolition of the pernicious advance system, & of the Law requiring two thirds Americans; the adoption of a better mode of shipping seamen; & an apprentice system— seem to be obvious.

Something must be done, as our National character & commerce are suffering great damage. I have had it from good authority that the rates of Insurance by American vessels have been materially increased, because of the inefficient crews they are known to have.

To carry out an apprentice system, an International arrangement would be necessary to reclaim deserters; For this no Treaty would be needed, as the merchant shipping act,[7] which I had the honor to forward at the time of its passage, contains a provision similar to our own Reciprocity Act—that on satisfactory evidence being given of facilities being granted for the arrest of deserters from British ships in any foreign country, Her Majesty may issue proclamation for like facilities being granted in England in favor of that country.

To put a stop to the violence & thieving on board ships on the high seas; and to remedy the mode of shipping seamen on this side, a Treaty would be necessary. In the first case to give the magistrates jurisdiction in all offences below those provided for in the Treaty. In the other to compel the seaman when shipped, to fulfil his contract, which would enable captains to dispense with shipping masters. And I submit whether there can be any national objection to giving the English local courts jurisdiction in minor offences, on the written application of the National Representative, & with the proviso that the accused should have the right of being tried by a Jury of his own countrymen.[8] It would certainly be vastly beneficial to our Commerce.

> With high respect
> I have the honor to be
> Your obed^t Servant
> Nathl Hawthorne.

Hon W^m L Marcy
Secretary of State

[*Another version in HW's hand:*]

> Consulate of the United States
> Liverpool 14 February 1857

Sir,

I have the honor to forward herewith a special report lately made by a society established in Liverpool for the relief of Foreigners in distress. The society is composed of the most influential and intelligent foreigners residing in Liverpool & their opinions are entitled to great consideration.

I also enclose a copy of resolutions adopted at a meeting of American Shipmasters lately held in Liverpool.

I have on several previous occasions called your attention to the system of Shipping Seamen for our merchant service and the evils resulting, & am constrained to do so again by the before mentioned papers having been forwarded to me (the first mentioned having also been published in the London Times & Local newspapers) & from the frequent occurrence of late of cases of gross cruelty occurring on board our vessels during the voyage from the US to Liverpool. Scarcely [MS blurred] from the US the Crew of which does not almost altogether consist [MS blurred] for which they shipped or rather [MS blurred] —mere landsmen. [MS blurred] shipmates [MS blurred] great debility [MS blurred] Latterly I have been [MS blurred] called on to investigate complaints made by such persons of assaults committed upon them by the inferior officers, or their Shipmates, or of their being plundered of the little clothing they brought on board.

A Despatch which accompanies this will inform you of a recent case of a man (by trade a Grocer & never before at sea except as a passenger to America) dying in the Liverpool Hospital, in consequence of ill usage received from the 2nd & 3^d mates & Boatswain of his vessel.

And unless this fatal result takes place, & in Liverpool, the perpetrators go unpunished, the authorities having no jurisdiction & the Treaty giving me none, unless I can make out a case of murder or assault with intent to commit murder or Robbery.

It would not be easy to say what would be the best [MS blurred] remedying the evils [MS blurred] manning our vessels, of which all the other evils are but branches—& [MS blurred] I speak of inefficient manning, I include the [MS blurred] the [MS blurred] for I am sorry to say the [MS blurred] Ships are almost equally in need of improvement with the seamen and are becoming [MS blurred]

[MS blurred] speedily, as our [MS blurred] commerce are

suffering great damage from the present system. I have it from good authority that the rates of Insurance by American vessels have been materially increased because of the inefficient crews they are known to have.

To carry out an apprentice system an International arrangement would be necessary to reclaim deserters, for this no Treaty is necessary as the Merchant Shipping Act, which I had the honor to forward at the time of its passage, contains a clause similar to our own Reciprocity Clause "that on satisfactory evidence being given of facilities being granted for the arrest of deserters in any foreign country Her Majesty may issue her proclamation for like facilities to be granted in England in favor of that country."

To put a stop to the violence & thieving on board ships on the high seas & to remedy the mode of shipping Seamen on this side, a Treaty would be necessary. In the first case to give the magistrates on this side Jurisdiction in all offences below those provided for in the Treaty. In the other to compel the Seamen when shipped to fulfill his contract, which would enable Captains to dispense with shipping masters. And I submit whether there can be any objection to [*MS blurred*] the English [*MS blurred*] courts jurisdiction in [*MS blurred*] National Representative [*MS blurred*] accused should have [*MS blurred*] certainly be vastly [*MS blurred*]

I am with High Respect
Your obedient Servant

1. NH enclosed a printed copy of "Special Report of the Managing Committee to the Members of the Society of Friends of Foreigners in Distress." Adopted at a meeting held on February 4, 1857, it was signed by F. Prange, Vice-President, and Edmund Pictet, Honorary Secretary. It read: "¶Ever since the foundation of the 'LIVERPOOL SOCIETY OF FRIENDS OF FOREIGNERS IN DISTRESS,' in 1851, the attention of the Committee has repeatedly been called to the sufferings inflicted upon Foreigners by the system in force at some of the ports of the United States for supplying the American mercantile marine with sailors. A large portion of the resources of the

Society has been applied to the relief of the victims of this evil system. ¶ But the evil has reached of late to such magnitude, and threatens such rapid increase, that the committee consider the sphere of their action ought no longer to be confined to the granting of assistance to the sufferers, but that it has become their duty to appeal to the authorities of both countries, in the hope that steps may be taken to attack the evil at its root. ¶ Hundreds of poor men of all nations are annually cast amongst us from the cause mentioned, in an utterly wretched condition, not only destitute of money and clothing, but too often in a ruined state of health from the revolting usage they receive on board the American vessels. Some of them have been carried off by force or strategem, leaving behind parents, wives, and children; others are enticed by the promise of good wages; and the great majority are turned away entirely destitute on their arrival in England. ¶ These are grave charges, and the Society must of course be expected to substantiate them; with this view the Committee have extracted from their books a list of cases which they have examined during the last year; they amount to 79, and since the beginning of the new year they have already had 27 cases. Only 37 of these have shipped of their own accord, whilst the remaining 69 had been brought over against their will. With two exceptions, they all complained of having been repeatedly and grossly assaulted and ill-treated during the voyage, and the fact that 82 of them were either obliged, on their arrival, to be sent to the hospital, or otherwise received medical assistance, sufficiently corroborates their complaints. ¶ All sorts of contrivances, it appears, are resorted to at New York to obtain Seamen for the American Packet Ships; for instance—the New York shipping agents advertise in English and in German, for 'young men who need not have been at sea before, to work as deck-labourers at fixed wages:' under this pretext they are decoyed on board, and when once there they are retained by force. Others engage of their own accord as ordinary seamen, cooks, carpenters, &c., but are alike deceived; others again are enticed into public houses, made drunk, and thus betrayed on board. It is on record that many have been offered work on board a steamer in the river, or to unload ships, and are thus prevailed upon to step into a small boat to be carried on board, which leaves them as soon as they are put on the deck of the ship, where they are retained forcibly. ¶ Amongst the applicants for relief there have been coopers, carpenters, cooks, waiters, clerks, and surgeons, who have been carried off in this nefarious way. Very soon after they are on board they are robbed of most of their effects, and there is no redress to be obtained; their remonstrances are laughed at or answered by ill-treatment, and the same means are employed to force them to go aloft and to do all that able seamen are expected to do. ¶ The cruelties which are practised upon these poor unprotected men on board of these ships would be incredible had they not been of late frequently confirmed by the proceedings in the Liverpool Police Court; but unfortunately, in redress for these ferocious assaults, committed upon the high seas, there is no practical remedy for these poor men on their arrival in this country. It has been proved in that court that on board of the 'Ocean Monarch' men have been forced to draw with their teeth iron nails from the deck into which they had been driven for that purpose, to the depth of two inches; that they have been compelled literally to lick up the dust from the deck of the cabin floor; and at the inquest held upon a Dutchman who had been beaten to death by the third mate and the boatswain of the 'Guy Mannering,' the surgeon who made the post mortem examination deposed 'that the head presented an enormously contused mass, the face was completely battered in, and there were from 70 to 80 contused wounds upon the feet, legs, thighs, and the back.' The hospitals of Liverpool record numerous instances of the lamentable condition in which the majority of these victims of savage ferocity are brought in. ¶ It may, perhaps, be pleaded in extenuation, that these men ship under false pretences as able seamen, and that when they are found on board to be only landsmen, the officers feel so annoyed and disappointed that they give vent to their vexation in ill-treatment. Although this would form no excuse whatever for the barbarous cruelties practised,

yet even this will not avail, for the shipping masters who are employed by the owners
to procure a crew, and who must be supposed to enjoy and to retain their confidence,
are perfectly aware of the condition and the quality of the men they engage at the
wages of 20 and 30 dollars per month; moreover, it is stated in a recent case heard
in the Liverpool Court, that two Germans and a Frenchman, who were decoyed on
board of the 'Albert Gallatin,' when the crew were mustered on deck, were objected
to as not being on the muster roll, and were proposed to be sent on shore; the first
mate, however, prevented this being done, stating that he would rather have these
three foreigners than three seamen already on the roll, no doubt thinking that the
former would prove the cheaper men, it being the practice in all cases that have been
brought before the Society, including the one in question, to turn off such unhappy
fellows on their arrival without paying them anything. Of the many cases which
have come under the notice of the Society it would be difficult to find any men that
could have passed themselves off as sailors, their outward appearance rendering it
impossible for them to impose upon the practised judgment of a seaman or shipping
master. ¶ It is, however, but justice, to exonerate the majority of the captains from
any participation in the actual ill-treatment; this has been generally practised by the
mates, boatswains, and crews. ¶ That such a system is fraught with the most
dangerous consequences to the shipping interest must be self-evident—an incompetent crew will always endanger the safety of a vessel; but it is in behalf of
Humanity that the Society have taken up this subject, and in that behalf they plead
forcibly, earnestly, and urgently, that the proper authorities should devise means for
putting an end to a system which, by its barbarity and cruelty, must prove a disgrace
to civilised nature" (Enclosure, Despatches, 13, NA). On February 12, John
Thomas Towson, secretary of the Liverpool Local Marine Board, sent a copy of the
Society's report to the Board of Trade, adding "I am directed to state that this Local
Board of their own knowledge can assure my Lords of the accuracy of the general
statement made in that Report, and to request that my Lords will consider whether
by any power of influence which they possess they could aid in checking so great an
evil" (Transcript, F.O. 5 / 684, PRO). James Booth forwarded the report on
February 23 to the Foreign Office, noting "My Lords are not aware that any thing
can be done in the matter but think it right to send the Papers for Lord Clarendon's
information" (MS, F.O. 5 / 684, PRO). The following day Clarendon noted on this
letter that Sir Francis Napier, newly appointed Minister to the United States, "must
be told." On February 27 the report was sent on to him with instructions "to take
such steps in this matter as you may think expedient" (Transcript, F.O. 5 / 684,
PRO). See C223.1.

2. The meeting was held on the evening of January 30 at the Royal Hotel; NH
presided and made a speech (943). Its resolutions deplored the recent public outcry
over shipboard abuses but dismissed allegations that negroes had been entrapped in
order to transport and sell them in a slave state [see C218.4], or that landsmen had
been offered "a bonus of $20 given them as an inducement to take a *free* passage" [see
n. 4 below] as "so absurd that they are hardly worth refuting." Nevertheless, the
ship masters conceded "That the present system of enlisting seamen has been from
its commencement the main and sole cause of the many and painful troubles which
occur in the River Mersey and on the outward passage from this port. . . . It is a
lamentable fact that both Masters and Seamen have been equally the dupes of *Land
Sharks*. We can find no better name for them. The one paying good money for
spurious material, and the other being robbed of his wages both at the commencement of the voyage and at the end. We therefore beg that, until some treaty of
reciprocity may be acomplished between H. B. Majesty's Government and the
United States, that we may be permitted to ship our crews through the regularly
appointed Shipping Agent at this port, or if that cannot be, that with the sanction
of the authorities we may be constituted our own Shipping Agents, that our seamen
may be shipped on board, thereby enabling the captain to examine the qualifications

of applicants. We also most humbly beg that the authorities of this port will represent our case to H. B. Majesty's government, that a treaty of reciprocity may be hastened with the United States, to fully meet the wants of this subject, and protect the immense commercial interest between the two countries." The ship masters also resolved to urge their employers in the United States to lobby for "a system of marine laws . . . that will efficiently protect their interest, as also the seamen who sail their ships." Particularly, they endorsed a system in which the government would appoint men of character and experienced shipping agents, making them "only responsible to the Government alone." They recommended "that the system of advances should be entirely abolished by inserting a clause in the [underwriters'] policy that any ship which pays advance wages shall, if lost, forfeit her insurance." Finally, they proposed a law imposing a fine for landlords allowing any seaman to be taken on board in a state of intoxication. In conclusion, the ship masters resolved "That copies of the foregoing Resolutions shall be sent to the Government of the United States, humbly soliciting that notice may be taken of it, and that we request the American Consul, Mr. Nathaniel Hawthorne, to forward the same" (Enclosure, Despatches, 13, NA).

3. See especially C51, Queries II.8, and C94. Compare also NH's letter of the same date to Bridge: "I have already, on more than one occasion, drawn the attention of the State Department to this subject. . . . The evil is now so great that it must soon be recognized and remedied; or we shall not be able to sail our ships" (946).

4. February 9, 1857, 12:6.

5. The immediate cause of these reports were public outcry over the death of a seaman aboard the *Guy Mannering* on January 14 (see note 1 above and C206) and the mutiny aboard the *James S. Bogart* on January 19 (C218). In addition, on January 26 the chief mate of the *Albert Gallatin* was tried for enticing foreigners on board the ship by "intimating . . . that they might obtain $20 a month merely as landsmen or 'deck labourers.' This money was received by the shippers, and it appeared that during the passage a system of cruelty had been practiced" (Liverpool *Mercury*, January 26, 3:4). During the trial, John Bridge Aspinall (1818–86), who represented the seamen "on behalf of the Society for the Protection of Foreigners in Distress," accused NH of "apathetic conduct . . . in regard to this class of cases in general, and ventured to assert that if these repeated acts of brutality were only properly represented to the United States' Government and people the American nation and mercantile marine would cease to be scandalized by their recurrence" (London *Times*, January 26, 9:1). On the same day, NH complained to Bennoch, "There is the devil to pay, just now, in my Consulate; and I am overwhelmed with an avalanche of mutiny, murder, and shipwreck . . . " (941). On January 31 NH commented to Ticknor, "I have had all sorts of trouble in my Consulate, lately;—indeed, I always do, but now more than ever. The Liverpool philanthropists are aroused about the enormities on board of our ships, and would like to have me run a-muck with them against the American shipmasters; and as I choose to take my own view of my own duty, they censure me pretty harshly" (943).

6. See Textual Note.

7. The act in question actually was The Foreign Deserters Act of 1852; NH corrected this error in C209.

8. This solution proved unacceptable to the American government, and no legal resolution was reached in NH's lifetime. In 1859, when Sir Richard Monckton Milnes (1809–85) raised the issue again (see 1044), the London *Times* commented, "Public opinion in America looks with singular indifference on deeds of violence, while there is the most extreme sensitiveness about any invasion of their national rights. Americans generally would rather allow Germans or mulattoes to be beaten by drunken captains to all eternity than recognize the claim of a British Court to punish an offence which does not fall within its jurisdiction. And yet this is the only

way in which the thing could be managed. . . . The plan of a mutual jurisdiction, by which offences committed on board the ships of either country should be tried at whatever port should be first reached after the commission of the act, would satisfy Englishmen perfectly, and their only fear would be that American tribunals would deal too leniently with our own ruffians; but that Americans would agree to this, and give the Judges of Assize for Lancashire jurisdiction over all American shipping entering the port of Liverpool is, as we said before, a matter of which we have very little hope" (August 3, 1859, 8:5–6). Compare NH's comments in *OOH*: "there will be no possibility of dealing effectually with these troubles as long as we deem it inconsistent with our national dignity or interests to allow the English courts, under such restrictions as may seem fit, a jurisdiction over offences perpetrated on board our vessels in mid-ocean" (pp. 33–34).

Consulate of the United States
Liverpool 13 Febry 1857

Gentlemen,

I am painfully conscious of the evils of the present system of shipping Seamen for the American merchant service, from the cases almost daily coming before me, of men, who, having been put on board vessels as seamen, have been subjected to the most cruel treatment at the hands of their irritated officers and shipmates, & plundered of their clothing.

I am glad the subject has enlisted your attention, & that you have determined to use your influence in procuring a remedy. American Ship owners can do much, as the prime source of the evil lies in the advance system of shipping seamen, & the want of a nursery for seamen.

At the same time it must be admitted the Laws on the subject want revising, & this will no doubt be attended to by our Government.

To put an end to the violence committed by officers & Seamen, & now so painfully common, some international arrangement is necessary, to give the magistrates jurisdiction. Such an arrangement is also needed to reclaim deserters, and to compel seamen shipped here to fulfil the contract they enter into; this would enable Masters to dispense with the services of unlicensed shipping masters.

This would also enable Seamen to be shipped through the sailors' Home.

I am very Respectfully
Your faithful Servant
Nath¹ Hawthorne

Messʳˢ Rathbone Broˢ & Co

1. William Rathbone, Sr. (1787–1868) was a former mayor of Liverpool and an eminent philanthropist and benefactor. His son, William Rathbone, Jr. (1819–85) was likewise an active philanthropist and champion of the lower classes (*DNB*). An influential member of the American Chamber of Commerce, the younger Rathbone was a social acquaintance of NH, who may have used him as a source for information in compiling C51 (Mays, pp. 79–80).

Consulate of the United States
Liverpool February 14th 1857

Sir

On the 16th Ult° a Coroners Jury found a verdict of Manslaughter against the 2nd and 3rd Mates and Boatswain of the American Ship Guy Mannering in the case of a man name unknown who died in the Liverpool Hospital from the ill usage received during the voyage from New York to Liverpool[2]

On this verdict the 3rd Mate Henry D Cutting and the Boatswain John Lewis were committed to Gaol and are to be tried at the next Liverpool Assizes to be holden in March   The 2nd Mate escaped and cannot be found

The Magistrates have always been of opinion that they had no Jurisdiction in such cases and were confirmed in that view by the English Secretary of State in a letter in reply some time since addressed to the Mayor of Liverpool[3]   The Coroner however contends that the death occurring in Liverpool gives Jurisdiction and is supported in that view by the Judges[4]

The case particularly as against the Boatswain at present seems a very bad one in which the perpetrators should not escape punishment   If the authorities here have no Jurisdiction they must certainly escape as I could not obtain their surrender to send them to the United States for trial the Treaty not including Manslaughter

In a despatch accompanying this I have ventured to make some suggestions on the subject of Jurisdiction in such cases

With high respect
I have the honour to be
Your Obedient Servant
Nath[l] Hawthorne.

Honorable W L Marcy
Secretary of State

1. This letter is the first of four (also C220, C238, C239) drafted by an unidentified second clerk. The text preserves his characteristic spellings and lack of punctuation.

2. The *Guy Mannering*, Captain Dollerd, arrived on the morning of January 14, and the seaman, a young Dutchman known only as "George," was removed to the Northern Hospital in a state of insensibility. He died later that day. His body, according to the Liverpool *Mercury*, presented "a frightful spectacle; the head and face appear to be 'mashed to a mummy,' the nose completely flattened and crushed, and the skull evidently fractured. Down to the extremities scarcely an inch of space appears between the bruises, cuts, and sores" (January 14, 1857 [second edition], 4:6). (See also C205.1.) At the inquest, evidence suggested that the deceased "had been a grocer, was put on board in a state of intoxication in New York as an able seaman, according to a very common practice which prevails among shipping agents at that port, and it is supposed that he had not previously been at sea." Other members of the crew had seen Lewis and Cutting, with John Carswell, the second mate, beat the deceased around the head and shoulders with a rope's end "until he could scarcely stand up. He was several times knocked down, and whilst down the second and third mates kicked him with their heavy sea boots about the head, sides, and all over his body." Lewis, when apprehended, admitted that "he had struck the deceased many a time, and asked the officer 'Do you think they will hang me?'" William B. Wall, surgeon of the Northern Hospital, confirmed that death was caused by congestion of the brain caused by the beatings, and the jury returned a verdict of manslaughter against the three officers. In addition they "expressed their indignation at the conduct of the captain in allowing the unfortunate deceased to be murdered by piecemeal day after day, and trusted that in future he would consider it to be his duty to repress such inhumanity" (Liverpool *Mercury*, January 16, 1857, 6:3).

3. See C156.1.

4. Lewis and Cutting were tried at the Spring Assizes, but Curry's contention of jurisdiction was overturned by a Court of Appeal; see C220.

Consulate of the United States
Liverpool 23 Febry 1857

Dear Sir,

The bearer William H Huntress is supposed to have been left behind by Capt Thomas H C Barstow of the Ship America of New York in violation of the Act of 23^{d} March 1825 sect 10. Depositions of himself & a witness, with my certificate, in the case, will be sent to the Secretary of State.[1]

I am
Your Obed^{t} servant
Nathl Hawthorne.

United States Attorney
for the Southern District
of New York

1. See C210.

Consulate of the United States
Liverpool 27th Februy 1857

Sir,

The present is to correct an error in my Despatch 83 dated
14 Febry. On the subject of reclaiming deserters, I refer to
the "Merchant Shipping Act" it should be "The Foreign
Deserters Act 1852."

Herewith I have the honor to enclose two pamphlets
Board's orders. Pages 16. 17. 18 of that for Febry–March
1856 contains an order in Council extending the benefit of
the Act to Chilian vessels.¹ On 28 July (pamphlet for August
pgs 11–12) another order is promulgated in lieu of the
preceding, the only difference being the omission in the latter
of the words "not being British subjects." No doubt it was
found that the Crews of Chilian vessels coming here, like our
own, were composed principally of persons who, according to
the English notion, are British subjects, & that the order was
consequently practically inoperative. The omission might be
obtained in favor of American vessels, with such a late
precedent.

With High Respect
Your obed Servt
Nathl Hawthorne.

Hon W^m L Marcy

1. The Order in Council, adopted on February 25, 1856, stated that "whereas it hath been made to appear to Her Majesty that due facilities will be given for recovering and apprehending Seamen who desert from British Merchant Ships in the territories belonging to the Republic of Chile . . . it is hereby ordered and declared that . . . Seamen, not being slaves, and not being British subjects, who desert from Merchant Ships belonging to subjects of the Republic of Chile, within Her Majesty's dominions, or the territories of the East India Company, shall be liable to be apprehended and carried on board their respective Ships" (Enclosure, Despatches, 13, NA).

United States Consulate
Liverpool 6th March 1857

Sir,

A penalty is supposed to have been incurred by Thomas H
C Barstow of New York commander of the ship America for
a violation of the tenth section of the Act of 3 Mar 1825 (V
4 U S Stat at Large pp 117) for leaving William Huntress a
seaman behind unlawfully and for which he is liable to be
prosecuted in my name as consul of the United States for this
Port.[2]

You, or the proper law officers of the United States, are
authorised, at their proper costs and charges, to institute in
my name a suit to recover the same for their use and benefit
and the same to control and to discharge according to Law in
such court having jurisdiction thereof as you or he shall deem
proper.

Witness my hand and consular seal
Nath[l] Hawthorne

Hon the Secretary of State

1. NH knew that Marcy had left office with Pierce on March 4, but had not yet
learned who would be his successor. Word of Lewis Cass's appointment and
confirmation arrived in England on March 21.

2. According to NH's certificate, Huntress applied to the Consulate on December

31 "in a very sickly condition" and claimed he could not obtain medical aid on the *America*. NH sent him to the hospital and informed Captain Barstow, who promised that Huntress would receive proper care if released to him. The following day, however, Huntress again applied to NH, claiming "that he had been taken from the Hosp[l] to DeCostas Shipping Office where he was requested to sign articles for another vessel. . . . " Huntress refused and was sent to a boarding house. When contacted, Barstow disclaimed knowledge of the proceedings and again promised to see that Huntress was taken on board. On January 26, Barstow claimed his ship's papers, stating that Huntress had been removed from the hospital, but five days later, after the ship had cleared, Huntress returned to the consulate, claiming that he had merely been moved to a boarding house and never taken on board (MS, Marine Extended Protest, 4, NA).

C211. TO MURRAY MCCONNEL AND WILLIAM L. MARCY, WASHINGTON

Consulate of the United States
Liverpool 7 March 1857

Sir,

With this by Steamer Africa I have the honor to forward the accounts of this Consulate for the Quarter ending 30th September 1856—viz

Disbursements for destitute Seamen ————£151.5.9
    at Exchange of 47³/₄[d] p $ ————————$760.39
For postages Newspapers &[c] ——————£40.12.8
    at Exchange of 47³/₄[d] p $ ————————$204.23

Very respectfully
Your obed[t] Servant

Murray M[c]Connell Esq
5th Auditor of the Treasury
Washington

Consulate of the United States
Liverpool 6 March 1857

Sir,

I have the honor to inform you that I shall forward by the Steamer sailing for New York to-morrow, to the 5th Auditor of the Treasury, the Accounts of this Consulate for the Quarter ending 30 September 1856 viz

For disbursements for dest: Seamen ————————£151.5.9
at Exchange 47³/₄ᵈ p $ ————————————$760.39
For postages Newspapers &ᶜ ————————£40.12.8
at Exchange 47³/₄ᵈ p $ ————————————$204.23

With high respect
I have the honor to be
Your Obed Servant
Nathˡ Hawthorne

Honorable Wᵐ L Marcy
Secretary of State
Washington
D.C

Consulate of the United States
Liverpool 10th March 1857

Gentlemen,

I have this day placed to your credit, with Mess[rs] Glynn Mills & Co, the sum of Two thousand and sixty eight pounds Ten shillings & Threepence (2068.10.3) sterling, being money due to the United States, & which you will please hold subject to the draft of the Secretary of the Treasury.

I enclose forms of receipt in triplicate, which please sign & return to me.[1]

I am Gentlemen
Your Obed Servant
Nath[l] Hawthorne

Mess[rs] Baring Bro[s] & Co
London

1. The Consulate's copybook contains a transcript of this receipt, dated March 11 (CO, 13A, 14, NA).

Consulate of the United States
Liverpool 13 March 1857

Sir,

I have the honor to forward herewith transcript of the Record of Treasury Fees of this Consulate for the quarter ending 30th Septem^r last, together with an account of fees shewing a Balance due the United States on the Quarter of $5633.36.[1]

I also forward an account current to 30 September shewing a total balance due from me to the United States on 1 Oct° of $9974.82.

In compliance with your instructions of 27 Aug, I have paid this total balance, in sterling £2068.10.3 @ 108½ per cent Exchange, to Messrs Baring Brothers & Co, whose receipt I herewith enclose.

I also forward duplicate of their receipt for £2050.3.5 paid for your draft of 27 Aug for $10500.

I am with high respect
Your obed^t Servt

Hon James Guthrie Esq

1. The Consulate collected a total of $7508.36 during this period; NH deducted only his salary (U.S. Treasury Fees, 1, NA).

Consulate of the United States
Liverpool 27 March 1857

Sir,

On the 14th Ulto I had the honor to forward copies of the Resolutions adopted at a meeting of American Shipmasters, and a Report of the Society for the relief of distressed foreigners in Liverpool, with reference to the mode of shipping seamen in American vessels and their treatment on board.

I have now the honor to forward a Report on the same subject since made by the American Chamber of Commerce, with the view of inducing American shipowners to move in the matter.[1]

I also enclose copies of depositions made before me, relating to the death of a man named Daniel M[c]Kay on board the Ship Wandering Jew, which occurred the day after crossing the Bar of the Mississippi, & was no doubt accelerated, if not occasioned, by the brutal treatment received from the first & third mates of the vessel, Kingsbury N Miller & W[m] W Owen, who both absconded as soon as the vessel entered the Mersey.[2]

The evidence not being such as would sustain a charge of murder, the two persons could not be given up under the provisions of the Treaty, but on being assured by the Police authorities that they would not object, if I chose to arrest the accused and send them back on my own responsibility, I employed officers to capture and put them on board a vessel, but up to this time they have not been found.

I am satisfied the Police could have found them had they

been very desirous of so doing, but acting without any evidence of legal authority made them lukewarm.

The case strongly shews the necessity for, either an extension of the provisions of the Treaty to all criminal offences, or an International arrangement, as I have before suggested,[3] for their trial in this country.

I am with high respect
Your obedient Servant
Nath[l] Hawthorne

Hon The Secretary of State
Washington

1. The American Chamber of Commerce had formed a subcommittee to deal with the abuses rising from the American shipping system. In March the subcommittee reported "that after conferring with the American Consul they have come to the conclusion that the evils arising out of the present system may to some extent be remedied by International arrangements between this Country and the United States and that it is desirable that steps should be taken without delay to induce the Governments of the two Countries to agree upon the necessary measures. ¶ [*Heading:*] —The chief points to be had in view appear to be— ¶ 1. To give the authorities of Great Britain subject in every case to the sanction of the American Minister or Consul jurisdiction over Seamen belonging to the American Vessels in British ports in cases of desertion refusal to work &c to the same extent as they now have in the case of British Seamen and to confer similar jurisdiction on the authorities of the United States in regard to Seamen belonging to British Vessels. . . . ¶ 2. To legalize the Shipping of Crews for American Vessels in British Ports in the manner now in use for British Vessels and to procure the passing of a law in the United States providing safeguards against the abuses of the system now prevalent there[.] ¶ 3. To give the authorities in Great Britain subject in every case to the sanction of the American Minister or Consul similar jurisdiction over offences committed at Sea on board American Vessels to that now exercised in cases occurring on board British Ships and vice versa with regard to British Vessels in American ports. ¶ The Sub-Committee would add that they are of opinion that the present System of making large advances to Seamen shipping in American Vessels is attended with very bad results both to the Shipowner and to the Seaman[.] How far the practice in question may be necessary to procure Seamen the Committee do not pretend to judge but they consider it probable that it is maintained more by the Shipping Masters for their own purposes than by the men who in the great majority

of cases derive but little benefit from the advance[.]" Following this report, the Chamber of Commerce resolved, on March 12, "to call the attention of the Chambers of Commerce at New York and other ports in the United States and of the Owners and Masters of American Vessels to the System alleged to be commonly practised for obtaining Crews and to the treatment of Seamen on board those Vessels. . . . pending the consideration of international arrangements on this subject the Chamber knowing that their views will be cordially reciprocated in the United States venture to appeal earnestly to the mercantile Bodies above mentioned to all American Shipowners and especially to Masters of American Vessels by whom the evils in question are severely felt to cooperate with them in repressing by all means in their power a system leading to results disgraceful to humanity and tending at once to tarnish the honor of the national Flag and to bring disrepute on the American Merchant Service" (MSS, Liverpool Public Libraries).

2. NH took depositions in this case on February 26. According to these, the *Wandering Jew* left New Orleans on January 16, at which time "the crew were mostly all drunk and the mates were hitting all round. . . . " According to Edward Moore, a seaman, Daniel McKay was beaten severely by the first and third mates when the ship was still in the Mississippi; "I dont know what for   They beat him with their hands and kicked him   He was afterwards standing at a tub washing the blood off when they came and said damn you why dont you wash yourself and they lifted him up and put him into it   they then carried him into the Forecastle and left him in his bunk in his wet clothes[.]" McKay died two days later; Augustus Luce, the ship's carpenter, recalled, "I saw him ten minutes before he died on deck near the Forecastle door   He could not speak so as to be understood   He was sitting down   I thought he had a fit[.]" Luce also noted that "The Captain was sick for about a fortnight so he couldn't get out" (MSS, Marine Extended Protest, 4, 111, NA).

3. In C205.

Consulate USA
Liverpool 27 March 1857

Sir,

James C Mathews was discharged sick on the 25 July from the Sarah G Hyde, & died on the 11th Aug. After payment of his expenses there was a balance remaining, which is payable to you, of $41.53. For this you should apply to the fourth Auditor of the Treasury at Washington.

The clothing was of trifling value, & having come out of a fever Hospital, I could neither dispose of it, nor induce any Captain to take it to the US. I therefore gave it away.

I am
Your obed Serv[t]
Nath[l] Hawthorne.

M[r] Jas F. Matthews
Brunswick
Me

---

1. According to U.S. Census records, James F. Mathews, 56, was a farmer at Brunswick. At that time his youngest son, James C., 15, was still living with him.

Consulate of the United States
Liverpool 2 April 1857

Gentlemen,

In reply to your Letter of yesterday, I beg to inform you, that my opinion is, that on satisfactory evidence being adduced to the Collector of the Port in the United States, where the Wools in question may arrive, that they had been shipped at Taganrog[1] with the bona fide intention of having them transported to a port in the United States, they would be entitled to entry at the *market value in the principal markets of Russia* at the date of exportation.

I am
Your obed[t] Servant

Mess[rs] Browne Shipley & Co

1. A Russian port on the Black Sea.

Consulate of the United States
Liverpool 2nd April 1857

Sir,

I beg to acknowledge the "Extract from the North Dock Division Report Book of the 31st Ulto," concerning the colored American Seaman Anthy Dubre, & to thank you for your kindness in sending it.

An order has been sent to the Hospital for the man's admission as an American seaman.

You will have the goodness to direct the Cabman to apply at this Office for the fare, if not already paid by the Captain.

I am
Your obed[t] Servant

Capt Greig
Head Constable

1. Captain (later Major) John James Greig (d. 1882) was Head of the Liverpool Police Force 1855–81 (Boase).

Consulate of the United States
Liverpool 16th April 1857

Sir,

On the 3^d Inst at the Chester Assizes a man named Campbell, by birth an Irishman, was convicted of shooting and wounding James Christie, a colored Seaman, on board the American Ship James L Bogart in this Port, & was sentenced to transportation for Life.

The Sentence is a severe one, but the circumstances of the case were of a peculiarly aggravated character.

The J L Bogart had shipped a colored crew at this port for Mobile, cleared for Sea, & anchored in the River, on Saturday the 17 Jany. The second mate, the man Campbell, was also shipped at Liverpool. As is commonly the case the Crew were not on board when the vessel went out of dock, & when subsequently got on board, were mostly in a state of intoxication. Two refused to go on board at all, & to supply their places, it appears from the evidence, that Christie & another were inveigled on board on the Sunday evening by a Shipping Agent under the pretence that she was an English vessel going to Antigua, & that on discovering the truth they refused to work, but were compelled to do so by the mates.

Early on Monday morning intelligence was brought from the vessel that a mutiny had occurred on board, that one of the Crew was shot and the chief mate badly wounded. After communicating with the Captain of the vessel (who was on shore & ignorant of what had been taking place) I sent off a body of Police. The wounded men were brought ashore &

placed in the Hospital.[1] The Crew were arrested on a charge of mutiny, & the 2nd mate on a charge of shooting Christie.

These charges were subsequently brought before the magistrates at Birkenhead, who dismissed the charge of mutiny, so far as it related to refusal of duty, as being one they were advised did not come within their jurisdiction, but remanded Jeremiah Jones one of the Seamen on the charge of assaulting the chief mate, Cha[s] S Furber, & committed Campbell, the second mate, for Trial for shooting Christie.[2]

The evidence of the Pilot & others shewed, that from the time of the vessel anchoring in the River, to the occurrences on Monday morning, the Crew had endured the most brutal usage from the two mates Furber & Campbell; & when at last they were driven to refuse work, they committed no violence until attacked by the mates with Pistols & other weapons, & that then they did no more than was necessary for self defense: The injury on the mate being by a blow with a weapon he himself had been using.[3]

The chief mate died in the Hospital on the 14th February, & a coroner's jury returned a verdict of justifiable homicide against Jerem[h] Jones.[4]

The severity of the punishment meted to Campbell will have a salutary effect in staying the acts of violence, now so common on board vessels.[5] He was well known for his brutality in former vessels. On board the Ship in which he came to Liverpool, a man had been found hanging dead in the Forecastle, under circumstances so suspicious that I demanded Campbell's surrender on a charge of murder & he was arrested under a warrant from the English Secretary of State.[6] The evidence proved gross cruelty, but the magistrates were of opinion that it did not warrant a committal for Trial on a charge of murder, & discharged him.

Furber the chief mate was also a man of very violent character, & was discharged from his last vessel for ill using the Crew. He was a native of New Hampshire, where he has respectable connexions, who have been informed of his death.[7]

> With high respect
> I have the honor to be
> Your Obed[t] Servant
> Nath[l] Hawthorne.

Hon Lewis Cass
Secretary of State

1. According to the Liverpool *Mercury*, "shortly after nine o'clock the report of firearms was heard on board, and soon after a flag of distress was seen floating from one of the masts, which had been hoisted by Joseph Harrison, the pilot in charge of the vessel." NH was informed, and he arranged to have a group of six officers dispatched to the ship to arrest the mutineers. "On board the officers found everything was quiet, and the crew looking over the side of the vessel, but on going to the forecastle deck they discovered a large pool of blood, a handspike, and part of an iron pump, also besmeared with blood. . . . The second mate was below, and upon being questioned by the officers he said, 'I shot him (Christie), and I am only sorry that the bullet did not go through his head and blow his brains out.' . . . The appearance of the crew indicated that a desperate affray had taken place, or that they had been the subjects of brutal treatment, as nearly the whole of them bore cuts and bruises" (January 21, 1857 [second edition], 2:6).

2. On January 20 the case was heard at the Birkenhead police court. Captain Conway preferred charges against the crew, who were represented by solicitors "retained by a well-known philanthropic gentleman of Liverpool" (*Mercury*). HW appeared for the Consulate. After evidence had been given, the magistrates dismissed the charge of mutiny, but asked the captain and HW if they wished to prefer any other charges. "The secretary to the American consul said that the charge was for an assault upon the chief mate, who now was at the point of death. Then there was a charge against Peter Campbell, the second mate, for shooting one of the men" (*Mercury*). After reexamination of witnesses, the magistrates remanded Campbell, along with the three crew members who had used deadly weapons (i.e., shearing knives).

3. Joseph Harrison, the pilot, testified at the hearing that abuse of the crew had begun on the evening they began to arrive on deck. "One of the men was put in irons; he was struck and kicked first, and then lashed between decks. On Sunday, the crew behaved themselves well, and he (the pilot) did not hear an insolent word from one of them; but, notwithstanding that, they were all (with the exception of three) locked up on Sunday night." The pilot concluded that "Every one of the crew, as he came on board . . . was illtreated by the officers." The cabin boy, James

Maharey, testified that on the morning of January 19 "the crew were ordered to their duty; the men replied that they would not work, as they were not going to Mobile, and they would not be abused. The first and second mates then procured pistols and a cutlass, and the crew seized handspikes and other weapons, and a dreadful struggle followed." On recall, the pilot added that the crew had initially "offered no violence, but simply reasoned with the mates about their being shipped for Mobile." Furber then fired over their heads, while Campbell shot directly at the men, wounding Christie, who nevertheless managed to knock Furber down with a handspike. Members of the crew then grabbed Furber's pistol and cutlass, and Campbell, his pistol jammed, retreated below deck.

4. Furber suffered a fractured skull in the affray and was not expected to live. He did survive this wound, however, but later suffered an attack of pleurisy and died on February 14. On the same day, during the coroner's inquest, evidence was given that the men had been "kidnapped . . . by means of a pretended shipping master" who had subsequently been sentenced to three months hard labor. Curry claimed that Christie and others "had been the victims of a diabolical plot" and that the colored seamen "considered they would be sold as slaves on the ship's arrival" (Liverpool *Mercury*, February 18, 1857, 2:6).

5. In sentencing Campbell, Baron William Watson (1827–99) said, "I have never heard such a case in all my life. You, with a murderous weapon in your hand, went about the decks of your vessel firing upon the crew. There is no kind of excuse to be found in the evidence, for God's mercy alone prevented you from murdering the man, in which case you would have been tried for that most fearful crime. I must mark your crime with such a punishment as will be a warning to all others. This is a land in which such things are not to be tolerated. I shall mark your crime with the highest punishment allotted by the law." The sentence, according to the London *Times*, "created considerable excitement in court" (April 4, 12:2), and in the following issue the *Times* devoted a full column to an editorial on the affair. After summarizing the facts of the case, the *Times* commented, "It appears almost incredible that such a murderous affair as this should have been got up, as it were, at a minute's notice, in a British river, and in broad daylight; nor will the astonishment of our readers be lessened when we add that the sentence seems to have taken the prisoner by surprise, as something unexpectedly severe. . . . It is to be hoped that the example so very justly made by Mr. Baron watson and the Chester jury may have its effect in deterring future offenders, and in improving the condition of those unfortunate men whom necessity or disaster may have subjected to such risks. . . . in these days of enlightenment and publicity, it will be surely hard, if humanity and economy together cannot make themselves heard in bringing about reform" (April 6, 1857, 9:2–3).

6. See C198; Campbell evidently had shipped on his previous voyage as "James H. Collins."

7. On February 27, 1857, HW wrote to John Furber, informing him of his brother's death and burial in St. James Cemetery (Letterpress copy, CO, 13A, 12–13, NA).

Consulate of the United States
Liverpool 8 May 1857

Sir,

On the night of the 29th Inst a collision occurred in the English Channel, 38 miles SW by W ¼ W of Tuskar, between the Ships Tuscarora of Philadelphia, & Andrew Foster of New York, which resulted in the total loss of the latter, but fortunately was not attended with any loss of life or personal injury.

The Tuscarora was going down channel, having sailed from Liverpool the previous day with a full complement of passengers (600) for Philadelphia; the Andrew Foster was coming up channel on her voyage from New York to Liverpool, & had no Passengers. The night is reported to have been dark and rainy, but the lights of each were seen by the other some fifteen minutes before the Collision. The Andrew Foster was close hauled on the wind, when she saw the lights of the Tuscarora two points on the port bow; the latter was going free. According to the Rule generally observed, & sanctioned by the English Admiralty Court, they should have passed each other on the port side, unless circumstances & the requirements of navigation rendered a departure from the rule necessary. The Rule seems to have been strictly observed by both, & the result was the collision. It is alledged on the part of the And^w Foster that the circumstances were such as required a violation of the Rule, but it is hard to define the precise point, when, in the exercise of his discretion, a master should assume the responsibility of violating a Rule so generally insisted on.[1]

The Andrew Foster sunk about an hour after the collision. The Tuscarora returned to Liverpool.

In connexion with the occurrence, I have to report the praiseworthy conduct of the master Thomas Perry, the mate Nicholas Perry, & the Crew, of the Schooner Little Fred of Plymouth, in rescuing the Crew of the Andrew Foster, & sharing with them their nearly exhausted stock of provisions and water.

It appears the Crew of the Andrew Foster when they found their vessel sinking, fired off Rockets, which were observed by the Little Fred, bound to Liverpool 90 days from Rio Grande. She bore up, & found the Crew in the Boats, & while taking them on board, the wreck drifted so nearly across her bow, as to place her in great danger, from which she was extricated by the skill of Captain Perry. Having had a long passage, she had been obliged to put into Cork for Provisions to enable her to reach Liverpool; so that she was ill provided for an addition of 40 people to her little company. What there was was freely shared for nearly three days, by which time it was almost exhausted, 40 Gallons of water & 3 pieces of Beef only remaining. They then hoisted a signal of distress, & subsequently fell in with the Steam Tug Fire King. The Captain of the Steamer was a contrast to Captain Perry. He demanded 30 Guineas for conveying the ship-wrecked crew to Liverpool but at last accepted an order from the Captain on his agents for £18, & the same day landed them in Liverpool.[2]

With high Respect
I have the honor to be
Your Obed[t] Servant
Nath[l] Hawthorne

Hon Lewis Cass
Secretary of State

1. The Marine Extended Protest, sworn by Captain Melvin Williams before NH on May 4, stated that at "11:45 being very dark with rain squalls we called all hands to shorten sail   That while clewing up Topgallantsails we saw a light about two points on the weather bow having ourselves the usual bright light at the Bowsprit end   The Stranger proved to be a ship standing down channel   Being close hauled on the wind on the starboard tack heading NE by E with the wind SE by E we kept along by the wind   The other vessel soon after kept away to cross our bow which brought her into collision with us and it is our belief if instead of keeping away at the time she did she had kept her course she would have gone clear of us to windward" (4, 66, NA).

2. In letters of May 25 and May 30, Assistant Secretary of State John Appleton (1815–64) acknowledged NH's report and informed him that, in return for their service to the *Andrew Foster*'s crew, the President had awarded Captain Thomas Perry $100, Mate Nicholas Perry, $50, and each of the crew, $20 (Instructions, 2, NA). On April 12, 1858, HW authorized Thomas W. Fox, U.S. Consul at Plymouth, to pay these sums to Captain Perry in Plymouth (Letterpress copy, CO, 13A, 39, NA).

Consulate of the United States
Liverpool 8th May 1857

Sir

Refering to my Despatch N° 82 dated 14th February I have the honour to inform you that the accused R D Cutting and John Lewis were tried at the Liverpool Assises on the 3rd of April when Cutting was acquitted and Lewis convicted   The Judge (Baron Martin) reserved sentence having doubts of the Jurisdiction[1]

The case was subsequently brought before the Judges sitting as a Court of Appeal in London and on the 2nd May it was decided that "had the death occurred at sea the case would not have been cognizable in this country and that the mere fact of the party not having died till he arrived at Liverpool did not alter the Law and therefore the conviction must be quashed"[2]

This decision though I have no doubt strictly correct will do much harm unless met by some such international arrangement as I have before suggested either for sending home persons guilty of crimes falling below the present Treaty or giving Jurisdiction to the Courts here to try them[3]

The latter would be by far the most efficacious as in the former case from the difficulty of inducing witnesses to return and prosecute conviction and punishment would be very uncertain.

With high Respect
I have the honour to be
Your Obedient Servant
Nathl Hawthorne.

Hon. Lewis Cass
Secretary of State

MAY, 1857

1. The trial actually occurred on March 28 before Sir Samuel Martin (1801–83), baron of the court of exchequer, a subdivision of the English court system "theoretically confined to matters of revenue, but in practice gradually extended to all kinds of cases . . . by means of the legal fiction that the wrong suffered by the plaintiff had rendered him unable to pay his debts to the king" (OED). Evidence showed that the second mate, John Caswell (who had absconded), had principally instigated the beatings, and that Lewis and particularly Cutting had acted under his express directions. Martin ordered an acquittal in Cutting's case and alluded to the ambiguous ruling made by the law officers in the case of Peter Connolly (see C156.1). After the jury had convicted Lewis of manslaughter, he concluded, "It is quite clear that your acts contributed partly towards the death of the deceased boy, but it is right that I should tell you that I have great doubt whether you can be indicted and tried by an English Court. I will upon the first opportunity take the opinion of a Court, consisting of at least five judges, upon the construction of the Act of Parliament, and you shall have the benefit of it. I can enter into the difficulty in which a man is placed who is acting under the orders of a superior officer, and, if the second mate had been here and found guilty, I should have felt it my duty to inflict the severest punishment upon him which the law allows, and I wish all persons in this court to hear me. . . . If the Court of Appeal should decide in your favour you will be discharged immediately their decision is made known" (London Times, March 30, 1857, 11:4). "As a criminal judge," DNB reports, Martin "did not shrink from imposing heavy sentences when demanded by justice, but his natural kindness of heart induced him not unfrequently to endeavor to obtain their mitigation."

2. This opinion, given by Justice Sir James Shaw Willes (1814–72), was reported in the London Times, May 4, 1857, 11:2.

3. See C205.

Consulate of the United
States of America
Liverpool 12 May 1857

Dr Sir,

I have given to Jacob Vincent a shipwrecked & destitute American Seaman, an order, as prescribed by Law, for a passage in the Empire State to New York. He informs me that he has presented it, & has been refused. That he went on board a second time when the Ship was going out, & was ordered ashore.

I beg to inform you of it that you may set the matter right; & have the man received on board. I send him with this, & must hold the vessel accountable if he be sent ashore again.

I am

Capt Briggs

1. The *Empire State* of New York, Captain L. J. Briggs, cleared Liverpool for New York on May 12, 1857 (Report of American Vessels, NA).

U.S. Consulate,
Liverpool, May 16th '57

Dear Sir,

Your letter, dated April 7th, is just received.[2] No person of
the name you mention has at any time been in my service, as
Secretary or otherwise; and it appears by the books of the
Consulate that no such person has ever been employed here.

Very Respectfully,
Nath[l] Hawthorne.

J. H. Herbert, Esq.
New York city.

1. Probably John H. Herbert, Weigher and Measurer at the New York Custom
House.
2. Unrecovered.

Consulate of the United States,
Liverpool, June 17th 1857.[1]

Sir,

There has recently appeared, in most of the English
newspapers, what purports to be a letter from the Secretary
of State of the United States to Lord Napier, British minister
at Washington, in response to a communication from his
Lordship on the treatment of American seamen.[2] In making
some remarks upon that letter, it is hardly necessary to say
that I do not presume to interfere in a discussion between the
Head of the Department, in which I am a subordinate officer,
and the Minister of a foreign power. But, as the above-
mentioned letter has been made public property, there is as
much propriety in my referring to it as to any other matter of
public importance, bearing especial reference to my own
official duties. I therefore take the liberty to address you, on
the supposition that this document expresses the opinion and
intimates the policy of our government respecting a subject,
on which I have bestowed much thought, and with which I
have had opportunities to become practically acquainted.

The sentiment is very decidedly expressed in the letter,
that the "laws now in force on the subject of seamen,
employed on board the mercantile vessels of the United
States, are quite sufficient for their protection."

I believe that no man, practically connected with our
commercial navy, whether as owner, officer, or seaman,
would affirm that the present marine laws of the United
States are such as the present condition of our nautical affairs
imperatively demands. Those laws may have been wise, and

• 143 •

effectual for the welfare of all concerned, at the period of their enactment. But they had in view a state of things which has entirely passed away; for they are based upon the supposition that the United States really possess a body of native-born seamen, and that our ships are chiefly manned by crews whose home is on our own shores. It is unfortunately the fact, however, that not one in ten of the seamen, employed on board our vessels, is a native-born or even a naturalized citizen, or has any connection with our country beyond his engagement for the voyage. So far as my observation extends, there is not even a class of seamen who ship exclusively in American vessels, or who habitually give them the preference to others. While the present voyage lasts, the sailor is an American; in the next, he is as likely to be sailing under any other flag as our own. And there is still another element of the subject, causing a yet wider discrepancy between the state of things contemplated by the law, and that actually existing. This lies in the fact, that many of the men shipped on board our vessels—comprising much the larger proportion of those who suffer ill-usage—are not seamen at all. Almost every ship, on her trip from New York to Liverpool, brings a number of returning emigrants, wholly unacquainted with the sea, and incapable of performing the duties of seamen, but who have shipped for the purpose merely of accomplishing their homeward passage.

On this latter class of men falls most of the cruelty and severity, which have drawn public notice and reprobation on our mercantile marine. It is the result—not, as one would naturally suppose, of systematic tyranny on the part of the constituted authorities of the ship—but of a state of war between two classes who find themselves, for a period, inextricably opposed on shipboard. One of these classes is composed of the mates and actual seamen, who are adequate to the performance of their own duty, and demand a similar efficiency in others; the second class consists of men who know nothing of the sea, but who have imposed themselves, or been imposed upon the ship, as capable of a seaman's duty. This deception, as it increases the toil and hardship of the real sailor, draws his vengeance upon the unfortunate impostor. In the worst case investigated by me, it appeared that there was not one of the sailor-class, from the second-mate down to the youngest boy, who had not more or less maltreated the landsmen.[3] In another case, the chief and second-mate, during the illness of the master, so maltreated a landsman, who had shipped as sailor, that he afterwards died in a fit.[4] In scarcely a single instance has it been possible to implicate the master as taking a share in these unjustifiable proceedings.

In both the cases, above alluded to, the guilty escaped punishment; and in many similar ones, it has been found that the sufferers are practically without protection or redress. A few remarks will make this fact obvious.

A consul, as I need not inform the Department, has no power (nor could he have, unless by treaty with the government in whose territory he resides) to inflict condign punishment for assaults and other outrages which may come under his official cognizance. The extent of his power (except in a contingency hereafter to be noticed) is, to enable the complainant to seek justice in our own courts of law. If the United States really possessed any native seamen, this might be effectual so far as they were concerned; for such seamen would naturally gravitate homeward, and would there meet the persons who had outraged them, under circumstances which would ensure redress. But the foreigner can very seldom be prevailed upon to return for the mere purpose of prosecuting his officers; and with the returning emigrant, who has suffered so much for the sake of obtaining a homeward passage, it is out of the question. In such cases, what is the Consul to do? Before the complainants make their appeal to him, they have ceased to be under the jurisdiction of his country; and they refuse to return to it in quest of a revenge, which they cannot be secure of obtaining, and which would benefit them little, if obtained. The perpetrators of these outrages are not men who can be made pecuniarily responsible, being almost invariably, as I have said, the lower officers and able seamen of the ship.

In cases of unjustifiably severe usage, if the master of the vessel be found implicated in the offence, the Consul has it at his option to order the discharge of the sufferer, with the payment of three months extra wages. But the instances of cruel treatment, which have come under my notice, are not of the kind contemplated by the act of 1840; not being the effect of the tyranny or bad passions of the master, or of officers acting under his authority, but, as already stated, of the hostile interests of two classes of the crew. To prevent these disorders would require the authority and influence of abler men, and of a higher stamp, than American shipmasters are now usually found to be. In very difficult circumstances, and having a vast responsibility of life and property upon their hands, they appear to me to do their best, with such materials as are at their command. So far as they lay themselves open to the law, I have been ready to inflict it, but have found few opportunities.

Thus, a great mass of petty outrage, unjustifiable assaults, shameful indignities, and nameless cruelty, demoralizing alike to those who perpetrate and those who suffer, falls into the ocean between the two countries, and can be punished in neither.[5] Such a state of things, as it can be met by no law now in existence, would seem to require new legislation.

I have not failed to draw the attention of the government to this subject, on several former occasions.[6] Nor has it been denied, by the last Administration, that our laws in this regard were defective and required revision; but the extent of those acknowledged defects, and of that necessary revision, was alleged as a reason why no partial measures should be adopted.[7] The importance of the matter, as embracing the whole condition of our mercantile marine, cannot be overestimated. It is not an exaggeration to say, that the United States have no seamen. Even the officers, from the mate downward, are usually foreigners, and of a very poor class; being the rejected mates and other subordinates of the British commercial navy. Men who have failed to pass their examination, or have been deprived of their certificates by reason of drunkenness or other ill-conduct, attain, on board of our noble ships, the posts for which they are deemed unworthy in their own. On the deterioration of this class of men necessarily follows that of the masters, who are promoted from it. I deeply regret to say, that the character of American shipmasters has already descended, many degrees, from the high standard which it has held in years past; an effect partly due, as I have just hinted, to the constantly narrowing field of selection, and likewise, in a great degree, to the terrible life which a shipmaster is now forced to lead. Respectable men are anxious to quit a service which links them with such comrades, loads them with such responsibility, and necessitates such modes of meeting it.

In making this communication to the Department, I have deemed it my duty to speak with all possible plainness, believing that you will agree with me that official ceremony is of little importance in view of such a national emergency as is here presented. If there be an interest which requires the intervention of Government, with all its wisdom and all its power—and with more promptitude than governments usually display—it is this. The only efficient remedy, it appears to me, must be found in the creation of a class of native seamen; but, in the years that must elapse before that can be effected, it is most desirable that Government should at least recognize the evils that exist, and do its utmost to alleviate them. No American statesman, being in the position which makes it his especial duty to comprehend and to deal with this matter, can neglect it without peril to his fame. It is a subject which requires only to be adequately represented in order to attract the deepest interest on the part of the public; and the now wasted or destructive energy of our philanthropists might here be most beneficially employed.[8]

In conclusion, I beg leave to say a few words on the personal bearing which the Secretary's supposed letter has upon my own official character. The letter expresses the opinion that the laws of the United States are adequate to the protection of our seamen, and adds that the execution of those laws devolves mostly on Consuls; some of whom, it suggests, in British ports, may have been "delinquent in the discharge of their duty." Now it is undeniable that outrages on board of our ships have actually occurred; and it is equally well-known, and I myself hereby certify, that the majority of these outrages pass without any punishment whatever. Most of them, moreover, in the trade between America and England, have come under my own Consular supervision and been fully investigated by me. If I have possessed the power to punish those offences, and, whether through sluggishness, or fear, or favor, have failed to exercise it, then I am guilty of a great crime, which ought to be visited with a severity and an ignominy commensurate with its evil consequences; and these, surely, would be nothing less than national. If I am innocent—if I have done my utmost, as an executive officer, under a defective law, to the defects of which I have repeatedly called the attention of my superiors—then, un-questionably, the Secretary has wronged me by a suggestion pointing so directly at myself. It trenches upon one of the few rights, as a citizen and as a man, which an office-holder might imagine himself to retain. I leave the matter with the Department. It is peculiarly unfortunate for me that my resignation is already in the hands of the President; for, going out of office under this stigma, I foresee that I shall be supposed to have committed official suicide, as the only mode of escaping some worse fate.[9] Whether it is right that an honorable and conscientious discharge of duty should be rewarded by loss of character, I leave to the wisdom and justice of the Department to decide.[10]

I am, Sir,
Most Respectfully,
Your obedient servant,
Nath[l] Hawthorne.

General Lewis Cass,
Secretary of State,
Washington,
D.C.

1. NH and his family had spent the last week of May touring Lincolnshire, but on May 29 NH received a letter from HW "with some perplexing intelligence," and he cut his tour short to return to the Consulate on June 4, "where I had an engagement that admitted of no delay" (EN, pp. 486, 494). This affair evidently did not involve Cass's letter, as letters to Ticknor and Bennoch written soon after (972, 974) indicate that he expected to set out again for Scotland by June 20. Publication of the letter, however, caused a further delay, and NH did not leave until June 26. He was absent again from the Consulate until July 17.

2. Sir Francis Napier (1819–98) had been appointed to the position in January. In previous positions in Austria, Italy, Turkey, and Russia, he had established a high reputation for diplomacy, and "in the United States he was considered to have been the most acceptable envoy they had up to that time received from Great Britain" (DNB). The British Foreign Office had sent Lord Napier the special report of the Liverpool Society of Friends of Foreigners in Distress, with instructions to take whatever actions he thought expedient (C205.1). On April 10 Napier wrote Cass, "The attention of Her Majesty's Government and of the British Public has been of late awakened by an evil which is reported to be extensive and increasing; I mean the irregularities attending the enlistment of Seamen on board the mercantile Vessels of the United States and the nature of their treatment when so employed. ¶ It is affirmed that in the Ports of this Country Her Majesty's subjects, and others, are not unfrequently decoyed on board American Ships, and retained against their will, that they are subjected to oppressive punishments, and that on reaching British Ports they are dismissed unpaid and cast upon the resources of local charity. ¶ It may be presumed that the abuses to which I allude are far from universal; the high character and attainments possessed by most of the persons in command of Merchant Vessels of the United States prompt us to believe that such frauds and severities have been perpetrated by subordinates, and it may be alleged in extenuation of the denial of wages, and summary discharge of men, that the latter frequently enter with pretended qualifications which are not justified by their previous experience. ¶ Enough, however, may be substantiated to prove the existence of malpractices which are stimulated by the great demand for labour at Sea and its high remuneration. The records of the Police Court at Liverpool those of the hospitals in the same city, and the reports of the 'Society of Friends of Foreigners in Distress' might be abundantly cited in evidence of the system complained of. ¶ In

bringing this subject forward under the sanction of the Earl of Clarendon I venture to express my hope that you may be enabled by consultation with the Secretary of the Navy and the Law Officers of the United States to suggest some remedial measure for these abuses should they be verified to your satisfaction on enquiry, and I can promise you the zealous cooperation of Her Majesty's Government for the same purpose within the limits of their authority" (MS, Notes from the British Legation, 34, NA). Cass responded on April 28, "I have the honor to acknowledge the receipt of Your Lordship's note of the 10th inst. stating that the attention of Her Majestys Government and of the British Public, has of late been awakened to the irregularities attending the enlistment of Seamen on board the mercantile vessels of the United States, and the nature of their treatment when so employed. Your Lordship expresses a hope that some remedial measure may be suggested for these abuses. ¶ In reply, I have the honor to state, that it is believed the laws now in force upon the subject of seamen employed on board the merchant vessels of the United States, are quite sufficient for their protection. The execution of these Laws in foreign countries, for the most part devolves upon Consuls. It is possible that these officers may, in some instances, have been delinquent in the discharge of their duty in Her Majestys Ports. This Department, however, is not aware of any such delinquencies; but, upon being satisfied of their existence, will not hesitate to apply the proper remedy. —A copy of the United States Consular Regulations is herewith transmitted, and Your Lordship is particularly referred to the 19th Chapter, entitled 'Duties of Consular officers in relation to seamen of the United States.' —From the great demand for sailors in our ports in proportion to their supply, and the improvidence and credulity which usually characterize them, they are necessarily exposed to imposition to a degree which probably no laws could prevent. —It is presumed that Seamen required for the British mercantile marine in Her Majesty's own ports are more or less subject to the same grievance. ¶ I should be glad to concur in any measures for the relief of this useful class of persons, but the Laws of this Country intended to prevent their mal-treatment are as effective, it is believed, as those of any other. —Instances may have occurred where offenders have escaped punishment, but this, I am persuaded, should be imputed to defective proof or other accident, and not either to any inadequacy in the Law itself, or to want of impartiality in its administration" (Transcript, F.O. 5 / 671, PRO). Napier forwarded this reply to Clarendon on May 3, commenting, "By the terms of the accompanying reply from General Cass Your Lordship will observe that there is not much prospect of the evil being mitigated by the intervention of the United States Authorities or by any new legislative enactment on the subject" (MS, F.O. 5 / 671, PRO). The Foreign Office, in turn, passed on a transcript of Cass's response to the Board of Trade, and on June 5 undersecretary Edmund Hammond wrote James Booth that Clarendon "has no objection to the Board of Trade communicating to the Liverpool Local Marine Board a copy of General Cass's reply" (Draft, F.O. 5 / 685, PRO). After first appearing in the Liverpool *Shipping and Mercantile Gazette*, Cass's letter (with no significant variants from the transcript) was published by the London *Times* on June 13 (12:6).

3. Perhaps a reference to the *Ocean Monarch* affair, investigated before Mansfield in November, 1856; see C203.1. One seaman testified that the officers "had the boys employed with penknives to run after the men and prick them in the back as they ran along the deck. . . . " Other witnesses claimed that they were made to dress as a female for the officers' amusement, pull nails out of the deck with their teeth, and lick coffee grounds and other dirt from off the deck. "When at sea," the Liverpool *Mercury* reported, "the mate made some of the men perform other disgusting acts which are not fit to be described" (November 14, 1856, 3:4). After a lengthy investigation, three of the officers were convicted of assaults committed within the Liverpool shipping channels, but Mansfield ruled no jurisdiction could be claimed for previous assaults.

4. A reference to the *Wandering Jew* affair; see C214.2

5. NH incorporated this sentence (with minor variations) into *OOH* (p. 33).

6. Especially C51 (Queries II.8), C94, C205, and C214.

7. See C94.3

8. Compare *EN*, p. 267.

9. Compare NH's characterization of Cass's letter in 993.

10. On June 19 NH told Ticknor, "I send by this steamer a despatch to Gen[l] Cass, on receipt of which he will feel much inclined to turn me out of office, without waiting till August 31st. It refers to a letter of his to Lord Napier, on the subject of the treatment of our seamen, in which he displays a shameful degree of ignorance of a matter which it is his duty to understand. If he does not grow wiser, it will not be my fault. I shall transmit you a copy of the despatch, to be set afloat in the American newspapers after I go out of office. This will be necessary in order to show that I have been zealous and faithful in the discharge of my duty; and it will also tend to enlighten the public on a matter of very great importance" (976). Cass received NH's despatch on July 2, but did not immediately respond. On September 17 NH thanked Bridge for a complimentary account of his work in the Washington *Union*, adding, "But for your paragraph, I should have thought it necessary to enlighten the public on the true state of the case . . . and I do not know but I may do it yet. . . . I shall send the Despatch to Ticknor, at any rate, for publication if necessary" (993). But on September 24 Cass formally accepted NH's resignation and informed him of Tucker's appointment, adding "it gives the Department pleasure, on your voluntary retirement, to express its acknowledgments for the valuable information and suggestions relative to our commercial interests, which you have, from time to time, communicated, and to assure you of its satisfaction with the manner in which you have discharged the laborious and responsible duties of the office" (*NHHW*, II, 163). In an accompanying letter, Cass said: "Your despatch, No. 90, of the 17th of June last, upon the maltreatment of seamen on board vessels of the United States, was duly received. The note to Lord Napier, which accompanied it, was correctly published in the English journals, but without the previous knowledge or consent of this Department. You seem to suppose that some of its expressions may have been intended to charge you with delinquency in your official duties towards seamen. No such intention, however, was entertained; and now that you are about to retire from your position, I am happy to bear testimony to the prudent and efficient manner in which you have discharged your duties. I owe it to myself, however, to add that I perceive nothing in the letter to Lord Napier which justifies the construction you have placed on it. On the contrary, while it admits that some delinquency, on the part of our Consuls, in executing the laws of the United States concerning seamen, is not absolutely impossible, it expressly disclaims all knowledge of such delinquency; and where offenders have escaped punishment, it attributes the escape to causes over which our Consuls could exercise no control. What you say with regard to the evils that afflict our commercial marine, it is not now necessary to consider; but you quite misapprehend my views if you suppose that I am insensible to the magnitude of these evils, or could have ever intended to deny their existence. I concur with you in opinion, however, that they are not so much chargeable to defective laws as to the want of that very class of persons whom the laws were made to protect. While, therefore, our statutes may be, and probably are, as well adapted to their objects as those of any other country, it is none the less true that our merchant service suffers constantly from the want of American seamen. How this want can be supplied, is a question to which, in my note to Lord Napier, it was not my purpose to reply" (*NHHW*, II, 161–62). Cass's letter arrived with Tucker, and on October 9 NH communicated to Ticknor the compliment to his "prudence and efficiency" (1005). See also NH's account of this exchange in *OOH*, pp. 32–33.

Consulate of the United States
Liverpool 25 June 1857

Sir,

I have the honor to acknowledge receipt of Circular N° 3 with its enclosure.[1]

With reference to the power I am supposed to have, of detaining persons charged with offences on board American vessels within the jurisdiction of the United States, I beg to inform you that I have no such power, when those offences fall short of any of the crimes specified in the Treaty of 1842, which they almost invariably do.

I enclose you copy of a Letter received by the Mayor of Liverpool from the English Secretary of State, some time since, in reply to one from him on the subject of a man charged with killing another on board an American vessel at Sea.[2] The opinion expressed by Sir George Grey has since been affirmed by the Superior Court, as I informed the Department.[3]

With great Respect
I am your obed^t Servant
Nathl Hawthorne.

To Hon Lewis Cass
Secretary of State

1. On December 30 Marcy had requested an opinion from Attorney General Cushing, concerning the powers and duties of consuls to detain American citizens accused of crimes and send them back to the U.S. Cushing responded with a lengthy opinion, which incoming Secretary of State Cass had printed up and circulated as Circular N° 3, dated May 29, 1857. Cushing admitted that he could find "nothing explicit" concerning consuls' criminal authority in the acts passed to date by Congress. Still, he observed that the master of a ship had power, recognized by international law, to arrest and detain a person committing criminal acts on shipboard, and when the ship touched in a foreign country, the consul had the power to make the master discharge the prisoner or allow him to detain the accused, "and in the latter case, he may have occasion to call on the local authorities to aid in detaining the party or in providing to send him home for trial." Cushing cited the new "Consular Regulations" as stating that "it will be the duty of the consular officer to require that the individual so accused, be delivered to him to be sent home for trial." But, Cushing stressed, primary responsibility for securing the prisoner belonged to the ship's master; the consul's authority "necessarily follows from that of the master" and the consul's duty is "to advise, aid, and, if need be, direct the master as to the further detention of the party as a criminal, and his immediate transmission to his country" (D, Instructions, 2, NA).

2. The case of Peter Connolly; see C156. Actually, the letter sent by NH recorded the Foreign Office's first opinion, which was superseded by a second, granting British courts jurisdiction because Connolly was a British citizen. Nevertheless, the law officers left no doubt that NH had no claim for jurisdiction, since "Manslaughter is not one of the offences in respect of which Extradition can take place."

3. The case of John Lewis; see C207.1, C220.

C225. TO LEWIS CASS, WASHINGTON

Consulate of the United States
Liverpool 25th June 1857

Sir,

On the 20th Instant the American Ship Vanguard cleared from this Port for New York with a colored crew. She did not proceed direct to Sea but anchored in the River. On Monday evening a serious affray occurred with the Crew, the greater part were sent ashore, one much injured, the vessel took on board another Crew and sailed early next morning.

On investigating the case it appeared that during the Saturday and Sunday the officers were very tyrannical, and had grossly illtreated the men. That the men under this provocation had refused duty, and declared they would not go in the Ship. That finally on the Monday evening an attempt appears to have been made to compel them to work, which led to acts of violence on both sides.

Not having the officers of the vessel before me, the evidence must of course be to a certain extent ex-parte, but I have no doubt whatever that the men were very badly treated before they refused duty.[1]

As there were steerage passengers on board during the occurrences, some of them will no doubt be able to give important testimony. I shall send as many of the Seamen as I can induce to go, and advise the District Attorney of the vessels they go by.[2]

With this I send copies of Depositions made before me, and of the report of the Police.

With great respect, Your Obed Servant
Nath[l] Hawthorne.

Hon Lewis Cass
Secretary of State

1. According to depositions, on June 24 NH took from William Valentine, the injured party, and from other seamen and witnesses, the two mates and carpenter had begun beating and threatening the seamen soon after they boarded. On Sunday morning, when the sailors refused to sing on command, the second mate singled out a group of troublemakers, Valentine among them, to "jig on the chain all day." The seamen retired to the forecastle, and when the mate asked them if they were going to obey his orders, they said "no we were not going to haul on a chain all day for merely refusing to sing   He said you are not agoing to do what you are told in this ship   We said yes we would do what we were told to do but we wouldnt haul on the chain all day on Sunday." The second mate and carpenter then attacked the group with handspikes, but when one of them grabbed the carpenter's spike, the two retreated and returned with the chief mate, armed with pistols. The men demanded to be put on shore, but, when the captain was summoned, he promised the men that they would be treated fairly, and the incident seemed cleared up. The next day, however, the shipping master came on board and pulled aside a number of seamen to be sent ashore as troublemakers. Valentine again demanded to leave the ship, telling the captain that "if he carried me to sea he would have to carry me dead for I would not go in the ship." The Captain refused, and the chief mate began shoving Valentine off the deck: "as soon as I turned my back to the mate I received a blow on the head which knocked me down   The Chief Mate got hold of me and continued to strike me with a pair of steel knuckles   I scrambled forward and when I got near the foremast the Captain his son (the third mate) and the carpentr came and each pointed a pistol at me and said raise your hand you son of bitch & we will put a ball through you   The chief mate kept striking me all the while with the steel knuckles[.]" The mate again asked Valentine if he would go in the ship, and he again refused, this time joined by most of the crew. The captain then promised to send for police to take them to shore, but when Valentine found he had not done so, he lowered himself by rope onto the steam tug escorting the *Vanguard*. The second mate and carpenter followed Valentine on board the tug, again knocking him down and kicking him in the face, until a group of seamen jumped over the ship's rail with knives drawn and chased the officers away. Valentine, unconscious, was taken back to the Liverpool Hospital. The other witnesses generally corroborated Valentine's testimony, although some of the men who had come with the shipping master testified that when the mate had shoved Valentine, he had drawn a knife and tried

to stab the mate. Another seaman recalled that the mate had told the men, "'This is a packet ship and I calculate to kill some of the niggers before we get across[.]'" (MSS, Marine Extended Protest, 4, 114, NA).

2. In a letter of July 10, HW sent word to McKeon that the Consulate was sending seven of the abused seamen, all blacks, to New York by various ships and steamers (Letterpress copy, CO, 13A, 24, NA). In a letter dated the same day, Cass sent a copy of NH's letter with the depositions to Attorney General Jeremiah S. Black (1810–83), "in order that such instructions may be given to the U.S. District Attorney at New York, as the case may seem to require" (MS, Attorney General's Papers, Letters Received / State Department, 2, NA). A note on the same letter indicates that on July 16 the Attorney General referred the matter to the Solicitor of the Treasury, "instructing him to investigate the matter." The *Vanguard* arrived in New York harbor on August 5, but there is no record of any further prosecution by the government.

US Consulate

Liverpool 9 July 1857[1]

Sir,

Referring to Mr Wilding's conversation, on friday last, with Mr Potberry,[2] I beg to hand you the papers left with me by Captain Adams of the American Ship Robert Parker, relating to materials saved from the wreck of said vessel, and brought to this port by the British ship "Bannockburn" Captain Bruce.[3] I will thank you for early information, respecting the possession and disposition of said materials

and am Respectfully

Your Obed Servant

Nathl Hawthorne.

To the Collector of Customs
Receiver of Droits
of Admiralty
Liverpool
2 Enclosures
Affid or Declaration of Master
Authority for me to settle

---

1. On this date NH was with his family in Edinburgh, so this letter must have been drafted by HW and sent to Scotland for NH's signature or, more likely, it was drafted after NH's return on July 17 and backdated.

2. One of the Liverpool Customs Officers; see C98.1

3. According to the Marine Extended Protest made by Captain Ebenezer G. Adams before Samuel Pearce on May 22, the *Robert Parker* of Portsmouth, N.H., had left Mobile on April 8 with a cargo of cotton. On April 22 she was struck by lightning, which set the cotton afire. After vainly trying to stifle the fire, the crew took to the boats, when the *Bannockburn* appeared on the scene. After loading their personal effects, the crew "returned to our own ship for more provisions which we succeeded in getting with great difficulty. . ." (4, 72, NA). See C239.

C227. TO M. F. MAURY,[1] WASHINGTON

US Consulate
Liverpool 18 July 1857

Dear Sir,

Herewith I beg to forward abstract Log of the British Bark Marion, London to Aden—Bombay and Liverpool, left with me by Capt Leighton.

I am frequently asked where your wind & current charts can be had in England, can you inform me?[2]

Your obed Servant

Lieut Maury

1. Lieutenant Matthew Fontaine Maury (1806–73) was Superintendent of the Depot of Charts and Instruments and of the Naval Observatory in Washington, D.C., (1842–61) (DNB).
2. Maury's *Wind and Current Charts*, then published for the Atlantic and Pacific Oceans, were used by captains to facilitate extremely fast passages. In addition, Maury advocated a uniform system for recording oceanographic data in ships' logs, and at the time was compiling a *Wind and Current Chart* for the Indian Ocean.

C228. TO CAPTAIN WILLIAM REED, *HORIZON*

US Consulate
Liverpool 18 July 1857

Dear Sir,

With reference to the complaints of Charles Harkin Oliver Nelson & John Smith, of their having been abused by your chief and third mates and Boatswain, I beg to inform you that unless those officers be sent away from the vessel I shall require you to discharge the before mentioned Seamen, & to pay them each three months extra wages. [1]

You will also understand that in the event of your discharging the officers, you will do it on your own responsibility, & subject to any claim they may make on account thereof hereafter.

I am
Your Obed Servant

Capt Reed
American Ship *Horizon*

---

1. According to depositions taken July 9 and 11, Harkin, Nelson, and Smith had each been severely beaten by the mates and boatswain. Nelson had been ordered to put his head between the steps of a ladder while the second mate lashed him, and he had also been ordered to carry a capstan bar around deck for four hours. Harkin recalled an incident when the boatswain struck him in the face with "the bite of a strap which he carried for the purpose"; Harkin grabbed it from him and drew his knife, cutting the boatswain slightly. For this, Harkin was put in irons for a while,

and, shortly after his release, the second mate told him "to go into the mainhatch house for a broom   I went and the chief mate 2nd mate and Boatswain came into the House aftr me and shut the door   The Boatswain then kicked me and knocked me down jumped onto me and kicked me   The second mate kicked me several times   The chief mate stood holding the handle of the door but never interfered." Smith testified to hearing Harkin beaten in the house and saw the boatswain strike Nelson often; in addition, he had been beaten and kicked around the head and face by the boatswain and chief mate, who told him "the best thing you can do now is to jump overboard you'll have no more peace on board this ship[.]" All three, joined by two other witnesses, agreed that the captain had stopped such incidents when he witnessed them, and after they had complained to him, most of the abuse stopped. Still, one testified, "the mates used to beat us whenever they could slyly and used to send us forward to do it." Smith concluded, "I would go in the ship if the chief and 2nd mates and Boatswain were to leave her it is my wish to make the voyage in her. The Captain is as nice a man as I should like to go with" (Marine Extended Protest, NA).

Consulate of the United States
Liverpool 18th July 1857

Sir,

I have the honor to address you on the subject of a vessel called the Rowena, now at this Port, in circumstances that suggest the propriety of the persons Registered as her owners being informed.

She belongs to Sanfrancisco where she is Registered in the names of A W Simpson and I. G. Jackson.

From such information as I have been able to obtain it appears, that she cleared from Sanfrancisco for Melbourne under the command of Captain Thomas. At Melbourne E R Burrows was endorsed by the Consul as master. From Melbourne she went to Calcutta, from thence to Hamburg; on which latter voyage she sprung a leak, & was obliged to put into St Helena; she reached Hamburg where she was repaired, & a Bottomry Bond entered into.[1] From Hamburg she went to Balize Honduras, where the Captain, unable otherwise to raise money to pay off the Hamburg Bond, executed another Bond in favor of a House in London, who are here represented by Messrs Holme & Slater. She then loaded for Liverpool, & eight days before sailing Captain Burrows died. There being no Consul the British authorities endorsed, 23 April 1857, Robert Quance, an Englishman, as master. She arrived here on the 1 Inst. The Crew also were foreigners, but treating them as American Seamen, I demanded and have obtained payment of their wages.

The Ship appears entirely abandoned to the Bondholders,

as far as I can see, and will probably be sold,[2] & I am not able to learn that any person represents the owners.

With high Respect
I am your Obed[t] Servant
Nath[l] Hawthorne

To Hon Lewis Cass
Secretary of State

1. A bottomry bond is a kind of mortgage, in which a ship's owner or master borrows money needed to complete a voyage, pledging his ship as security (*OED*).

2. On January 9, 1858, the consulate reported to the Department of the Treasury that the register of the *Rowena* had been cancelled, an act usually indicating transfer of ownership to British hands (Letterpress copy, CO, 11A, 3, NA).

C230. TO JOHN MCKEON, NEW YORK

United States Consulate
Liverpool 21 July 1857

Dear Sir,

This will be delivered to you by Robert H Haynes and Dan¹ Donovan two American Seamen, who were, according to their affidavits of which I enclose copies, seriously maltreated on board the American Ship Arctic Captain Zerega, which sailed hence for New York on the night of the ninth or morning of the 10th of July inst.¹ They state that the assaults were witnessed by several of the Crew and steerage passengers who have gone to New York in the Ship. I shall send copies of the Depositions & a statement of the case to the Department of State by the next steamer.

I am Resp^y
Your Obed^t Servant
Nath¹ Hawthorne.

The United States Attorney
District of New York

1. On July 20, NH took depositions from Robert H. Haynes, a native of South Carolina, and from Daniel Donovan, an Irish-born citizen of Boston. Haynes testified that he was sober when he boarded the *Arctic* on July 9. Shortly afterwards he was helping rig the jibboom "when I received a blow on the eye from the second mate (Kelly) which rendered me insensible and I remember nothing more until I

found myself going ashore with the shipping master who sent me to the Hospital. I had given the mate no provocation whatever. I had never spoken to him and dont know what he struck me for." Donovan testified that at the same time he was helping with the rigging "when the second mate came and asked me what I was standing there for I told him when he up fist and knocked me down and then kicked me about the head and face with his Boots[.]" Donovan then deserted the ship and applied to the Consulate, which sent him to the Hospital. William B. Wall certified on the same day that Haynes had been admitted with bruises around his eyes and a broken nose, and that Donovan had been admitted with a bruised eye and some twenty bruises and abrasions "which might have been inflicted by kicks" (MS, Marine Extended Protest, 4, NA).

US Consulate
Liverpool 30 July 1857

Dear Sir,

I yesterday passed forward two men, Thomas Noble & Thomas Hitchen, who stated that they had been left by the Susquehanna, being ashore on leave when she sailed. The first mentioned I sent per steamer to Cork, at a cost of 10/6, the other, Hitchen, by way of Dublin, at a cost of 17/8. As these sums are I presume properly chargeable to the men, perhaps Mr Rittenhouse[2] will have their receipts taken, and send me the money.

I am very respectfully
Your Obed Servant
Nathl Hawthorne.

Capt Sands USA
Commanding Frigate
"Susquehanna"

1. Captain Joshua Ratoon Sands (1795-1883) had served with distinction in the U.S. Navy during the War of 1812 and the Mexican War. Promoted to Captain in 1854, he commanded the *Susquehanna*, which was assisting in the unsuccessful attempt to lay a submarine telegraph cable from England to North America (*DAB*).

2. Purser of the *Susquehanna* and a descendant of David Rittenhouse (1732–96), pioneer astronomer and first director of the U.S. Mint (Moran, I, 70).

Consulate of the United States
Liverpool 31 July 1857

Sir,

I have the honor to enclose herewith copies of Depositions made before me, and a medical certificate in the case of two men admitted into the Hospital at this place suffering from injuries inflicted by the second mate of the ship Arctic Captain Zerega of New York.[1]

The Arctic cleared at this office on the 10th of July and the names of Hugh Haynes and Daniel Donovan appear on the list of persons shipped at Liverpool.

It appears from the statements of the men and enquiries I have made that the Captain was not on board during the occurrences complained of, and the men will likely have been reported as deserters.

The men were sent by me in the Steamer "Ericsson" which sailed for New York on the 22nd Inst, and directed to apply to the District Attorney, to whom I sent a statement of the case and copies of the Depositions and medical certificate.

With high Respect
I have the honor to be
Your Obed' Servant
Nath' Hawthorne

Hon Lewis Cass
Secretary of State

1. See C230.

US Consulate
Liverpool 1 August 1857

Dear Sir,

I beg to forward herewith copies of Depositions made
before me in the Case of Richard Lyons a seaman left behind
from the Am Ship Ashburton.[1]

Lyons shipped on board the Calhoun for New York &
applied for these copies. There not being then time to prepare
them, I promised to forward them to you.

The conduct of Lyons was very bad. He went on board
drunk, beat one of the steerage passengers, & raised a fight
among the Crew. For the assault on him by the shipping
master's runner he was told he could obtain redress here, if
he was entitled to any, but he refused to prosecute. Of the
manner of his being subsequently left behind, the Depositions will inform you. He stated that he intended to sue the
Captain & wanted these copies of the Depositions, but I don't
think it a case for a Government prosecution.

Resp^y Your Obed Servt
Nathl Hawthorne

The District Attorney
New York

1. On July 21, Lyons testified that he had come to Liverpool on board the *Ashburton*, Captain Bradish. When the ship left the Liverpool dock, before departing the port, he and some of the crew and steerage passengers were, by his admission, "much the worse for Liquor[.]" After Lyons quarreled with them, the shipping master's runner told him he must go ashore, followed him onto the tug alongside, and "licked me with his fists." Lyons immediately applied at the Consulate for a note to rejoin the ship, "and was told I was too much in liquor and must get sober first[.]" The next day he received a note and presented it to the captain, who "opened it swore at me and said he would lick me[.]" The captain went with Lyons to the Consulate and, after seeing NH, told Lyons that if he went in his ship, he would have to go in irons. Lyons said he was willing to ship on those terms and was fitted for handcuffs, but when he went to the pier at the time appointed by the captain, he found that the boat had left for the *Ashburton* five minutes before (MS, Marine Extended Protest, 4, NA).

C234. TO CAPTAIN WILLIAMS,[1] AZ

U.S. Consulate
Liverpool 1 Aug 1857

Sir,

I beg to inform you that after a careful consideration of the several statements made before me in the case of Francis M Wheeler and M McDonald,[2] deserters from your vessel, I am bound to conclude that their desertion was caused by the ill usage to which they were subjected during the voyage, and order their discharge, with the payment of three months extra wages, according to the Law of 20th July 1840.

I am
Your obed Servant
Nath[l] Hawthorne

Capt Williams
Ship AZ

1. Unidentified; the consulate's "Report of American Vessels" and later correspondence identify the captain as George Green (NA). The AZ had arrived on July 21.
2. NH had taken depositions in the case on July 22; see C235.

C235. TO LEWIS CASS, WASHINGTON

Consulate of the United States
Liverpool 14th Aug 1857

Sir,

I have the honor to transmit herewith the Certificate of
Registry of the ship AZ of New York, which I felt it my duty,
under the 28th section of the Act of 1856, to refuse to the
master on his refusal to pay the three months extra wages for
two of his Crew, whose discharge I had ordered under the 17
section of the Act of 1840.

The AZ arrived here on the 21 of July, and on the following
morning Fred M Wheeler, and Mich^l McDonald, Cook &
Steward, applied to me for relief. In consequence of the
statements they made to me, I sent for the Captain, and took
their affidavits and those of two of the Crew, separately, in
his presence.[1]

In reply he alledged, that they were grossly incompetent to
perform the duties they had shipped for. He admitted that he
had beaten them some, but not in the cruel manner described. He accounted for the injuries they were covered
with, by saying that they had inflicted them on each other in
fighting, and produced his officers and one of the Seamen to
contradict their statements.[2] They went farther than the
Captain, and were oblivious of any beating whatever, but
were equally ignorant of any fighting between the Cook and
Steward. I send you copies of the several affidavits (Enclosure N° 2).

In all cases of this kind, depending entirely on the evidence
of Seamen (who seem to have their own peculiar notions on
the subject) it is extremely difficult to arrive at the truth,[3]

• 171 •

but looking at the evidence before me in this case, the admission of the Captain, and the condition of the men described in the accompanying copy of surgeon's certificate (enclosure N° 3), I was forced to the conclusion that Wheeler and McDonald had been very cruelly used by the Captain, and were entitled to their discharge.[4] I trust the Department will arrive at the same conclusion, and sustain me in the course I have adopted.[5] If a master be allowed to ill use, or knowingly suffer others to ill use, those under his command, on the plea, alledged in this case, that the victims are incompetent, the consequences would be deplorable.[6]

I shall send the men home by the Atlantic on the 19th Instant for New York, with instructions to apply to the District Attorney.

With high respect
I have the honor to be
Your obed^t Servant
Nathl Hawthorne.

To Hon Lewis Cass
Secretary of State

---

1. On July 22 NH took evidence from Wheeler and McDonald. Wheeler, the AZ's steward, complained of a long series of abuses: "I found some beans in the Locker in the Galley spoiled and I hove them overboard   The day after the Captain asked me about them   I told him that they were spoiled and I had hove them overboard   He called the Cook aft and flogged us both with a piece of Ratlin   A day or two after the Captain was having his cup of Coffee before breakfast and asked me which coffee I had made it from   I told him that in the Bag when he hove the pot coffee and all at me   Some days after the Captain told me to kill a chicken and make some soup   I did so cutting the chicken in pieces   The Captain flogged me with a rope for not putting the chicken in whole   Another time he found fault with a pudding I made and flogged me with a rope. . . . The Captain caused this injury to my nose   I was orderd to clean some window blinds and after I had done them the Captain went to look at them   He asked me if I could do them no better than

that I said I could not with salt water that I could do them better if I was allowed fresh water and soap He then took up one of [the window blinds] and struck me on the nose with it I went forward to wash the blood off my nose when I came aft he asked me what I went forward for to shew myself to the passengers bleeding I told him I had been to wash the blood off I then went into the pantry and he followed me and struck me on the nose with something he had in his hand I believe steel or brass knuckles." Charles Seymour, a seaman, corroborated Wheeler's testimony, saying he had seen the captain strike the steward with a window sash and "had frequently seen the Captain beat the steward before that I have seen the steward bleeding several times from the violence of the Captain[.]" McDonald, the cook, testified to a similar string of beatings: "about nine days after we sailed from New York as near as I can recollect the Captain called and told me to take some water to the chickens I said the mate had the Tin giving water to the pigs He told me to bring it in my cap I said it would not hold it He came down off the House struck me in the face and then kicked me I then went aft into the pantry about my work the mate followed me and struck me over the eye cutting me where the mark is now The next day I believe the Captain found some fault about the binnacle Lamps being dirty and came with a Rope to beat me I begged him not to beat me as I was very sick He beat me with the rope and then made me go down on my knees and gave me some Castor Oil he then took the Lampfeeder and poured a quantity of Lamp Oil down my throat. . . . He used to make us carry wooden Guns about the decks and play leap frog with handspikes to make fun for the passengers and was constantly beating us I have left the Ship because I was afraid of my life to stop in her[.]" Seaman George Balldridge attested to to the lampfeeder incident and confirmed that "I have during the voyage seen the Captain beat the Cook and Steward frequently with a piece of Ratlin Stuff I have seen him give them water to drink out of the dogs can" (Enclosure, Despatches, 13, NA).

2. James Neville, chief officer of the AZ, testified, "I am unaware of the Cook & Steward having been ill used during the voyage I refuse to say whether I have struck them or not[.]" Adams Davis, second mate; Peter C. Green, carpenter; Walter Franklin, third mate; and William Warner, seaman; all stated that they knew nothing about the injuries and never saw them receive any blows from any person.

3. Compare NH's apparent recollection of this case in *OOH*, pp. 31–32.

4. Surgeon Wall certified that Wheeler's right arm, thigh, and back were covered with contusions and abrasions, that his left shoulder was badly contused, and that his nose was fractured: "I am of opinion that these injuries must have been very serious." He also stated that McDonald had "received ten contusions of the back which appear to have been inflicted by a rope."

5. On October 5, Assistant Secretary Appleton reported to Tucker that the AZ's Register had been returned to the owners on payment of the extra wages to Wheeler and McDonald. The owners, however, were forced to pay an extra duty on tonnage because the ship had sailed without its papers, and this, the State Department ruled, "will not be returned, as the owners must be held responsible for the conduct of the Master, who, as reported to this Department by the late Consul, was guilty of great cruelty and hardship towards the above-mentioned seamen. ¶ The course pursued by the late Consul in this case meets the entire approval of the Department" (MS, Instructions, 3, NA).

6. A fragmentary draft of this sentence survives in NH's hand; see textual note.

United States Consulate
Liverpool 18 August 1857

Sir,

    Whereas Frederick M Wheeler and Michael McDonald having deserted from the ship AZ of New York George Green Master in this port and I on enquiring into the facts being satisfied that such desertion was caused by the ill usage inflicted by said George Green did on the 1 day of Aug 1857 order the discharge of said Frederick M Wheeler and Michael McDonald with the payment of 3 months extra wages pursuant to the 17 section of the Act of 20 July 1840 and said George Green having refused payment of such extra wages and sailed for New York without his ship's Register you or the proper Law Officer of the United States are authorised at their proper cost and charges to institute in my name a suit to recover the same and the same to control and to discharge according to Law in such Court having jurisdiction thereof as you or he shall deem

United States Consulate
Liverpool 18 Aug 1857

Sir

This will be delivered by Frederick M Wheeler and Michael McDonald two American seamen who deserted from the American Ship AZ of New York, and whose discharge was ordered by me under the 17 sect of Act 30 July 1840. The master refusing to pay the extra wages I detained his papers and he sailed without them, for New York 13 Aug.

The papers, with statement & depositions in the case, were sent to the Secretary of State by the last steamer.

I send you by this steamer authority to prosecute in my name, if it be necessary.

I am very respectfully
Your obed^t Servant
Nathl Hawthorne

The United States Attorney
New York

Consulate of the United States
Liverpool [18 Sept 1857][1]

Sir

I forward herewith certain depositions taken before me in the case of George Maudluff Steward of the Ship "Castine" You will perceive by them that while the Ship was lying in the port of Castine in April last the Master Captain James Simpson committed a violent and bloody assault upon the person of the Steward without any adequate cause[2] Captain Simpson himself in a personal interview which I had with him substantially admitted having perpetrated the assault and was unable to justify it on any more definite grounds than an alleged insolence in the look or tone of the Steward. The injuries sustained by the latter were serious, as was evidenced by the scars still remaining on his head and arm[3]

There appears to have been no other ill treatment of the Steward on the part of the Captain until after the Ship arrived in Liverpool when in consequence of his making complaint of the above facts to me Captain Simpson again violently assaulted him and the Steward deserted from the vessel[4]

As the first and more desperate assault was committed in one of our own ports and as the Steward then (whether through ignorance or for whatever other reason) failed to bring the case before a magistrate I might perhaps have felt myself justified in passing the matter over provided there had been no evidence of an enduring Malevolence on Captain Simpsons part. But the second assault appeared to me to imply that the Captain cherished a resentment against the Steward which might on slight occasion break forth in further violence and this impression was strengthened by the tone of the Captain's remarks made personally to myself in reference to the reason and the facts

Under such circumstances I considered that my duty required me to view the second assault in the light thrown on it by the first; and I therefore ordered the discharge of the Steward with payment of three months advance wages, conceiving it better for both parties that they should be separated   Captain Simpson declining to comply with the order as regarded the payment of advance wages I refused to deliver the Ships register[5]   I feel it proper to say that Captain Simpsons general treatment of his crew appears to have been unexceptionable and that he seemed to me on the whole a kind hearted man, but to be afflicted with a temper easily kindled to violence and not easily pacified.

The man being colored I could not send him to New Orleans where the vessel has gone and have sent him to Boston[6]

> With high respect
> I have the honor to be
> Your obed Serv[t]
> Nath[l] Hawthorne.

Hon Lewis Cass

---

1. The date, omitted by the unidentified second clerk, is taken from HW's cover for the letter, on the verso of the second sheet. NH had remained near Liverpool through August, but had admitted to Ticknor that he performed "very little service" (988). When no successor had arrived by the end of the month, he stayed on in office, but on September 15 learned that Tucker had been appointed to fill his place (991). By September 17 he had made plans to leave "in a day or two" for Paris (993).

2. On July 16 George Maudluff testified to NH that he had joined the *Castine* at Castine, Maine, around April 24. Shortly afterwards, Captain Simpson asked him for some soft bread. Maudluff admitted that he had baked none, but sent a boy to buy some on shore. "I told the Captain I had sent the boy for some bread but he would not listen to me called me a damed black son of a bitch and said he would kill me struck me several times with his fist then took down a pair of tormentors and struck me several times on the arm cutting it badly The tormentor slipped out of his hand and he then took an axe and struck me with it on the head He made another blow at me with it and it slipped out of his hand He then took a billet of wood and hove it at me in doing this he knocked a pot of hot coffee over which fell on me and scalded me He said go aft and wait on the Table I said I was not fit He said go you black son of a bitch or I'll kill you[.]" Christopher C. Gloss, cook of the ship, witnessed the scene and corroborated Maudluff's testimony (Enclosure, Despatches, 13, NA).

3. According to Maudluff, he complained about the assault to NH, "and in answer to the question why I had not applied to a magistrate at Castine said because I did not know such a person in there and was a stranger[.]" NH told him not to take his discharge until Simpson had seen the consul. "The next afternoon the captain came on board and said what parcel of damned stuff and lies have you been telling the Consul I said I had told no lies he said hush and struck me tore my collar and threatened to mash me up There was no one present it being in the pantry I was getting his dinner and he told me he did not want any damned dinner and that he would not pay me a damned cent and would take me in the Ship I went ashore as soon as I could and applied at the Consulate and stated what had happened[.]" Gloss could not corroborate this exchange, but did confirm that after the captain had gone into the cabin with Maudluff, "a few minutes after I saw the steward come out of the Cabin greatly excited and his shirt all torn[.]"

4. On July 23 ten crew members of the *Castine* made a declaration "at the request of Captn James Simpson" that Maudluff had made no complaints of ill treatment and "tho we saw him daily and constantly there was no appearance of rough usage or violence on his person[.]" They also claimed that both at Castine and at St. Johns, where the ship stopped, Maudluff had been allowed on shore and had had ample opportunity to to make complaints against the captain there if he had wished to do so. They concluded "that during the whole voyage we have experienced the kindest treatment from Captain Simpson and have no cause whatever of complaint and we can confidently assert that Captain Simpson has always treated the steward with every kindness up to the time of the steward leaving the vessel[.]"

5. On September 10 Simpson formally protested NH's actions in a statement sworn before a Liverpool Notary Public. He again denied mistreating Maudluff and stated "that he disproved the said charge in the presence of the said Consul by the evidence of ten of the crew of the said vessel"; being compelled to leave for New Orleans without his register, Simpson held NH and all others concerned "responsible for all losses damages and expenses and for any seizure or detention of the said vessel either in this port or elsewhere which may arise or occur in consequence of the said vessel having sailed without her Certificate of Registry" (Official Correspondence Inward, NA). See C235.5. On November 21, Secretary of Treasury Nowell Cobb wrote to F. H. Hatch, Collector of Customs at New Orleans, instructing him to deliver the *Castine*'s papers to the owners "upon the payment of the sum demanded by the Consul. . ." (Transcript, Instructions, 3, NA).

6. The last page of the Consulate's letterpress volume records a slightly variant text of this last paragraph. See textual note.

US Consulate
Liverpool 18 Sept 1857

Dear Sir,

Annexed please find account of nett proceeds of materiel saved from your Ship the Robert Parker, and enclosed Mess[rs] Brown Shipley & Co's draft for $56.38 equivalent of Balance.[2]

The Captain of the Robert Parker never reported in any way whatever, that anything had been saved from his vessel, until the day previous to his leaving here, when he informed me that the Captain of the salving vessel had refused to deliver to him, or pay for, any of the property saved. The consequence was much difficulty & delay in settling the matter.

I am
Resp[y] Your obed Serv[t]

Ichabod Goodwin Esq
Portsmouth

1. Ichabod Goodwin, merchant, had an office at 82 Market St., and a residence at 34 Islington St. (*Portsmouth City Book and Directory*, 1856–57).

2. See C227. The letterpress book also includes a memorandum recording that on September 16 NH received £12.9.6 from the Receiver of Droits of Admiralty. After deducting 5% commission and car fare, he bought a draft from Brown Shipley & Co on Boston for £11.15.0 or $56.38 (Letterpress copy, CO, 13A, 33, NA).

C240. TO MURRAY MCCONNEL, WASHINGTON

Consulate of the United States
Liverpool
September [26?] 1857[1]

Sir

I regret that the preparation of my Quarterly accounts has been delayed by the protracted illness of the clerk who had them in Charge.[2]

They will be proceeded with as speedily as the difficulties of the case will permit, it having been necessary to instruct another person in the Method of this peculiar class of accounts under the disadvantage of receiving no assistance or explanation from his predecessor[3]

I hope and except to forward them at a very early date

I have the honor to
be Your Obt Serv[t]
Nath[l] Hawthorne
Consul

To
The Fifth Auditor
Dep[t] of State
Washington

1. The number after "September" is illegible in copy; it is conjectured from 1001.

2. NH left Liverpool on September 24, intending to meet his family and accompany them to Paris. But two days later NH wrote Ticknor, "I was telegraphed

back from Leamington on account of the severe illness of Mr. Wilding, who is prostrated with a nervous fever, attended with delirium. This has thrown a load of business upon me, making it impossible for me to leave at present. The worst effect of it is (so far as I am concerned) that it will cause an embarrassing delay in the adjustment of my accounts, and the arrangement of my financial concerns" (1001). NH turned over the Consulate to Tucker on October 12 and left Liverpool for good on October 16.

3. Compare NH to Ticknor, October 9: "Mr. Wilding's illness has most seriously inconvenienced me by the delay of my accounts; for they are of a peculiar class, and it has been necessary to instruct another person how to make them up without aid or advice from him; and he held all the clues in his hands. However, this difficulty is in a fair way to be surmounted; and I shall soon know how I stand with the Treasury Department" (1005).

C241. TO MURRAY MCCONNELL AND LEWIS CASS,
WASHINGTON

[Liverpool
20 November 1857

[Submitting accounts of Liverpool consulate.]

US Consulate
Liverpool 20 Nov 1857

Sir

I have the honor to inform you that I have this day
forwarded to the 5th Auditor of the Treasury the Accounts of
this Consulate for the Quarter ending 31 Decr 1856 viz
Disbursements for Destitute Seamen
£427.8.7 @ 47½^d per dollar————————$2159.64
Department of State for Postages &^c
£52.7.4 @ 47½ ———————————————$264.59
And for the half year ending same date for Expenses
receiving & transmitting Despatches————$242.00[1]

With high Respect
I have the honor to be
Your obed^t Servant
Nathl Hawthorne

Hon Lewis Cass
Secretary of State

1. NH evidently had drawn against his account on November 1 for $76.87. On January 13, Edward Stubbs wrote that his draft had been honored, but that according to the accounts as submitted, he was due only $70.85. "This amount," he concluded, "deducted from your dft, leaves due, by you, a balance of $6.02; and stands against [you] on the books of the Treasury" (MS, Instructions, 3, NA).

United States Consulate
Liverpool 4 Decr 1857

Sir,

I have the honor to inform you that I shall forward by same
Steamer with this accounts of this Consulate for the quarter
ending 31st March 1857^1 viz
    Disbursements for Dest Seamen–£525.9.5 or $2627.55.
    Department of State for Postages
        Newspapers &^{c}————————£29.18.2 $149.54
calculated at 48^d p dollar. I enclose Brown Shipley & Co's
Certificate of Exchange.

With high Respect
I am Your obed^t Servant
Nathl Hawthorne

Hon Lewis Cass
Sec^y of State
Washington

1. On July 27 the Department of Treasury had informed NH that the accounts
ending March 31, 1857 were overdue and ordered him to transmit them "without
further delay" (D, Instructions, 2, NA).

United States Consulate
Liverpool 10 Dec[r] 1857

Sir,

I have the honor to inform you that by same steamer with this I shall forward to the 5th Auditor of the Treasury the accounts of this Consulate for the Quarter ending 30 June 1857 viz
For disbursements for Destitute Seamen
£314.5.2 equal to ————————————————$1571.29
Department of State for Postages &[c]
£46.17.10 equal to ————————————————$234.45
Also an account for Expenses incurred receiving & transmitting Despatches half year ending same date————$242.00
I also forward Mess[rs] Brown Shipley & Co's Certificate of Exchange.[1]

I am with great Respect
Your obed[t] Servant
Nath[l] Hawthorne.

Hon Lewis Cass
Secretary of State

1. On February 18, 1858, the newly appointed First Comptroller, William Medill, responded that NH's accounts for this quarter and for the preceding one had

been adjusted and that NH owed the Treasury $180.98, since his charge for loss by Exchange had not been "accompanied with the necessary vouchers showing that you actually sustained the loss charged for. . . . ¶ The certificate of Brown Shipley & Co. in relation to the rate of Exchange at their respective dates are doubtless correct, but that fact does not authorize the accounting officers to allow the same to you, inasmuch as they afford no proof that you actually sustained the loss claimed by you in the sale of your draft. ¶ The accounting offices are authorized to allow only *actual losses* by Exchange sustained by Diplomatic and Consular Agents of the Government and claims for supposed or mere constructive loss cannot be entertained. ¶ The Certificate of the Banker or Merchant who negotiated your Drafts, that he purchased them at an actual loss to you of the sum charged in your a/c current, will be deemed sufficient to authorize the payment of the suspension, provided the Gold Standard of the U. States (viz: $23^{22}/_{100}$ grs. of pure gold to the dollar,) is adopted as the basis of computation" (MS, Instructions, 3, NA). On May 5, HW wrote NH, "I have been in communication with Baring, who informed me that you did not sell them your drafts, but only sent them out for collection; but they have furnished me with a statement which I think must satisfy the very particular Comptroller. I will forward it from here to Washington" (MS, Berg). HW received no immediate response and thought the matter settled, but in 1861 the Treasury informed HW that nearly all of NH's claims for losses by exchange had been disallowed. On November 14, HW wrote NH that "At this distance of time it is difficult to get at the accounts and vouchers among the mass of dusty accumulations, and one's memory affords but little help." HW located vouchers for $5.80, but added, "I fear you will have to submit to the loss of the remainder, unless you can attack the present Comptroller more successfully that I did the other. It is a manifest injustice, as of course you had to pay Baring's commissions for collecting the drafts, and interest on the money advanced to pay the accounts" (*NHHW*, II, 166).

United States Consulate
Liverpool 24 Decem^r 1857

Sir,

I have the honor to inform you that by same steamer with this I shall forward to the fifth Auditor of the Treasury the accounts of this Consulate for the Quarter ending 30 Sept 1857

For Disbursements for destitute Seamen ———$535.52

Department of State for Postage &^{c} ———$118.18

Also for the portion of Quarter from 1st to 11 Oct^r

For Disbursements for destitute Seamen ———$160.89

Department of State for Postages &^{c} ———$38.79

Also for Expenses incurred for receiving and transmitting Despatches from 1 July to 11 Oct^o inclusive 103 days @ £100 per annum ———————$136.56

I enclose herewith Messrs Brown Shipley & Co's Certificate of Exchange.

With high Respect
I have the honor to be
Your obed^t Servant
Nathl Hawthorne

Hon Lewis Cass
Secretary of State

C245. TO LEWIS CASS, WASHINGTON

United States Consulate
Liverpool 31 Decr 1857

Sir,

I have the honor to forward herewith my accounts for
Office Rent from 1 Jany to 11 October 1857, and for Salary
from 12 Oct° (when I delivered the Consulate to my
Successor) to 10 November 1857—30 days, to which I am
entitled under the Act of Aug 1856.[1] For the respective
amounts I have this day drawn upon you in favor of Messrs
Baring Brothers & Co London.[2]

I have the honor
to be with high regard
Your obed^t Servt
Nathl Hawthorne.

Hon Lewis Cass
Secretary of State
Washington

1. These amounts respectively came to $616.43 and $583.56 (*FIN*, p. 629).
2. NH's 1858 pocket diary records that HW forwarded these last two letters to
NH in London, where he and his family were "awaiting the settlement of my official
accounts in order to go to the continent. The delay has been much greater than I
expected." The accounts arrived on January 1, and, after signing them, NH
"Returned the accts through Mr. Miller" (*FIN*, p. 575). NH left England on
January 5. On January 23, Appleton responded, "Your draft for $583⁵⁶/₁₀₀,

purporting to be for Office rent from 1st January to the 11th October, has been presented and paid; and the amount is charged to you on the books of the Treasury, where it will so remain until you render an account with voucher by which you may obtain a corresponding credit. These should have preceded or accompanied the draft" (MS, Instructions, 3, NA). HW wrote NH on May 5, "What will you do? I have obtained a voucher for what you actually paid, including rate, and enclose amended account for your signature, if you should determine to claim the amount, which I certainly should do" (MS, Berg).

EDITORIAL APPENDIXES

TEXTUAL NOTES

C147A. Paraphrase, Parke-Bernet Galleries Catalogue, April 18–19, 1944, item 493. LS [in HW's hand, signed by NH?], 1 page, small quarto. Address: To Collector of Customs, N.Y.

C148. Letterpress copy, CO, 10A, [58], NA. In HW's hand, unsigned in copy. In ¶1 sentence 1, HW interlined in pencil 'Master of the Ship Burlington of that place'; in ¶2, he altered 'accordingly' to 'according to'. The copied version includes unfilled blanks after ¶1 'p' and above 'U S Consul' where NH would have signed the letter. At end of letter text, a period is supplied. Publ., Byers, p. 305.

C149. Letterpress copy, CO, 12A, 285 (bottom), NA. In HW's hand, unsigned in copy. After 'you can take', HW altered 'him' to 'them'.

C150. Letterpress copy, CO, 12A, 285 (top), NA. In HW's hand, unsigned in copy. In sentence 1, 'Letter' is emended from 'Lettr'. At end of letter body, a period is supplied.

C151. Letterpress copy, CO, 12A, 286 (top), NA. In HW's hand, signed by NH. Interior address not copied but transcribed by HW in pencil at bottom of letter.

C152. Letterpress copy, CO, 12A, 286 (bottom), NA. In HW's hand, signed by NH. In sentence 1, 'whic[h]' (2nd) is supplied at end of page.

C153. Letterpress copy, CO, 12A, 287, NA. In HW's hand, unsigned in copy. In date, '185[6]' is supplied at edge of page.

C154. Letterpress copy, CO, 12A, 288, NA. In HW's hand, unsigned in copy. In sentence 2, HW altered 'be' from 'by'. In same sentence, 'contain[ed]' is supplied at edge of page, and a period is supplied.

C155. Letterpress copy, CO, 12B, 81, NA. In HW's hand, signed by NH. At end of ¶2, a period is supplied.

C156. MS, H.O. 45 / 6330, PRO. In HW's hand, signed by NH. HW's comma after second 'Driver' has been moved inside the close double quotes. Other text: Letterpress copy, CO, 12A, 289 (bottom), NA (unsigned). In Letterpress copy, the top address and date were not copied, and the date alone was transcribed in pencil by HW at the top of the page; also, in letterpress copy a blank is left where 'Peter Connolly' appears in MS.

C157. Letterpress copy, CO, 12A, 289 (top), NA. In HW's hand, signed by NH. After 'immediately', the word 'communicate' is supplied. A period is supplied at end of letter text.

C158. MS, Despatches, 13, 'Nº 58' [sic], NA. In HW's hand, signed by NH. Cover: 'U S Consulate / Liverpool 25 Jany 1856 / Nath¹ Hawthorne / Nº 58 / one Enclosure / Received — / Henry N Johnson a / Prisoner sent in Ship / Cultivator to New York'. Note: 'Recd 11. Feby. Mr. Abbott / See letter to the / Comptroller Dec. 26'. In ¶1, HW cancelled 'f' before 'of which'; in ¶3, he altered 'mo' to 'having'. Other text: CO, 10A, 'N[MS blurred]', NA (unsigned). Publ., Sweeney, p. 253; SAR 1979, pp. 356–57; Byers, p. 305.

C159. Letterpress copy, CO, 12A, 290–91, NA. In HW's hand, unsigned in copy. In ¶1 sentence 1, HW's dittography 'I have / I have sent' is emended.

C160. Letterpress copy, CO, 12A, 292, NA. In HW's hand, signed by NH. In ¶2, HW interlined 'I believe' before 'the only'. At edge of page, letters are supplied: ¶1: 'striki[ng]', 'Americ[an]', 'York[.]'; ¶2: 'Citizen[.]'.

C161. MS, Despatches, 13, [60], NA. In HW's hand, signed by NH. Cover: 'U S Consulate / Liverpool 1 February 1856 / Nath¹ Hawthorne / N° 60 / Received — / Advising rescue of crew of / Am Bark Olivia by English / Bark Emperor.' Note: 'Recd 22nd Feby. Mr Abbott. / Ansd 25 ″ / Reported to the Pres- / ident on 25 ″'. A second hand has bracketed the letter text from ¶1 'the rescue . . . ' to ¶3 '. . . windbound.' and again from ¶5 'The master . . . ' to ¶5 '. . . deserves mention.' The same hand also pencilled two small 'x's' in ¶5, under 'telegraphed' and beside 'Sᵗ John'. In ¶1, HW left a space for Captain Ferguson's first name, but never filled it in; in ¶6 sentence 2, he altered 'than' to 'that'. In ¶2 sentence 1, 'boisterous' is emended from 'boisteroous'; in sentence 2, 'of' is supplied before 'water' and 'vessel' is emended from 'vessels'; at end of sentence 3, a period is supplied; in ¶3 sentence 5, 'speak in' is emended from 'speak of'. Other text: CO, 10A, 'N° 60', NA (signed). Publ., Sweeney, pp. 255–57; SAR 1979, pp. 357–58.

C162. MS, Despatches, 13, 'N° 62', NA. In HW's hand, signed by NH. Cover: (crowded into right and left margins of second recto) 'U S Consulate / Liverpool 5 Feby 1856 / Nath¹ Hawthorne / N° 62 / On the Receipt & transmⁿ / of Despatches, & expeses [*sic*]'. Note: 'Recd 26. Feby. Mr Abbott. / Ansd 1 March'. In ¶5 sentence 1, HW interlined 'might' after 'such vigils'. At the end of ¶7, HW left extra room after 'where or how.' and before 'By employing'. As HW appears to have been crowded for space on the final verso of this letter, this extra space has been interpreted here as a paragraph break. In interior address, HW cancelled 'Wᵐ' after 'Hon'. In ¶5 sentence 1, after 'attention during', 'the' is emended from 'to'. In ¶7 sentence 3, 'Despatch' is emended from 'Despach'. Other text: CO, 10A, '62', NA (signed). Publ., Sweeney, pp. 262–65; *SAR* 1979, pp. 359–61; Byers, pp. 306–07.

C162A. Letterpress copy, CO, 12A, 293, NA. In HW's hand, signed by NH. Second page of letter, containing close and interior address, copied in mirror image on same page as the body; HW also pencilled 'Y O S / N H' and interior address at bottom of page. In ¶2, before 'I was', HW altered 'I' to '&'; in ¶3, he altered 'advise' to 'advice'; in ¶6 sentence 3, after 'must be', he cancelled 'after'; in ¶7, he altered 'the' to 'this'. At edge of page, letters are supplied: ¶1: 'receive[d]'; ¶2: 'wa[s]'; ¶5: 'consignee[s.]'; ¶6 sentence 1: 'agen[t]', 'respect-in[g]'; sentence 2: 'ma[y]', 'recommend[.]'; sentence 3: 'un-question[ed]', 'must b[e]', 'du[ly]'. Image of second page is very faint; in interior address, '[Ca]pt' and '[S]hi[p]' are sup-plied from HW's transcript at foot of page. In ¶1, 'Letter' is emended from 'Lettr' and HW's dittography '2ⁿᵈ mate mate' is emended; in ¶6 sentence 3, 'after' is emended from 'aftr'.

C163. Letterpress copy, CO, 12A, 295, NA. In HW's hand, signed by NH. At edge of page, letters are supplied: heading, 'Stat[es]', '185[6]'; body, 'nominate[d]', 'surveyor[s]', 'attend-in[g]', 'tomorr[ow]', 'Bisse[t]', 'wit[h]'.

C164. Letterpress copy, CO, 12A, 297, NA. In HW's hand, signed by NH. In sentence 1, HW altered '1855' from '1856'. At edge of page, letters are supplied: date: 'State[s]'; ¶2: 'interes[t]'. In sentence 1, 'in' is supplied after 'succeeded'.

C165. MS, Despatches, 13, 'N° 63', NA. In HW's hand, signed by NH. Cover: 'U S Consulate / Liverpool / 22 Feby 1856 / Nathˡ Hawthorne / N° 63 / Received — / Advising the Rescue of crews / of Brig Crusader & Schooner / Mayflower by British Barks Sarah—& Baticola'. Note: 'Recd 11th March Mr Abbott.' A second hand has bracketed the letter text from ¶1 'the Crusader' to end of ¶3; a second close bracket appears at end of ¶5. In ¶2 sentence 2, HW altered 'falled' to 'fallen';

in ¶6, he interlined 'money'. A period is supplied at the end of ¶4. Other text: CO, 10A, 'Nº 63', NA (signed). Publ., Sweeney, pp. 266–67; *SAR* 1979, pp. 362–63.

C166. Letterpress copy, CO, 12A, 299, NA. In HW's hand, signed by NH. At edge of page, letters are supplied: ¶1 sentence 1, 'you woul[d]'; ¶2 sentence 1, 'produc[e]'.

C167. Letterpress copy, CO, 12A, 300, NA. In HW's hand, signed by NH. At edge of page, letters are supplied: date, '185[6]'; ¶1, 'America[ns]'; ¶2, 'reques[t]', 'suc[h]'; ¶3, 'plac[e]', 'desir[e]'.

C168. Letterpress copy, CO, 12A, 301 (bottom), NA. In HW's hand, unsigned in copy. In sentence 1, after 'the Duty', HW interlined '&c' without a caret. In sentence 1, 'addressed' is expanded from 'add^d'. At edge of page, letters are supplied: sentence 1, 'had bee[n]'; sentence 2, 'conten[ts]'. Second line of interior address is barely visible at bottom of page; it has been reconstructed from HW's usual styling.

C169. MS, Essex. In HW's hand, signed by NH. Periods are supplied at ends of ¶1 and ¶3, and in ¶2, a comma is supplied after 'Messrs Henry'. Other text: Letterpress copy, CO, 10B, 'Nº 41', NA (signed).

C170. Letterpress copy, CO, 10B, 'Nº 42', NA. In HW's hand, unsigned in copy. Interior address is partially blurred; 'Treas[ury]' is supplied. In ¶2 sentence 1, 'November' is emended from 'Novembr'.

C171. MS, Despatches, 13, 'Nº 64', NA. In HW's hand, signed by NH. No cover. Note: 'Recd 21. April. Mr Abbott.' In sentence 4, HW superseded a comma with a closing parenthesis. In sentence 1, an apostrophe is supplied for 'steamer's'. Other text: CO, 10A, 'Nº 64', NA (unsigned). Publ., Sweeney, pp. 268–69; *SAR* 1979, p. 363.

C172. (i). Letterpress copy, CO, 10B, 'N° 43', NA. In HW's hand, unsigned in copy. HW cancelled an extra '5' after '$142.95'. At end of letter text, a period is supplied. (ii). MS, Despatches, 13, 'N° 65', NA. In HW's hand, signed by NH. Cover: 'US Consulate / Liverpool 11 April / 1856 / Nath¹ Hawthorne / N° 55 / [*rule*] / one enclosure / Received — / Advising accounts / for Destitute Seamen / Postages &c'. Notes: 'Recd 26. April. Mr Abbott.' [*right margin*] 'Certificate sent to the Agent. Apr. 20.' At end of letter text, a period is supplied. Other text: CO, 10A, 'N° 65', NA (unsigned). Publ., Sweeney, p. 270; SAR 1979, p. 364. (iii). Letterpress copy, CO, 10B, 'N° 45', NA. In HW's hand, signed by NH. (iv). MS, Despatches, 13, 'N° 66', NA. In HW's hand, signed by NH. Cover: 'US Consulate / Liverpool 26 April / 1856 / Nath¹ Hawthorne / N° 66 / Received — / Advising drafts / for accounts for / Quartr ending 31 Decr'. Note: 'Recd 12. May. Mr Abbott.' HW originally numbered this despatch '45', then cancelled the numeral and added '66'. In date, HW altered '1856' from '1855', and at start of letter text, he altered '1855' from '1856'. Other text: CO, 10A, 'N° 66', NA (signed). Publ., Sweeney, p. 271; SAR 1979, pp. 364–65.

C173. Letterpress copy, CO, 12A, [303] (top), NA. In HW's hand, unsigned in copy. In ¶2 sentence 1, HW cancelled 'The' before beginning again with 'Such'. Interior address not copied but transcribed by HW in pencil at bottom of page.

C174. Letterpress copy, CO, 10B, '44', NA. In HW's hand, signed by NH. In ¶2, after 'Quarter of $', HW left a blank; after copying the letter, he pencilled the sum into the letterpress copy. In first line of date, MS is blurred; '[United States]' has been supplied; in ¶2, a comma is supplied after 'my salary' and a period is supplied at end.

C175. CO, 10A, [67] (first leaf, to ¶4 sentence 1 '. . . Iron purchased') and CO, 10B, '46' (second leaf, to end), NA. In

HW's hand, signed by NH. HW noted at bottom of first leaf, 'for conclusion see / other side' and at top of second leaf, 'For beginning see other side'. Publ., Byers, pp. 307–08.

C176. MS, Despatches, 13, 'Nº 68', NA. First leaf of a sheet; second, with copy of letter and cover, was evidently detached at the Department. In HW's hand, signed by NH. Note: 'Recd 7. June. Mr Abbott.' A second hand, in ¶1 sentence 1, interlined 'some time since' after 'I gave'; the same hand also pencilled a horizontal line above 'I gave' and a close parenthesis at end of ¶3. The interlined reading is rejected as a departmental annotation. In ¶3 sentence 2, HW altered 'that' to 'those'. Periods are supplied at ends of ¶1 and ¶2. Other texts: CO, 10A, '68', NA (unsigned); Transcript, Despatches, 13 (bound immediately following the MS), NA. Publ., Sweeney, pp. 272–73; *SAR* 1979, pp. 365–66.

C177. Letterpress copy, CO, 12B, 82, NA. In HW's hand, signed by NH. HW noted on this copy, 'No answer being rec^d / Copy sent 30 May'. See Historical Notes. In interior address, HW cancelled 'To' before 'G M'. In ¶1, his dittography 'of / of the United' is emended. At end of letter text, a period is supplied. Other text: Transcript (in HW's hand), F.O. 5 / 656, PRO.

C178. Letterpress copy, CO, 12A, fourth unnumbered folio pasted on back of [303], NA. In HW's hand, signed by NH.

C179. Letterpress copy, CO, 12A, third unnumbered folio pasted on back of [303], NA. In HW's hand, signed by NH. At start of letter text, HW left a blank after 'M^r', and NH filled in the name 'William H. Dougherty,' After 'obliged to refuse', HW altered 'him' to 'his'. A comma is supplied after 'bearer of this', and 'naturalized' is expanded from 'naturl^d'.

C180. MS, F.O. 5 / 656, PRO. In sentence 2, after 'ten days', HW cancelled 'so that' and continued '& I should'. In sentence 1, after 'Stevens', HW's comma is emended to a close parenthesis, and 'surrender' is emended from 'sur-rendr'. A period is also supplied for sentence 1. Other text: Letterpress copy, CO, 12B, 84, NA. First line of heading and last line of interior address not copied.

C181. MS, William L. Marcy Papers, Vol. 70, No. 48470 Library of Congress. In NH's hand.

C182. MS, Despatches, 13, '69', NA. In HW's hand, signed by NH. Cover: 'US Consulate / Liverpool 27th June 1856 / Nathl Hawthorne / [*rule*] / N° 69 / Three enclosures / Received — / Prisoner on a charge of murdr / with two witnesses sent in / the Mary E Balch for New / York 20 June 1856'. Notes: [*top*] 'Recd 12. July Mr Abbott. / See letter to Comptroller Dec. 26.' [*right margin*] 'Enclosures sent to / the <Audit> Comptrol / lor Dec. 26'. In the margins, HW has written brief headings describing the topics covered: ¶1, 'Prisoner / forwarded'; ¶2, 'Witnesses / sent'; ¶3, 'Copies of / Depositions / N° 1'; ¶4, 'Copy of / certificate / to Captain / N° 2 / To pay for / Passages'; ¶5, 'Money ad- / vanced to one of / Witnesses / N° 3 / Difficulty of / detaining the / Witness'. These legends have not been included in the text. In ¶1 sentence 1, HW altered 'master' to 'Master'; in ¶4 sentence 1, he altered 'to' to 'on behalf', squeezing the second word into the bottom right corner of first recto. In ¶3 sentence 1, an apostrophe is supplied for 'Prisoner's'. Other text: CO, 10A, '69', NA (unsigned). Publ., Sweeney, pp. 274–75; *SAR* 1979, pp. 366–67.

C183. Letterpress copy, CO, 12A, first unnumbered folio pasted on back of [303], NA. In HW's hand, signed by NH. In ¶1, after 'pursuant to', 'the' is supplied.

C184. (i). Letterpress copy, CO, 10B, '48', NA. In HW's hand, unsigned in copy. Interior address not copied but transcribed by HW in pencil at foot of first folio. In ¶1, after first sum, HW cancelled 'F' and wrote 'Accompanied' over it. (ii). MS, Despatches, 13, 'N° 70', NA. In HW's hand, signed by NH. Cover: 'US Consulate / Liverpool 18 July 1856 / Nath¹ Hawthorne / N° 70 / [*rule*] / Received / Advising forwarding / of accounts.' Note: 'Recd 31. July. Mr Abbott'. Other text: CO, 10A, '70', NA (unsigned). Publ., Sweeney, p. 277; *SAR* 1979, p. 367. (iii) Letterpress copy, CO, 10B, 'N° 51', NA. In HW's hand, unsigned in copy. (iv) MS, Despatches, 13, [71], NA. In HW's hand, signed by NH. Cover: 'US Consulate / Liverpool 15 Aug 1856 / Nath¹ Hawthorne / N° 71 / Received — / Advising drafts for / Disbursements for Seamen / & for Postages &ᶜ.' Note: 'Recd 29. Aug. Mr Abbott.' In ¶2, HW cancelled 'Messrs' before 'Wᵐ D Ticknor'. At end of ¶1, an apostrophe is supplied for 'Co's'. Other text: CO, 10A, '71', NA (signed). Publ., Sweeney, pp. 277–78; *SAR* 1979, p. 368.

C185. Letterpress copy, CO, 10B, '49', NA. In HW's hand, unsigned in copy. In letter text, HW interlined 'attempt at' after 'crime of'.

C186. (i). Letterpress copy, CO, 10B, '52', NA. In HW's hand, signed by NH. Before third sum, HW interlined 'expenses incurred in' with a caret. A period is supplied at end of letter text. HW copied this letter over a pencilled draft of the same letter (no substantive variants). (ii). MS, Despatches, 13, 'N° 72', NA. In HW's hand, signed by NH. Cover: 'US Consulate / Liverpool 26 Aug / 1856 / Nath¹ Hawthorne / N° 72 / [*rule*] / Received — / Advising accounts / forwarded to 5ᵗʰ Auditor'. Note: 'Recd 16. <April> Septr. Mr Abbott.' HW first omitted the second dollar sum, then squeezed it in below the line beneath '£29.12.9'; here it is printed on the line after the pound sum. Other text: Letterpress copy, CO, 10A, '72', NA (signed). HW copied this letter over a pencilled draft of the same letter; substantive variants: sentence 1, 'fifth' for '5ᵗʰ'; '30ᵗʰ June' for '30 June'; first dollar sum missing; second pound and dollar sums missing. Publ., Sweeney, pp. 278–79; *SAR* 1979, p. 368. (iii). Letterpress copy, CO, 10B, 'N° 54', NA. In HW's hand, unsigned in copy. A period is supplied at end of letter text. (iv). MS, Despatches, 13, 'N° 73', NA. In HW's hand, signed by NH. Cover: '1856 / US Consulate / Liverpool 25 Sept^r / Nathl Hawthorne / N° 73 / One Enclosure / Advising drafts for / Disbursements. / Received—' Note: 'Recd 13th Octr. Mr Abbott.' In ¶1 sentence 1, HW altered 'have' to 'had'. Other text: CO, 10A, 'N° 73', NA (unsigned). Publ., Sweeney, pp. 279–80; SAR 1979, p. 369.

C187. Letterpress copy, CO, 13A, 1, NA. In HW's hand, signed by NH. A period is supplied at end of letter text.

C188. Letterpress copy, CO, 10B, [53], NA. In HW's hand, signed by NH. In ¶1, 'half' is supplied before 'year ending same date' (see C186, ¶2). In ¶3, 'a' is supplied before 'sum'; in ¶4 sentence 2, an apostrophe is supplied for 'Barings''; in ¶5 sentence 2, HW's apparent 'beforementioned' is read as two words, following his customary usage.

C189. MS, Despatches, 13, 'N° 74', NA. In HW's hand, signed by NH. Cover: '1856 / US Consulate / Liverpool 26 Sept 1856 / Nathl Hawthorne / N° 74 / 2 enclosures. <A> Transmitting a report / of Committee of House / of Commons on "Local / charges upon shipping" / & a notice respecting Lights / & Buoys in approachs [sic] to Liver- / pool / Received —'. Note: 'Recd 13. Octr. Mr Abbott.' At end of ¶2, at a page break, HW left a long space, then wrote 'Our / Our' twice, apparently as a catchword; the space is interpreted as a paragraph break, and only the first 'Our' is printed here. Other text: Letterpress copy, CO, 10B, 'N° 74' (erroneously placed after Treasury 'N° 54'), NA (signed). Publ., Sweeney, pp. 280–81; SAR 1979, pp. 369–70.

C190. MS, Despatches, 13, [75], NA. In HW's hand, signed by NH. Cover: '1856 / U.S. Consulate / Liverpool 3^d Oct 1856 / Nathl Hawthorne / [rule] / N° 74 [sic] / [rule] / One

Enclosure / Received— / Forwarding copy of advertisement / for designs for New Government / offices in London'. Note: 'Recd 16. Octr. Mr Abbott.' A departmental clerk also pencilled at the top of the advertisement transcript, 'Please copy.' Other text: Letterpress copy, CO, 10B, '75' (erroneously placed after Treasury 'N° 54'), NA (unsigned). Publ., Sweeney, pp. 281–82; SAR 1979, p. 370.

C191. MS, Despatches, 13, [76], NA. In HW's hand, signed by NH. Cover: 'US Consulate / Liverpool 10 Oct° 1856 / Nath¹ Hawthorne / N° 75 [sic] / [rule] / Received — / Reply to Despatch of / 15 Sept 1856 respecting / Despatches forwarded by / Persia 5 Aug passing thro' / Post Office'. Note: 'Recd 27. Octr Mr Abbott.' In ¶2 sentence 1, HW interlined 'the' before 'Persia'. Other text: CO, 10A, 'N° 76', NA (unsigned). Publ., Sweeney, pp. 283–84; SAR 1979, p. 371.

C192. Letterpress copy, CO, 13A, 2, NA. In HW's hand, signed by NH. HW pencilled a draft of the letter on the copybook page (no variants).

C193. MS, Despatches, 13, [77], NA. In HW's hand, signed by NH. Cover: 'US Consulate / Liverpool 24 Oct 1856 / Nath¹ Hawthorne / N° 75 [sic] / [rule] / Received — / Advising appointment / of Mʳ Alfred Davy as / Consular Agent at / Manchester.' Note: 'Recd 10. Novr. Mr Abbott. / Ansd 11 ″ '. A period is supplied at end of letter text. Other text: CO, 10A, '77', NA (signed). Publ., Sweeney, p. 285; SAR 1979, pp. 371–72.

C194. Letterpress copy, CO, 13A, 3, NA. In HW's hand, signed by NH.

C195. MS, Despatches, 13, [78], NA. In HW's hand, signed by NH. Cover: '1856 / US Consulate / Liverpool 7 Nov / Nath Hawthorne / N° 78 / Received — / Forwarding specimen / of "Sorghe".' Note: 'Recd 24. Novr. Mr Abbott. / Ansd 16 Decr / Bag of seed / retained by / the Secretary / for distribution.' A period is supplied at end of letter text. Other text: CO, 10A, '78', NA (unsigned). Publ., Sweeney, pp. 285–86; *SAR* 1979, p. 372; Byers, p. 308.

C196. MS, Despatches, 13, [79], NA. In HW's hand, signed by NH. Cover: '1856 / US Consulate / Liverpool 21 Nov / Nath¹ Hawthorne / N° 79 / Received — / Reporting loss of Ships / Samuel M Fox—Silas / Wright—& Louisiana of / New York.' Note: 'Recd 8. Decr. Mr Abbott.' In ¶5 sentence 1, HW altered 'n' to 'so'. Other text: CO, 10A, '79', NA (unsigned) Publ., Sweeney, pp. 287–88; *SAR* 1979, p. 373.

C197. Letterpress copy, CO, 13A, 4, NA. In HW's hand, signed by NH. At end of ¶1, '1855' is emended from '1856' and a period is supplied.

C198. Letterpress copy, CO, 13A, 5, NA. In HW's hand, signed by NH. In ¶1 sentence 2, HW cancelled 'have' before 'demand the surrender'.

C199. Letterpress copy, CO, 13B, 2, NA. In HW's hand, unsigned in copy. A period is supplied at end of letter text.

C200. MS, Despatches, 13, [80], NA. In HW's hand, signed by NH. Cover: '1856 / US Consulate / Liverpool 19 Decʳ / [*rule*] / Nath¹ Hawthorne / [*rule*] / N° 80 / [*rule*] / Received / Acknowledging receipt / of newspaper & pamphlets / containing statutes.' Note: 'Recd 5. Jany. Mr Abbott.' Other text: CO, 10A, '80', NA (signed). Publ., Sweeney, p. 289; *SAR* 1979, p. 374.

C201. MS, Essex. In HW's hand, signed by NH. A period is supplied at end of letter text.

C201A. Letterpress copy, CO, 13B, 3–4, NA. In HW's hand; ¶2 sentence 2 and close not copied but transcribed by HW. In ¶1 sentence 1, HW's unusual abbreviation 'Eng' is expanded to 'English' and his comma after 'Magician' has been moved inside the close quotation marks; at end of sentence 4, close quotation marks are supplied; signature is emended to NH's usual form from HW's 'N. Hawthorne'.

C202. Letterpress copy, CO, 13A, 6, NA. In HW's hand, signed by NH. In sentence 1, HW altered 'clothing' to 'clothes'. In sentence 2, 'matter' is emended from 'mattr'.

C203. MS, Resignations and Declinations File, 1857–1867, Record Group 59, NA. In NH's hand. Notes: 'Mr Young.' [*On second verso*] '13 Feby 1857 / Resignation of / Consul Hawthorne / of Liverpool to / take effect 31 / August'.

C204. MS, Despatches, 13, '81', NA. In HW's hand, signed by NH. Cover: '1857 / US Consulate / Liverpool 13 Feby / N Hawthorne / Consul / N° 81 / Received — / Informing of loss of / Ship Confederation'. Note: 'Recd 5. March Mr Abbott.' In ¶1 sentence 1, HW altered initial 'o' to 'near' and squeezed a comma in before it; in ¶2 sentence 1, he interlined 'next morning' before 'she struck'. At end of ¶1, a period is supplied. At start of ¶3, HW's repetition of 'The / The' at a page break is omitted as a catch word. In ¶1 sentence 1, HW's dittography 'of / of' is emended; in ¶3 sentence 4, his dittography 'an / another' is emended, and his 'beforementi-/ tioned' is emended to 'before mentioned'. Other text: Letterpress copy, CO, 10A, '81', NA (unsigned). Publ., Sweeney, pp. 290–92; *SAR* 1979, pp. 374–75.

C205. (i). MS, Despatches, 13, '83', NA. In HW's hand, signed by NH. Cover: '1857 / US Consulate / Liverpool 13 Feby / N. Hawthorne / N° 83 / Two enclosures / Received — / Enclosing papers on / the subject of shipping / seamen'. Note: 'Recd 5. March Mr Abbott.' A separate note in the Despatches volume reads 'Sent to Mr. Flagg Sept. 28.' (Edmund Flagg was the State Department's Superintendent of Statistics [Sweeney, p. 298].) In ¶5 sentence 1, HW left a blank in right margin after 'entire', evidently intending to ask NH for clarification; neither he nor NH filled it in (letterpress version, unfortunately, is illegible at this point). In ¶4 sentence 2, HW altered 'as' to 'once'; in sentence 3, after 'occurs', he superseded a dash with a comma; in ¶8 sentence 3, he altered 'seamen' to 'seaman' and 'this' to 'his' (compare [ii]); in sentence 3, he first wrote 'juryman' then cancelled 'man'. Periods are supplied at end of ¶1, ¶3 sentence 3, and ¶6 sentence 1. Publ., Hall, pp. 19–21; Sweeney, pp. 294–95; *SAR* 1979, pp. 375–77, Byers, pp. 309–10. (ii). Letterpress copy, CO, 11B, 1–3. In HW's hand; unsigned in copy. In ¶6, sentence 3, HW interlined 'they' after 'crews'; in ¶7, he cancelled 'from' before 'in any'. Both the top and bottom portions of all three pages are badly blurred, as is the right margin. At bottom of first copybook page, ¶3 sentence 2, after 'Scarcely', three words are illegible, then three-fourths of a line after 'consist', then two words after 'or rather', and one line after 'landsmen'. At the top of the second page, two and a half lines are too faint to read; after 'shipmates' another line is illegible, and after 'debility', another line, but no ¶ break is visible here (compare [i]); after 'have been', one word is illegible. At bottom of second page, ¶6 sentence 1, after 'best', two words are illegible, then two more after 'evil', one word after 'branches—&', two words after 'include the', one word after following 'the', and one word after 'say the'. At top of third page, eight full lines are too faint to read, and three words after 'as our'. At bottom of third page, ¶8 sentence 4, one word is illegible after 'objection to', one word after 'English', two-thirds of a line after 'jurisdiction in', four words after 'Representative', and four words after 'vastly'. In dateline, '[Consulate of the United States / Liverpool] 14 February 18[57]' has been reconstructed according to HW's conventional usage. At edge of page, letters and punctuation are supplied: ¶2 sentence 1, 'Liverpool[.]'; ¶3 sentence 1, '[your]', 'ag[ain]', 'to m[e]', 'Tim[es]'; last sentence, 'per-[sons]', 'the[y]'; ¶4 sentence 1, 'befor[e]', 'Liverp[ool]', 'ma[tes]'; ¶5 sentence 1, 'Liverp[ool]', 'juris[diction]', 'm[urder]'; ¶6 sentence 1, 'speak [of]', 'equal[ly in]'; sentence 2. 'th[e] present'; sentence 3, 'increase[d]'; ¶7 sentence 1, 'arres[t]', 'count[ry."]'; ¶8 sentence 1, 's[eas]', 'would b[e]'; sentence 2, 'this [side]'; sentence 3, 'In [the]', '[which] would'; sentence 4, '[sub]mit'. A period is supplied for ¶1.

C206. Letterpress copy, CO, 13A, 7–8, NA. In HW's hand, signed by NH. At page break, ¶4, 'arrange[ment]' is supplied. At end of ¶4, a period is supplied, and in ¶5, an apostrophe is supplied for 'sailors' '. Publ., Hall, p. 21; Sweeney, p. 293.

C207. MS, Despatches, 13, 'Nº 8<1>2', NA. In a second, unidentified clerk's hand, signed by NH. Cover: 'US Consulate / Liverpool 13 Feby / 1857 / N. Hawthorne / Nº 82 / Received — / Informing of committal / of <2ⁿᵈ&> 3ᵈ mate ↑ & Boatswain ↓ of the / Guy Mannering for / manslaughtr'. Note: 'Recd 5. March Mr Abbott.' Other text: Letterpress copy, CO, 10A, '82', NA (unsigned). Publ., Hall, pp. 19–20; Sweeney, pp. 295–96; *SAR* 1979, pp. 377–79.

C208. Letterpress copy, CO, 13A, 11, NA. In HW's hand, signed by NH.

C209. MS, Despatches, 13, 'Nº 84', NA. In HW's hand, signed by NH. Cover: '1856 [*sic*] / US Consulate / Liverpool 27 Feby / Nathˡ Hawthorne / [*rule*] / Nº 84 / [*rule*] / Two Enclosures / [*rule*] / Received — / Correcting an error in / Despatch Nº 83—& enclosing / two orders in Council relative / to the reclamation of deserters / [*rule*]'. Note: 'Recd 17. March Mr Abbott'. A separate note in the Despatches volume reads 'Sent to Mr. Flagg Sept 28'. Periods are supplied at ends of ¶1 and ¶2 sentence 3 (inside HW's close quotation marks). Other text: Letterpress copy, CO, 13B, 5 (signed). Publ., Hall, pp. 20–21; Sweeney, pp. 299–300; *SAR* 1979, p. 379.

C210. Letterpress copy, CO, 13B, 8, NA. In HW's hand, signed by NH. In ¶2, 'jurisdiction' and in close, 'seal' have been conjectured from parallel language in C148; copy is blurred and illegible. Interior address is blurred but legible, but HW has pencilled above it more clearly 'Secy of State'. Periods are supplied at ends of ¶1 and ¶2.

C211. (i). Letterpress copy, CO, 13B, 7, NA. 'N° 58'. In HW's hand, unsigned in copy. (ii). MS, Despatches, 13, 'N° 85', NA. In HW's hand, signed by NH. Cover: '1857 / US Consulate / Liverpool 6 March / N. Hawthorne / N° 85 / Received — / advising / Transmitting accounts / for Seamen—& Depart / of State to 5th Auditor'. Note: 'Recd 25th March Mr Abbott'. In dateline, HW interlined 'March' above cancelled 'Febry'; in sentence 1, he cancelled 'for' before 'inform'. Other text: Letterpress copy, CO, 13B, 6 (unsigned). Publ., Sweeney, p. 302; SAR 1979, p. 380.

C212. Letterpress copy, CO, 13A, 14. In HW's hand, signed by NH. A period is supplied at end of letter text. In interior address, at a blur in MS, 'B[r]os' is supplied.

C213. Letterpress copy, CO, 13B, 9, NA. 'N° 59'. In HW's hand, unsigned in copy. A period is supplied at end of ¶2. Interior address is badly blurred and illegible, and HW has pencilled above it 'Treasury'; 'Hon [James Guthrie] Esq' has been supplied. Although NH knew Guthrie had left office, presence of 'Esq' in copy indicates HW wrote a personal name here. Compare C211 (ii), addressed to Marcy, even though C210 was addressed to 'Secretary of State'. The following Treasury letter (a form letter not printed), dated March 21, was addressed 'Honorable / The Secretary of the Treasury / Washington / D.C'.

C214. MS, Despatches, 13, 'N° 86', NA. In HW's hand, signed by NH. Cover: '1857 / US Consulate / Liverpool / 27 March / N. Hawthorne / N° 86 / [rule] / Two enclosures / [rule] / Received — / Report of Liverpool Chamber / of Commerce on subject of / Seamen—& depositions / relating to the death of a / Seaman on board Ship Wandering / Jew transmitted.' Note: 'Recd 13. April. Mr Abbott.' A separate note in the Despatch volume reads 'Sent to Mr. Flagg. / March 27. 1857'. In ¶2 sentence 1, HW altered 'r' to 'Report'. In ¶3, HW's apparent dittography at a page break, 'entered the Mersey. ¶The / entered the Mersey ¶The evidence' is omitted as a catch phrase. Other text: Letterpress copy and transcript, CO, 11B, 4–5 (unsigned). HW pencilled ¶1 and most of ¶3 into the copybook where the original had not copied clearly. Publ., Hall, p. 22; Sweeney, pp. 303–04; *SAR* 1979, pp. 380–81; Byers, pp. 310–11.

C215. Letterpress copy, CO, 13A, [unnumbered folio between 31 and 32], NA. In HW's hand, unsigned in copy. At ends of ¶s 1 and 2, periods (absent in both texts) are supplied. The signature and second line of interior address are accepted from Transcript, as is the period at end of ¶1 sentence 2; otherwise the text follows the wording and accidentals of the letterpress copy. Other text: Transcript, CO, 13A, 15, NA. In HW's hand (pencil), signed (in ink) by NH. The following substantive variant is rejected: '11 Aug' for '11ᵀᴴ Aug'.

C216. Letterpress copy, CO, 13A, 17, NA. In HW's hand, unsigned in copy. In interior address, 'Shipley' is supplied from the volume's index; copy is blurred and illegible.

C217. Letterpress copy, CO, 13A, 16, NA. In HW's hand, unsigned in copy. In ¶1, HW's comma after 'Ulto' has been moved inside the close quotation marks.

C218. MS, Despatches, 13, 'Nº 87', NA. In HW's hand, signed by NH. Cover: (squeezed onto bottom of second verso) 'Nº 87 / [*rule*] / 1857 / US Consulate / Liverpool 16 April / N. Hawthorne / Nº 87 / [*rule*] / Received — / Petr Campbell transported / for Life for shooting a / Seaman on board American / Ship J. L. Bogart'. Note: 'Recd 2nd May. Mr Abbott'. In ¶1 sentence 1, HW altered 'Irish' to 'Irishman'; in ¶3 sentence 3, he altered 'on' to 'not on'. In ¶5, a comma is supplied after 'second mate'. In ¶6, 'he' is supplied before 'himself'. Other text: Letterpress copy, CO, 11B, 6–9 (unsigned), NA. Publ., Sweeney, pp. 310–12; *SAR* 1979, pp. 381–82.

C219. MS, Despatches, 13, 'N° 88', NA. In HW's hand, signed by NH. Cover: '1857 / [*rule*] / US Consulate / Liverpool 8ᵗʰ May / N. Hawthorne / [*rule*] / N° 88 / [*rule*] / Received — / Advising loss of <'An'> Ship / "Andʷ Foster" & rescue of / crew by schooner Little / Fred.' Note: 'Recd 23d May. Mr Abbott. / Ansd 25 / ″ <29> 30'. Another hand has pencilled a bracket at the start of ¶4. A separate note in the Despatch volume reads 'To the Captain $100 / Mate 50 / Each of the crew 20'. In ¶1 sentence 1, 'Ships' is emended from 'Ship's'. Other text: Letterpress copy, CO, 11B, 10–12 (signed), NA. Publ., Sweeney, pp. 314–15; *SAR* 1979, pp. 383–84.

C220. MS, Despatches, 13, 'N° 89', NA. In second clerk's hand, signed by NH. Cover: '1857 / US Consulate / Liverpool 8 May / N. Hawthorne / [*rule*] / N° 89 / [*rule*] / Received — / Conviction of Jno Lewis / for manslaughter quashed / by the Judges in court of / appeal.' Note: 'Recd 23d May. / Mr Abbott.' In ¶2, the clerk cancelled 'and' before 'did not'. Other text: Letterpress copy, CO, 11B, 13–14 (signed), NA. Publ., Sweeney, pp. 316–17; *SAR* 1979, pp. 384–85.

C221. Letterpress copy, CO, 13A, 18 [bottom], NA. In HW's hand, unsigned in copy. In ¶ 1 sentence 1, 'Seaman' is emended from 'Seamen'. In interior address, 'Briggs' is supplied from the Consulate's Report of American Vessels; letterpress copy is blurred and illegible.

C222. MS, Pearson Collection, Yale. In NH's hand.

C223. MS, Despatches, 13, 'N° 90', NA. In NH's hand. Cover: '1857 / U. S. Consulate / Liverpool / Nathˡ Hawthorne / [*rule*] / N° 90 / [*rule*] / Received — / Treatment of Seamen / [*rule*]'. Note: 'Mr Abbott. Recd 2nd <June> July'. In ¶3 sentence 1, at right margin, NH first wrote 'acquai-', wiped it out, and wrote 'con-' of 'con- / nected' over it; in ¶6 sentence 4, NH first wrote 'sed' then wiped out the 'd' and finished 'seldom'; in ¶7 sentence 3, he began 'inf' then wiped out the 'f' and added a hyphen, finishing 'fluence' on next line; in ¶10 sentence 2, he interlined 'intervention of' before 'Government'; in sentence 3, he wrote 'now' over wiped-out 'wa'; in ¶11 sentence 9, he began 'unf' then wiped out the 'f' and added a hyphen, finishing 'fortunate' on next line; he then wrote 'for me' over wiped-out 'that'. In ¶10 sentence 5, 'beneficially' is emended from 'be- / necially'. Other texts: Letterpress copy of Transcript, partially in HW's hand, partially in an unidentified hand, CO, 11B, 15–27 (concludes 'S^d Nathl Hawthorne' in HW's hand). Substantive variants rejected: ¶1 sentence 3, 'my official' for 'my own official' [compare *NHHW* text]; ¶3 sentence 8, 'This is' for 'This lies'; ¶ 9 sentence 8, 'fields' for 'field'. Also, *NHHW*, II, 153–61 (perhaps using as copy-text a now unknown draft or transcript). Substantive variants rejected: ¶1 sentence 2, 'a Department' for 'the Department'; sentence 3, 'my official' for 'my own official'; ¶2 end (no ¶); ¶3 sentence 2 'These' for 'Those'; ¶3 sentence 7, 'aspect' for 'element'; end (no ¶); ¶4 sentence 2, 'a result' for 'the result'; end (no ¶); ¶6 sentence 2 'a complainant' for 'the complainant'; sentence 3 'insure' for 'ensure'; end (no ¶); ¶7 sentence 1, 'month's' for 'months'; sentence 3 'now found' for 'now usually found'; end (no ¶); ¶8 sentence 1, 'and to those' for 'and those'; ¶9 sentence 2, 'revision. But' for 'revision; but'; sentence 6, 'examinations' for 'examination'; sentence 8, 'it held' for 'it has held'; end (no ¶); ¶11, sentence 3, 'testify' for 'certify'; sentence 5, 'these' for 'those'; 'those' for 'these'; 'an effect' for ' in effect'; ¶10 sentence 4, 'and deal' for 'and to deal'; ¶11 sentence 2, 'these' for 'those'. Publ., Sweeney, pp. 319–26; *SAR* 1979, pp. 385–89; Byers, pp. 312–16.

C224. MS, Despatches, 13, 'N° 91', NA. In HW's hand, signed by NH. Cover: '1857 / US Consulate / Liverpool /

Nathl Hawthorne / 25 June / N° 91 / 1 Enclosure / Received
— / Acknowledging receipt / of Circular N° 3 on the sub-
ject / of detaining persons charged with / offences on b^{d}
American vessels'. Note: 'Recd 9. July. Mr Abbott'. Other
text: Letterpress copy, CO, 11B, 28 (signed), NA. Publ.,
Sweeney, p. 330; *SAR* 1979, pp. 389–90.

C225. MS, Despatches, 13, [92], NA. In HW's hand, signed
by NH. Cover: '1857 / US Consulate / Liverpool / 25 June /
Nathl Hawthorne / N° 92 / Two enclosures / Received — /
Revolt on board Am^{n} / Ship Vanguard.' Note: '92 Recd 9.
July. Mr Abbott. Please copy / Ansd 10 ″ / Enclosures sent
to <Fift> Atty Gen July 10.' In ¶3, HW altered 'man' to
'men'. A period is supplied for ¶3. Other text: Letterpress
copy, CO, 11B, 29–30 (unsigned), NA. Publ., Sweeney, pp.
332–33; *SAR* 1979, pp. 390–91.

C226. Letterpress copy, CO, 13A, 22, NA. In HW's hand,
signed by NH. In dateline, HW altered 'July' from 'June'. In
list of enclosures, 'Master' is emended from 'Mastr'.

C227. Letterpress copy, CO, 13A, 25, NA. In HW's hand,
unsigned in copy. In ¶1, HW's unusual abbreviation 'Br BK'
is expanded to 'British Bark'.

C228. Letterpress copy, CO, 13A, 26, NA. In HW's hand,
unsigned in copy. In ¶1, apparent 'beforementioned' has been
read as two words, following HW's customary usage.

C229. MS, Despatches, 13, 'N° 93', NA. In HW's hand,
signed by NH. Cover: 'N° 93 / [*rule*] / US Consulate /
Liverpool 18 July / [*rule*] / Nathl Hawthorne / [*rule*] / N° 93
/ [*rule*] / Received — / Infor<ation>ing the Department / of
Ship Rowena of San fran / cisco being <here> ↑ in Liverpool
↓ in possession / of British Bondholders.' Note: 'Recd 3.
Augst Mr Abbott'. In ¶3 sentence 5, 'Liverpool' is emended
from 'Liver / pool'. Periods are supplied for end of ¶2 and for

¶3 sentences 1 and 2. Other text: Letterpress copy, CO, 11B, 31–32 (unsigned), NA. Publ., Sweeney, pp. 333–34; *SAR* 1979, pp. 391–92.

C230. Letterpress copy, CO, 13A, 28, NA. In HW's hand, signed by NH. In sentence 1, HW altered 'ninth' from 'te'; in sentence 3 he interlined 'shall'. In sentence 1, 'Donovan' is supplied from C232; Letterpress copy is blurred and illegible.

C231. Letterpress copy, CO, 13A, 30, NA. In HW's hand, signed by NH. In sentence 3, after 'perhaps', HW interlined 'Mr Rittenhouse' above erased 'your'. In sentence 3, 'taken' is conjectured; copy is blurred and illegible.

C232. MS, Despatches, 13, 'N° 94', NA. In HW's hand, signed by NH. Cover: '1857 / U.S. Consulate / Liverpool—— / 31 July / N. Hawthorne / N° 94 / [*rule*] / 2 Enclosures / [*double rule*] / Received — / Reporting assaults / committed by second / mate of ship Arctic / on two Seamen.' Note: 'Rec^d 14th Aug Mr Abbot'. In ¶2, HW interlined 'Daniel' above cancelled 'Donald'. Other text: Letterpress copy, CO, 11B, 33–34 (unsigned), NA. Publ., Sweeney, p. 335; *SAR* 1979, p. 392.

C233. Letterpress copy, CO, 13A, 31, NA. In HW's hand, signed by NH. In ¶3 sentence 2, HW cancelled 'and' after 'drunk'. In ¶3 sentence 3, 'master['s]' is supplied at edge of page. In ¶2 sentence 1, 'Lyons' is emended from 'Lyon's', and in ¶3 sentence 5, 'don't' is emended from 'dont'; at end of ¶3, a period is supplied.

C234. Letterpress copy, CO, 13A, 32, NA. In HW's hand, signed by NH.

C235. MS, Despatches, 13, '95', NA. In HW's hand, signed by NH. Cover: '1857 / US Consulate / Liverpool / 14 Aug / Nathl Hawthorne / N° 95 / Three enclosures / Received — / Transmitting Certificate / of Registry of Ship "AZ" / with documents relating to / discharge of two Seamen.' Note:

'Recd 14. Septr. Mr Abbott. / Referred to Sec. of T. with Register. / See Mr. Cobb's letter of Oct 2d'. In ¶2 sentence 2, HW altered 'his' to 'the' before 'Crew'. In ¶4 sentence 3, HW first wrote 'When a master ill uses', then erased 'When', replacing it with 'If', interlined 'be allowed to', and erased final 's' of 'uses' to produce 'If a master be allowed to ill use'; in same sentence, he altered 'suffers' to 'suffer'. In ¶2 sentence 1, a comma is supplied after 'Steward'. Other text: Letterpress copy, CO, 11B, 35–37 (unsigned), NA. On f. 34 is a faint copy of a note in NH's hand containing a fragment of a draft of ¶4 sentence 3: 'on the pl[ea] <of> alledged in the / [ca]s[e] that the victims were incompetent / <[*unrecovered*] the> <such ill u[sa]ge> / <[*unrecovered*]> the consequences would / be <fr> [d]eplorably <in the present> / <[*unrecovered*]> with the present seamen / [*unrecovered*] seamen'. As the original note appears to have been no more than 2 × 4½ inches in size, it is unlikely to have been part of a complete draft by NH; but it may represent an addition NH wished to insert into the letter when HW drafted the final copy. Publ., Sweeney, pp. 338–39; *SAR* 1979, pp. 393–94; Byers, p. 317.

C236. Letterpress copy, CO, 11B, 38, NA. In HW's hand, second page with possible continuation, close, and signature not copied.

C237. Letterpress copy, CO, 11B, 39, NA. In HW's hand, signed by NH. At edge of page, letters are supplied: ¶1 sentence 2, 'mas[ter]', 'pap[ers]'. In ¶3, 'steamer' is emended from 'steamr'.

C238. MS, Despatches, 13, [99], NA. Dateline, interior address, and ¶'s 1–4 in second clerk's hand, ¶5 and complementary close in HW's hand, signed by NH. Cover: 'US Consulate / Liverpool / 18 Sept 1857 / N. Hawthorne / N° 99/ 2 Enclosures / Concerning illtreatment / of Steward of Ship Castine'. Note: 'Recd 3d Octr. Mr Abbott. / Referred with register to the Secre- / tary of the Treas Nov 20.—See his letter / of Nov 21.' The manuscript has been corrected in a hand and ink resembling NH's signature; these corrections are accepted as authorial: ¶1 sentence 3, 'insolence' for 'indolence'; ¶3 sentence 2, 'reason' over an erased word; ¶4 sentence 1, 'separated' for 'seperated'; sentence 3, 'but' for 'and'. The same hand in ¶1 sentence 3 added a period after 'Steward' and altered following 'the' to 'The'; in sentence 4, he added a comma after 'serious'; in ¶4 sentence 1, he added a semicolon after 'first' and a comma after 'wages'. In ¶5, HW altered his own 'is' to 'has'. In ¶2, 'violently' is emended from 'volently'. Sweeney (p. 44) speculates the loss of three despatches between 'N° 95' and 'N° 99'. But since the State Department did not acknowledge any such despatches or request information on missing letters, the gap is more likely the result of confusion in the office during the interregnum between NH and Tucker. Other text: Letterpress copy and Transcript in HW's hand, CO, 11B, 40–43 (signature not copied). Third folio not copied but transcribed (in a variant text) in pencil by HW: 'kindly & humane ¶ The Steward being colored I <can> could not send him to New Orleans wher[e] the ship has gone & have sent him to Boston. / I am with Great Res / Your Obed Serv' / NH' Publ., Sweeney, pp. 347–48; SAR 1979, pp. 394–95; Byers, pp. 319–20.

C239. Letterpress copy, CO, 13A, 34, NA. In HW's hand, unsigned in copy. In ¶1 sentence 1, HW wrote 'materiel' over cancelled 'yo'.

C240. Letterpress copy, CO, 11B, 44, NA. In second clerk's hand, signed by NH. Number of date is illegible; close is badly blurred and torn at the bottom; it is reconstructed with help of parallel language in C238: 'I [have the honor] to / [be Your Obt] Serv' / Nath¹ Hawthorne / Co[nsul]'

C241. (i) Paraphrase, Sotheby's catalogue 4744E, 2 December 1981, item 485. LS [probably in HW's hand, signed by

NH], 1 page, folio. Address: to M. McConnell [sic], 5th Auditor of the Treasury. (ii) MS, Despatches, [unnumbered; follows Tucker's Despatch 'N° 4'], NA. In HW's hand, signed by NH. No cover. Note: 'Recd 5. Decr. Mr Abbott.' In ¶1 sentence 1, HW cancelled 'Ste' after 'forwarded to'; before third sum, he altered 'rec' to 'Expenses'. Publ., Sweeney, p. 355; *SAR* 1979, pp. 395–96.

C242. MS, Despatches, [unnumbered; follows C241], NA. In HW's hand, signed by NH. No cover. Note: 'Recd 22nd Decr. Mr Abbott. / Enclosure sent same day to Auditor'. In dateline, HW altered '2' to '4' before 'Dec'. A period is supplied at end of letter text. Publ., Sweeney, pp. 355–56; *SAR* 1979, p. 396.

C243. MS, Despatches, [unnumbered; follows an intervening Tucker despatch, also unnumbered], NA. In HW's hand, signed by NH. Cover: '1857 / United States Consulate / Liverpool 10 Decr / Nath¹ Hawthorne / late Consul / N° __ / One Enclosure / Received / Accounts of disbursements / Postages &ᶜ forwarded'. Note: 'Recd 26. Decr. Mr Abbott.' After first sum, HW first wrote 'Also account for receiving' then cancelled it and continued on the line below. A period is supplied at end of letter text. Publ., Sweeney, pp. 356–57; *SAR* 1979, pp. 396–97.

C244. MS, Despatches, [unnumbered; follows C243], NA. In HW's hand, signed by NH. No cover. Note: 'Recd 20. Jany Mr Abbott. / No certificate enclosed.' After fourth sum, HW drew a short dash to the right margin and put a dollar sign there; then he cancelled the sign and wrote 'from' over the dash. Immediately after 'annum' he began another dollar sign, then cancelled this with a long dash to the right margin, completing '$136.56.' there. Before the two sums for 'Department of State', dollar signs are supplied, and a period is supplied at end of letter text. Publ., Sweeney, p. 357; *SAR* 1979, p. 397.

C245. MS, Despatches, [unnumbered; follows C244], NA. In HW's hand, signed by NH. No cover. Note: 'Recd 25. Jany Mr Abbott. / Referred with enclosures same day to Agent.' On the cover, another hand has noted, '1976 / Hawthorne at / 31 Dec 1857 / With a/ct for Salary / and Office rent'. In sentence 1, HW altered first 'I' in '11 October' from a '3'. A period is supplied at end of letter text. Publ., Sweeney, p. 358; *SAR* 1979, p. 397; Byers, p. 321.

WORD-DIVISION

1. End-of-the-Line Hyphenation in the Centenary Edition

Possible compounds hyphenated at the end of a line in the Centenary text are listed here if they are hyphenated within the line in the copy-text. Exclusion from this list means that a possible compound appears as one unhyphenated word in the copy-text. Also excluded are hyphenated compounds in which both elements are capitalized.

143.12   above-mentioned

2. End-of-the-Line Hyphenation in the Copy-Texts

The following possible compounds are hyphenated at the ends of lines in the copy-texts. The form adopted in the Centenary Edition, as listed below, represents Hawthorne's, Marcy's, or Wilding's predominant usage as ascertained by other appearances or by parallels within the copy-texts.

26.5	out-sailing	147.28	seamen
26.32	alongside	148.8	seamen
66.13	shipwrecked	162.11	Sanfrancisco

3. *Special Cases*

The following possible compound is hyphenated at the end of line in both copy-text and Centenary Edition. It appears here in the adopted Centenary form which is obscured by line-end hyphenation.

146.35   overestimated

CONSULAR LETTERS NOT PRINTED

The following list contains all known letters sent out from the Liverpool Consulate during Hawthorne's tenure that are not included in the Centenary's text. Most of them fall into two large groupings: forty-six letters both drafted and signed by HW and twenty-nine form letters cancelling ships' registers, twenty of them signed by NH. Also included are two letters drafted by HW and signed by NH's Vice-Consul, Samuel Pearce, and three letters unsigned in copy but probably signed by HW or Pearce.

For reference purposes, each letter is numbered in chronological order; if two letters were dated on the same day, they are numbered in alphabetical order of the recipient. The name and address (if known) of the recipient is then given, followed by the letter's date. The status of the letter's author is then described: if HW both drafted and signed the letter, the note reads "By HW." Otherwise, the descriptions previously given are used: "In HW's hand, signed by NH"; "In HW's hand, unsigned in copy"; and, in the two instances noted above, "In HW's hand, signed by Pearce". A brief précis of the letter's subject matter is then presented, with a cross reference (when relevant) inside brackets to consular letters, personal letters, or to entries in *EN*. Finally, the location of the copy-text is described, using the same format as the Textual Notes.

1. To Thomas Aspinwall, London, August 4, 1853. By HW. Requests money for Hector Frazer, a seaman trying to rejoin his vessel. Letterpress copy, CO, 12A, 197, NA.

2. To Thomas Aspinwall, London, August 12, 1853. By HW. Requests money for Frazer and two other seamen. Letterpress copy, CO, 12A, 198, NA.

3. To James Guthrie, Washington, October 14, 1853. In HW's hand, signed by NH. Cancels registers of *Chenamas*, *Gibraltar*, *John & Lucy*, and *South Carolina*. Letterpress copy, CO, 10B, 'N° 1', NA.

4. To Mrs. Wilson Auld, New Orleans, October 31, 1853. By HW. Forwards her deceased husband's effects and details his medical and funeral expenses [see C8]. Letterpress copy, CO, 12A, 209–10, NA.

5. To James Guthrie, Washington, January 20, 1854. In HW's hand; unsigned in copy. Cancels registers of *Liberia Packet*, *Rolling Wave*, *Switzerland*, and *M. R. White*. Letterpress copy, CO, 10B, 'N° 5', NA.

6. To James Guthrie, Washington, April 7, 1854. In HW's hand; unsigned in copy. Cancels registers of *Advance*, *Ozark*, *Pemaquid*, *Trieste*, *Franklin*, *Mayflower*, *Oswingo*, *Red Jacket*, and *Chipman*. Announces loss of *Pantheon*. Letterpress copy, CO, 10B, 'N° 8', NA.

7. To James Guthrie, Washington, May 6, 1854. In HW's hand; signed by NH. Cancels registers of *Austin & Ellen* [see C39–41], *Ralph C Johnson*, *Miltiades*, *Princeton*, *Rip Van Winkle*, and *S. V. Given*. Letterpress copy, CO, 10B, 'N° 9', NA.

8. To James Guthrie, Washington, May 20, 1854. In HW's hand; signed by NH. Cancels registers of *Lightning* and *Ocean Chief* [see C34, C36–37, C44]. Letterpress copy, CO, 10B, 'N° 10', NA.

9. To James Guthrie, Washington, July 13, 1854. In HW's hand; signed by NH. Cancels registers of *Mary Pleasants*, *Shenandoah*, *Dakotah* and *Ohio*. Letterpress copy, CO, 10B,

'N° 13' [first], NA. This letter is cancelled in copybook with a diagonal pencilled line.

10. To Catharine Wilson, Philadelphia, August 22, 1854. In HW's hand, signature cut off at bottom (see 11 below). Requests proof that she is the wife of a deceased seaman so that she can claim his effects [see C65]. Letterpress copy, CO, 12A, 220, NA.

11. To Mr. B. Donnelly, Philadelphia, August 22, 1854. By HW. Reports that Mrs. Wilson has requested her husband's effects. Letterpress copy, CO, 12A, 221, NA.

12. To Philip T. Heartt, U.S. Consul, Glasgow, September 16, 1854. By HW. Requests information on a seaman who has applied for relief. Letterpress copy, CO, 12A, 228, NA.

13. To James Guthrie, Washington, September 29, 1854. In HW's hand; signed by NH. Cancels registers of *Virginia*, *Pamgustuk*, *Mary Crocker*, *Sea Slipper*, *Wm. R. Hallett* [see C59], and *Shackamaxon*. Letterpress copy, CO, 10B, 'N° 15', NA.

14. To James Guthrie, Washington, November 29, 1854. In HW's hand; signed by NH. Cancels registers of *Howard*, *Stormaway*, and *Blue Jacket*. Letterpress copy, CO, 10B, [18], NA.

15. To James Guthrie, Washington, December 29, 1854. In HW's hand; signed by NH. Cancels registers of *Knickerbocker*, *Champion of the Seas* [see C37.3], and *James Baines* [see EN, pp. 89–91]. Letterpress copy, CO, 10B, [19], NA.

16. To James Guthrie, Washington, January 12, 1855. In HW's hand; signed by NH. Cancels register of *Benin*; reports loss of *Pride of the Seas*. Letterpress copy, CO, 10B, 'N° 21', NA.

17. To James Guthrie, Washington, February 2, 1855. In

HW's hand; signed by NH. Cancels registers of *Mary Spring* and *St. Lawrence*. Letterpress copy, CO, 10B, [23], NA.

18. To James Guthrie, Washington, February 16, 1855, In HW's hand; signed by NH. Cancels registers of *Commodore Perry*, *Blanche Moore*, and *Amancipado*. Letterpress copy, CO, 10B, '24', NA.

19. To Godfrey Rider, Provincetown, March 9, 1855. By HW. Provides information on the travel and stated destination of a delinquent ship's captain. Letterpress copy, CO, 12A, 240, NA.

20. To James Guthrie, Washington, March 24, 1855. In HW's hand; signed by NH. Cancels register of *Nathaniel Hooper*. Letterpress copy, CO, 10B, '25', NA.

21. To James Guthrie, Washington, April 7, 1855. In HW's hand; signed by NH. Cancels registers of *Royal Arch*, *Oswingo*, and *Starlight*. Letterpress copy, CO, 10B, '26', NA.

22. To James Guthrie, Washington, May 4, 1855. In HW's hand; signed by NH. Cancels registers of *Young Brander* and *Japan* [see C90]; reports loss of *North Carolina* in collision with *Robert* [see C88–89]. Letterpress copy, CO, 10B, '27', NA.

23. To J. Franklin Pierce, New York, June 16, 1855. By HW. Details bags and parcels sent on steamer; warns him to make sure that despatch bags carry the usual seal to prevent difficulties with customs officials. Letterpress copy, CO, 12A, 251, NA.

24. To Captain Berry, *Courser*, June 26, 1855. By HW. Warns him not to pay discharged seamen partly in clothing; asks to see him about a seaman who has applied for medical aid. Letterpress copy, CO, 12A, 252, NA.

25. To John Miller, London, June 27, 1855. In HW's hand; unsigned in copy (NH was on vacation, so Pearce must have

signed this letter). Assures him that the despatch bags sent to Liverpool in April were duly forwarded in charge of the Despatch Agent. Letterpress copy, CO, 12A, 253, NA.

26. To Captain Weeks, *Pelican State*, July 6, 1855. By HW. Warns him to put a stop to paying his crew partly in clothing. Letterpress copy, CO, 12A, 254.

27. To Wingate Hayes, Providence, R.I., July 13, 1855. By HW. Informs him that his citation and copy of libel have been dealt with as requested. Letterpress copy, CO, 12A, 255, NA.

28. To M. Joseph Nitier, French Consul at Liverpool [see *EN*, pp. 9–10], July 17, 1855. In HW's hand, signed by Pearce. Assures him that his charges [against a captain for misappropriating material from a derelict French vessel] will be investigated. Letterpress copy, CO, 12A, 256, NA.

29. To Captain Yates, *Flora*, July 17, 1855. By HW. Requests to see him concerning M. Nitier's charges. Letterpress copy, CO, 12A, 257, NA.

30. To M. Joseph Nitier, French Consul at Liverpool, July 20, 1855. In HW's hand, signed by Pearce. Summarizes testimony of Captain Yates and concludes that there was no wrongdoing involved. Letterpress copy, CO, 12A, 258–61 (first), NA. Copybook also holds a rough draft in HW's hand.

31. To Messrs. Stitt Brothers, Liverpool, July 21, 1855. By HW. States that the consulate is not liable for having attached the wrong oath to an invoice. Letterpress copy, CO, 12A, 261 (bottom), NA.

32. To Thomas Hodgson, Plumbland, July 27, 1855. By HW. Regrets that the consulate has no funds to assist his return to the U.S. Letterpress copy, CO, 12A, 262, NA.

33. To Henry M. Little, Portsmouth, July 27, 1855. By HW.

Informs him that his papers cannot be found at the consulate. Letterpress copy, CO, 12A, 263, NA.

34. To James Guthrie, Washington, August 10, 1855. In HW's hand; unsigned in copy. Cancels registers of *Oneco*, *Childe Harold*, and *Donald McKay*. Letterpress copy, CO, 10B, 'N° 30', NA.

35. To G. E. Marsden, August 22, 1855. By HW. Warns that affidavits cannot be verified at the consulate without the usual fee. Letterpress copy, CO, 12A, 268, NA.

36. To James Arrott, U.S. Consul, Dublin, September 7, 1855. By HW. Informs him that his letter [concerning seamen rescued from the *John Bright*] has been referred to the U.S. Consul at Bristol. MS, Enclosure, Arrott to Marcy, November 15, 1855, Consular Despatches, Dublin, NA; Letterpress copy, CO, 12A, 265 (second; pagination in copybook erroneously skips from 269 back to 264), NA.

37. To Mrs. Elsa Champion, Lyme, Ct., September 7, 1855. By HW. Informs her of her son's death and requests proof of her identify so she can claim his wages and effects [see 1154]. Letterpress copy, CO, 12A, 264 (second), NA.

38. To James Arrott, Dublin, September 12, 1855. By HW. Identifies owners of *John Bright* and promises to contact them [see C160]. MS, Enclosure, Arrott to Marcy, November 15, 1855, Consular Despatches, Dublin, NA.

39. To Richard E. Eaton, Secretary, Arklow Marine Society, September 20, 1855. By HW. Regrets that the Liverpool Consulate cannot repay him for saving the *John Bright* seamen, nor will the owners do so; suggests that he apply to Arrott. MS, Enclosure, Arrott to Marcy, November 15, 1855, Consular Despatches, Dublin, NA; Letterpress copy, CO, 12A, 267 (second), NA.

40. To James Guthrie, Washington, September 21, 1855. In

HW's hand; signed by NH. Cancels registers of *Granite State* and *Break o'Day*. Letterpress copy, CO, 10B, [33], NA.

41. To David Scott, Acting U.S. Consul, Cork, October 8, 1855. By HW. Requests information on Mr. [Mc]Knight of *Wandering Jew*; also gives advice on transmission of accused mutineers to Liverpool for extradition [see C130–32]. Letterpress copy, CO, 12A, 268 (second), NA.

42. To Captain J. J. Comstock, *Baltic*, November 29, 1855. By HW. Warns him to receive two seamen turned ashore or else incur a fine and jail sentence. Letterpress copy, CO, 12A, 279, NA.

43. To James Guthrie, Washington, December 14, 1855. In HW's hand; unsigned in copy. Cancels register of *Sharon*. Letterpress copy, CO, 10B, 'N° 36', NA.

44. To James Guthrie, Washington, January 11, 1856. In HW's hand; signed by NH. Cancels register of *Grecian*. Letterpress copy, CO, 10B, 'N° 38', NA.

45. To James Guthrie, Washington, February 2, 1856. In HW's hand; signed by NH. Cancels registers of *Astracan* and *Olivia* [see C161]. Letterpress copy, CO, 10B, '39', NA.

46. To John Alexander, Esquire, Clerkenwell Public Court, February 13, 1856. By HW. Provides information on an alleged American seaman and promises to find him the means to return home. Letterpress copy, CO, 12A, 294, NA.

47. To Hugh Keenan, U.S. Consul, Cork, February 14, 1856. By HW. Advises him on how to handle discharges of foreign seamen from American ships. Letterpress copy, CO, 12A, 296, NA.

48. To William Robertson, Esquire, Pembroke Dock, February 22, 1856. By HW. Encloses an Extended Protest on the loss of the *Great Duke* and asks him to show it to the mate and

have him correct it if necessary. Letterpress copy, CO, 12A, 298, NA.

49. To James Guthrie, Washington, March 1, 1856. In HW's hand; signed by NH. Cancels registers of *Horizon* and *Constitution*. Letterpress copy, CO, 10B, '40', NA.

50. To M. Laird, Esquire, March 4, 1856. By HW. Promises to show him the commercial treaties between the U.S. and France. Letterpress copy, CO, 12A, 301 (top), NA.

51. To Captain Sawyer, *Thorndike*, March 4, 1856. By HW. Warns him not to pay his crew partly in clothing. Letterpress copy, CO, 12A, 302 (top).

52. To Edward de Leon, U.S. Consul General, Alexandria, Egypt, March 24, 1856. By HW. Advises him of shipment of hunting rifles under bond. Letterpress copy, CO, 12A, unnumbered folio between 301 and 302, NA.

53. To John Dunn, Esquire, Belfast, April 7, 1856. By HW. Advises him that he has not yet received instructions to pay his claim for subsistence of shipwrecked seamen on board his vessel. Letterpress copy, CO, 12A, 302 (bottom), NA.

54. To Captain Ross, May 2, 1856. By HW. Warns him to discharge or provide for a seaman in the hospital. Letterpress copy, CO, 12A, [303] (bottom), NA.

55. To George M. Dallas, May 31, 1856. By HW. Requests action on request for warrant for Charles Stevens [see C177]; warns that unless a reply is forthcoming, local authorities will release Stevens. MS, F.O. 5/656, PRO.

56. To George M. Dallas, June 10, 1856. By HW. Acknowledges receipt of warrants for arrest and extradition of Stevens [see C182–83]. Letterpress copy, CO, 12B, [84], NA.

57. To James Guthrie, Washington, June 11, 1856. In HW's

hand; unsigned in copy. Cancels register of *Henry Pratt.* Letterpress copy, CO, 10B, 'N° 47', NA.

58. To Captain Jacob T. Woodbury, *Mary E. Balch*, June 18, 1856. By HW. Authorizes him to convey Stevens to the U.S. for trial. Letterpress copy, CO, 12B, second unnumbered folio pasted on back of [303], NA.

59. To Captain McManas, *Emeralda*, July 5, 1856. By HW. Warns him to receive a seaman on board and return him to the U.S. Letterpress copy, CO, 11B, 1 (top), NA.

60. To James Guthrie, Washington, July 18, 1856. In HW's hand; unsigned in copy. Cancels register of *Southport.* Letterpress copy, CO, 10B, '50', NA.

61. To George M. Dallas, London, September 1, 1856. By HW. Requests passports for a party of Americans. Letterpress copy, CO, 13B, 1, NA.

62. To James Guthrie, Washington, November 4, 1856. In HW's hand, signed by NH. Cancels registers of *George A. Hopley* [see C94.2] and *Catharine*. CO, 10B, '55', NA.

63. To James Guthrie, Washington, December 12, 1856. In HW's hand; signed by NH. Cancels registers for *Louisiana* and *Samuel M. Fox* [see C196]. Letterpress copy, CO, 10A, 'N° 56' (but located after Despatch 79), NA. On the 10B side, at foot of '55', HW pencilled a cross reference to this letter.

64. To Unknown Recipient (interior address is illegible), February 19, 1857. By HW. Gives general advice to a captain whose ship has wrecked. Letterpress copy, CO, 13A, 9, NA.

65. To James Guthrie, Washington, February 20, 1857. In HW's hand; unsigned in copy. Cancels registers of *Sea Lion, Northern Empire, Capitol, James Buchanan,* and *Adriatic.* Letterpress copy, CO, 13A, 10, NA.

66. To John F. Furber, ?, New Hampshire, February 27, 1857. By HW. Informs him of the death of his brother due to injuries incurred during the *James L. Bogart* mutiny [see C218]. Letterpress copy, CO, 13A, 12, NA.

67. To Secretary of the Treasury, March 13, 1857. In HW's hand; unsigned in copy. Cancels register of *Ithona*. Letterpress copy, CO, 13B, 10, NA.

68. To Secretary of the Treasury, March 21, 1857. In HW's hand, signed (in pencil) 'N Hawthor' in HW's hand. Cancels register for *Ambassador*. Letterpress copy, CO, 11A, 1, NA.

69. Fragment, to U.S. Vice Consul, Cardiff, April 28, 1857. In HW's hand; verso not copied. Syntax resembles letters drafted by HW. Provides information on a destitute seaman who has applied for relief. Letterpress copy, CO, 13A, 18 (top), NA.

70. To J. B. Browning? (interior address is blurred and almost illegible), May 13, 1857. By HW. Refuses to allow officers to be stationed aboard the *Universe*. Letterpress copy, CO, 13A, 19 (top), NA.

71. To Secretary of the Treasury, Washington, May 20, 1857. In HW's hand; signed by NH. Cancels register of *Euroclydon*. Letterpress copy, CO, 11A, 2, NA.

72. To Captain Libbey, May 23, 1857. By HW. Warns that he will decide tomorrow on the case of two seamen abused on board his ship. Letterpress copy, CO, 13A, 19 (bottom), NA.

73. To Thomas W. Fox, U.S. Consul, Plymouth, May 28, 1857. By HW. Informs him that a seaman forwarded with funds has refused to return to the U.S. and has disappeared. Letterpress copy, CO, 13A, 20, NA.

74. To Thomas W. Fox, U.S. Consul, Plymouth, June 2, 1857. In HW's hand; unsigned in copy (see 70 above).

Acknowledges receipt of draft on account of vanished seaman. Letterpress copy, CO, 13A, 21 (top), NA.

75. To Rev. Henry Leader, June 2, 1857. By HW. Acknowledges receipt of letter with document found in a bottle; promises to forward it to the owners of the vessel indicated, who will investigate the charges made. Letterpress copy, CO, 13A, 21 (bottom), NA.

76. To Hugh Keenan, U.S. Consul, Cork, July 6, 1857. By HW. Confirms authenticity of bill of lading for bags of rice shipped on board an American ship. Letterpress copy, CO, 13A, 23, NA.

77. To John McKeon, U.S. Attorney, New York, July 10, 1857. By HW. Advises him that seamen abused on board *Vanguard* have been sent by steamer to him [see C225]. Letterpress copy, CO, 13A, 24, NA.

78. To Messrs E. E. and W. J. Babcock, July 21, 1857. By HW. Sends receipt for effects of deceased American. Letterpress copy, CO, 13A, 29, NA.

79. To Captain J. R. Sands, *Susquehanna* [see C231], July 21, 1857. By HW. Communicates apology from Commandant of Liverpool North Fort for not returning salute. Letterpress copy, CO, 13A, 27, NA.

80. To U. S. Consul General, Calcutta, September 18, 1857. By HW. Encloses papers of *Golconda*, left behind by mistake. Letterpress copy, CO, 13A, 35, NA.

INDEX

Abbotsford, Scotland, XV, 607; XVIII, 495

Abbott, Jacob, XVI, 1, 2, 594; *Marco Paul's Adventures in Pursuit of Knowledge*, XVI, 1; "Rollo Books," XVI, 2

Abbott, John S. C., XVI, 594

Abby Blanchard (ship), XIX, 318

Aberdeen, Scotland, XVII, 365

Abolitionists, XVII, 231, 245; XVIII, 8, 89, 109, 115–16, 227, 458, 482, 584, 589–90, 595

Acadia, Nova Scotia, Canada, XVI, 220

Accra, Ghana, XVI, 91

Adair, Robert, letter to, XVI, 391; correspondence of, XVI, 391

Adams, Alvin, XVI, 204

Adams, Augustus, XVI, 692; XVIII, 323, 469

Adams, Capt. Ebenezer G., XX, 157–58, 179

Adams, Henry, XVIII, 548; correspondence of, XVII, 51; *The Education of Henry Adams*, XVII, 51

Adams, John, XV, 638; XVII, 13

Adams, John Quincy, XV, 26–27; XVI, 183; XVII, 13

Adams, Joseph Henry Jr., letter to, XVI, 77; references to, XVI, 79, 80

Adams, Joseph Henry, XVI, 77

Adams, Joseph, XV, 256

Adams, Capt. Samuel, letter to, XIX, 346

Adams, Mrs., XV, 167, 169

Adams & Co. Express, Baltimore, XIX, 231

Addington, Henry Unwin, correspondence of, XIX, 91

Addison, John E. W., XVII, 592

Addlestone, Surrey, XVII, 466

Aden, Arabia, XX, 159

Admiralty, British, XIX, 118

Admiralty Court, British, XIX, 301; XX, 136

Aeschylus, XV, 365

Aesthetic Papers, Boston, XV, 23; XVI, 267, 299

Africa, XV, 38, 686; XVI, 25, 26, 27, 76, 78, 82, 91, 97, 189, 683, 686; XVII, 433

Africa (ship), XX, 122

The African Repository, Washington, XVI, 638

Afton, William F., letter to, XVI, 651

Agassiz, Jean Louis Rodolphe, XVI, 250; XVIII, 107, 336

Agrippina, Empress of Rome, XVIII, 318

Aikens, Mr. and Mrs., XVIII, 647

Aikin, Berkley (pseud. of Frances Aikin Kortright), letter to, XVIII, 468; *The Dean: or the Popular Preacher*, XVIII, 468; *The Old, Old Story, Love*, XVIII, 469

Aikin, James, XVII, 127

INDEX

Aikin, John, *Geographical Delineation*, XV, 136
Aikin, John (1747–1822), XVII, 52
Ainley, Capt. Richard, XIX, 190, 193, 223; XX, 99
Ainsworth, Capt. Allen C., XX, 90
Ainsworth, Catherine Calista, letter to, XV, 270
Ainsworth, Peter, XVII, 61, 74
Ainsworth, Mrs. Peter, XVII, 61, 74
Ainsworth, Thomas, letter to, XIX, 347
Akers, (Benjamin) Paul, XVIII, 143, 144, 386; *Milton*, XVIII, 143; *Pearl-Diver*, XVIII, 143
Albany, N.Y., XV, 224, 616, 617; XVI, 341, 671; XIX, 367; Albany Female Academy, XVI, 613
Albany *Argus*, XVIII, 65
Albert, Prince Consort of England, XVIII, 78
Albert, Mr., XVI, 680
Albert Gallatin (ship), XVIII, 11; XIX, 33, 92, 387, 388–89; XX, 110, 111
Albery (seaman), XIX, 253
Albion, N.Y., XVIII, 414
Alchemy, XVIII, 593
Alcott, Abba May Sewall (Mrs. A. Bronson), XVI, 531, 542; XVIII, 431
Alcott, Abigail May, XVIII, 476
Alcott, Amos Bronson, XV, 20, 28, 32, 309, 474, 506, 539; XVI, 248, 261, 531, 541, 542, 548, 567, 568; XVIII, 127–28, 319, 481, 529, 575; correspondence of, XV, 309; XVIII, 128, 530; journal of, XVII, 242; XVIII, 302, 363–64, 423, 432; *Conversations on the Gospels*, XV, 32
Alcott, Anna Bronson, XVI, 172–73, 349. *See also* Pratt, Anna Bronson Alcott (Mrs. John B.).
Alcott, Louisa May, XVIII, 431, 511, 529, 533
Aldershot, Hampshire, XVII, 37, 482; XVIII, 181

Aldrich, Charles, XVIII, 643
Aldrich, Thomas Bailey, letter to, XVIII, 559; *Poems*, XVIII, 559; "Père Antoine's Date-Palm," XVIII, 559
Alexander the Great, XV, 399
Alexander, Charles (seaman), XX, 55–56, 58–60, 62–63, 64
Alexandria, La., XVIII, 65
Alfred, Prince of England, XVIII, 355
Alfred Tyler (ship), XV, 365
Allen, John, XVII, 10
Allen, Thomas, XV, 448
Allen, William, XV, 159, 161, 171, 173, 174, 182, 194–95, 232; correspondence of, XV, 172; *American Biographical and Historical Dictionary*, XV, 161, 232
Allen, William (seaman), XIX, 92
Allen, William Brockway, XV, 529, 535, 540, 560, 655; correspondence of, XV, 529
Allibone, Samuel Austin, *Critical Dictionary of English Literature and British and American Authors*, XVI, 487
Allingham, Catherine, correspondence of, XVII, 180
Allingham, J. T., *The Weathercock; or, What Next?*, XV, 123
Allingham, William, letters to, XVII, 180, 359; references to, XVII, 201, 372; correspondence of, XVII, 180, 360; *Day and Night Songs*, XVII, 202, 360; *Diary*, XVII, 181; *The Music Master*, XVII, 372; *Poems*, XVII, 181, 202, 373
Allston, Washington, XV, 32, 474, 695; XVI, 49, 62, 354; "Elijah in the Desert," XVI, 49; "Uriel in the Sun," XVI, 62
Almy, John Jay, XVI, 684
Ambriz, Angola, XVI, 189
America (ship), XVII, 106, 114, 233, 297; XIX, 101, 118, 133, 135, 306, 362, 366, 367; XX, 117, 120–21

INDEX

Bacon, Leonard, letters to, XVII, 528; XVIII, 31, 69, 79, 85, 99; references to, XVII, 76, 84, 563, 565, 566; XVIII, 66–68, 74, 80, 102; correspondence of, XVII, 530; XVIII, 69–70, 79

Bacon, Theodore, XVIII, 351

Badajoz, Estramadura, Spain, XVIII, 425

Baden, Germany, XVII, 515

Badger, Ada. See Shepard, Ann Adaline

Badger, Henry Clay, XVIII, 178, 528

Bahama Islands, XIX, 266

Bahia, Brazil, XV, 203

Bailey, Gamaliel, XVI, 506, 518; XVII, 111, 162

Bailey, Mrs. Gamaliel, XVII, 111

Bailey, Mary Otis, letter to, XVIII, 344

Bailey, Philip James, XVII, 523

Baines, James, XIX, 139–41, 151

Baines, James & Co., XIX, 80, 131, 138, 288

Baines, Thomas, *History of the Commerce and Town of Liverpool*, XIX, 220, 226

Baker, Georgina Crossman, letter to, XVIII, 148

Baker, Nathaniel B., XVI, 561

Baker's Island, Salem, Mass., XV, 126

Balaklava, Russia, XVII, 381

Baldwin, Mrs. Ann, XVIII, 68, 82, 85

Ball, Nahum, XV, 409

Ball's Bluff, Va., Battle of, XVIII, 422

Ballardvale, Andover, Mass., XVI, 181, 277

Ballard Vale Company, XX, 36

Balldridge, George (seaman), XX, 173

Ballou, Maturin Murray, XVIII, 415; *Ballou's Pictorial*, Boston, XVIII, 415

Ballyshannon, Ireland, XVII, 180

Balmain & Hill, Liverpool, XIX, 356

Baltic (ship), XVII, 101; XVIII, 118; XIX, 304, 305; XX, 6, 9

Baltimore, Md., XV, 162; XVI, 546, 615, 618, 638; XVII, 431; XVIII, 435, 628, 637; XIX, 231, 274–75, 276, 292, 344; XX, 49

Baltimore & Ohio Railroad, XVIII, 443

Bancroft, Elizabeth Davis Bliss (Mrs. George), XV, 284; XVI, 66, 158, 165

Bancroft, George, letters to, XV, 283, 508, 515; references to, XV, 54, 76, 260, 279, 287, 365, 382, 389, 410, 419, 500, 501, 502, 507, 699; XVI, 66, 85, 89, 102, 113, 114, 123, 143, 147, 278, 279, 374; XVIII, 447, 636; correspondence of, XV, 284, 390; XVI, 90, 93, 103, 114, 131, 143, 151; *History of the United States*, XV, 261

Bangor, Me., XVI, 55, 223; XVIII, 471, 487; Penobscot House, XVIII, 471

Bangor, Wales, XIX, 69, 99, 105, 205, 209

Bank of England, XVII, 380; XVIII, 128

Banks, Gen. Nathaniel Prentiss, XVIII, 336

Bannockburn, Battle of, XVIII, 390

Bannockburn (ship), XX, 157–58

Barbary, XV, 52

Barbauld, Mrs. Anna Letitia, XVII, 52

Baring Brothers Bank, London, letters to, XIX, 330; XX, 124; references to, XVI, 299; XVII, 143, 146–47, 152, 172, 177, 186, 193, 200, 214, 218, 239, 297, 312, 328, 335, 342, 353, 361, 373, 389, 499, 553, 557; XVIII, 133, 152, 161–62, 191, 192, 206, 211, 245, 297; XIX, 41, 117, 120; XX, 76–77, 125, 186, 188

Barker, Elise, XV, 527, 541

Barker, Jacob, XVI, 299

INDEX

Boston *Advertiser*, XV, 268, 281, 297, 365, 471, 547, 558, 598, 610; XVI, 239, 282, 515; XVII, 423; XVIII, 423
Boston *Advocate*, XV, 603
Boston *Almanac*, XVI, 64
Boston Athenaeum. *See* Athenaeum, Boston
Boston *Atlas*, XV, 50, 237; XVI, 151, 279
Boston Book, XV, 309, 524
Boston *Chronotype*, XVI, 380
Boston *Commonwealth*, XVI, 506, 653
Boston *Courier*, XV, 85, 245, 246; XVI, 97; XVII, 423; XVIII, 185, 272
Boston Custom House. *See* Custom House, Boston
Boston *Evening Transcript*. *See* Boston *Transcript*
Boston *Gazette*, XVI, 598
Boston *Globe*, XVI, 537
Boston *Journal*, XVI, 608; XVIII, 439, 469
Boston *Liberator*, XVII, 231
Boston *Miscellany of Literature and Fashion*, XV, 22, 598, 619, 644; XVI, 86, 159
Boston *Morning Post*. *See* Boston *Post*
Boston *Museum*. *See* *Boston Weekly Museum and Literary Portfolio*
Boston *Post*, XV, 314, 406, 416, 471, 493, 603, 680; XVI, 96, 356, 515, 587, 589, 591, 617; XVII, 297
Boston *Quarterly Review*, XV, 602
Boston *Round Table*, XVII, 20
Boston & Salem Stage Co., XV, 11–14, 105, 116, 130, 141, 146, 161, 197, 229, 254, 256
Boston Tea Party, XV, 309
Boston *Times*, XVI, 545, 560; XVII, 228; XIX, 88
Boston *Transcript*, XV, 227, 297, 489; XVI, 32, 274, 549, 608; XVII, 131, 248, 372, 390, 423, 486; XVIII, 55, 59, 325, 415–16, 557, 606

Boston *Traveler*, XVI, 97; XVII, 423
Boston Weekly Magazine, XV, 314
Boston Weekly Museum and Literary Portfolio, XVI, 300, 404, 488
Boulogne, France, XVIII, 136
Bowditch, Nathaniel, *The New American Practical Navigator*, XIX, 196
Bowdoin College, Brunswick, Me., XV, 5, 13, 17, 19, 34, 35, 37, 38, 41, 42, 52, 89, 137, 144, 145, 151, 153, 155–57, 159–61, 165, 167–71, 173–75, 177–95, 225, 233, 249, 252, 254, 265, 307, 323, 688; XVI, 2, 17, 84, 91, 177, 178, 346, 523, 524, 551, 579, 588, 593, 607, 616, 650; XVII, 131, 270, 269, 299, 321, 536; XVIII, 334, 511, 661; Athenaean Society, XV, 41, 159, 175, 223, 307; XVI, 178; Maine Hall, XV, 169; Peucinian Society, XV, 41, 161
Bowdoin Port-Folio, XV, 307
Bowen, Abel, XV, 679
Bowen, Anna Gilman, letter to, XVIII, 628
Bowen, Charles, XV, 236
Bowen, Charles H., letter to, XVIII, 341
Bowen, Charles J., XVIII, 628
Bowen, Levi K., XIX, 252
Bowman, Mr., XVIII, 65
Bowness, Westmoreland, XVII, 368
Boyd, Joseph B., letters to, XV, 259, 260; XVI, 394
Boys' and Girls' Magazine, Boston, XV, 693, 698; XVI, 1
Bradburn, George, XVI, 379
Bradbury, James Ware, XV, 38; XVI, 344
Bradbury, Wymond, XV, 644
Bradbury & Soden, Boston, XV, 644
Bradford, Alden, XV, 240, 243
Bradford, George Partridge, letter to, XVII, 149; references to, XV, 532, 545, 648, 670; XVI, 47–48,

54, 55, 107, 563; XVII, 160, 280, 351; XVIII, 408, 471, 481, 488, 505; correspondence of, XV, 546
Bradish, Capt., XX, 169
Bradley, Rev. Caleb, XV, 111, 115
Brady, Matthew B., XVIII, 443, 453
Brailsford, Rev. Willson, letter to, XVII, 164
Braintree, Mass., XVII, 13
Braman, Jarvis, XV, 477
Bramwell, Jane, XVII, 539, 550; XVIII, 28
Brattleboro, Vt., XVI, 174; XVIII, 407
Bray, Caroline Hennell (Mrs. Charles), XVIII, 223
Bray, Charles, XVIII, 223
Bray, Berkshire, England, XVII, 124
Brazer, Rev. John, XV, 217
Brazil, XV, 204; XIX, 180
Bremer, Fredrika, XVI, 350; XVII, 216; XVIII, 141; *An Easter Offering*, XVI, 350, 354; *Homes of the New World: Impressions of America* XVI, 354
Brenholm, Capt., XIX, 69
Brentano, Clemens, *Des Knabens Wunderhorn*, XV, 267
Bridge, Charlotte Marshall (Mrs. Horatio), letters to, XVI, 634, 684; references to, XVI, 165, 190, 193, 229, 271, 312, 313, 330, 334, 356, 357, 368, 407, 463, 495, 503, 510, 566, 607; XVII, 123, 187, 188, 208, 212, 215, 285, 294, 333, 497; XVIII, 101, 381, 412, 443, 444, 450, 526, 554
Bridge, Edward Theodore, XVI, 592
Bridge, Horatio
—letters to: XV, 262, 681, 686; XVI, 25, 65, 75, 78, 89, 91, 92, 96, 100, 102, 108, 113, 120, 122, 141, 144, 147, 188, 190, 192, 195, 311, 329, 355, 357, 368, 406, 461, 495, 503, 604; XVII, 187, 200, 203, 207, 212, 229, 253, 284, 287, 292, 298, 322, 327, 333, 337, 374, 376, 385, 496, 504, 587; XVIII, 8, 18, 100, 303, 317, 380, 412, 427, 450, 451, 526, 553, 661
—references to: XV, 5, 6, 7, 8, 21, 37–41, 51, 67, 71, 178, 254, 267, 268, 271, 285, 286, 288, 460, 584, 695, 700; XVI, 60, 67, 68, 70, 73, 82, 84, 86, 94, 98, 127, 131, 156, 165, 196, 229, 271, 296, 333, 334, 349, 365, 398, 479, 500, 505, 510, 546, 592, 634, 635, 684, 685; XVII, 7, 9, 10, 49, 190, 215, 221, 226, 264, 316, 325, 334–35, 364, 372, 382, 408, 471, 507; XVIII, 14, 37, 90, 179, 223, 382, 410, 436, 443, 444, 452, 641; XIX, 4, 47, 49, 50; XX, 101, 111, 151
—correspondence of: XV, 285–86; XVI, 75, 81, 101, 120–21, 143, 296, 313, 330–31; XVII, 8, 316; XVIII, 554, 555–56, 593
—1843–44 journal: XVI, 27, 189, 196
—*Journal of an African Cruiser*: XV, 40–41, 71, 683; XVI, 26, 66, 75, 80, 82, 84, 86, 89, 91, 92, 94, 96, 97, 102, 105, 108, 113, 122, 124, 127, 136, 139–41, 152, 158, 170, 188, 194, 195, 242, 312, 355, 356–58, 368, 406, 638; XVII, 15; XIX, 6
Bridge, James, XV, 38, 177
Bridge, Marion, XVI, 503, 607, 635; XVII, 187, 213, 285, 327, 333
Bridge, Samuel James, XVI, 188, 190, 194, 195, 566, 604, 607, 684
Bridget (Peabody cook), XV, 637
Bridgman, Laura Dewey, XV, 576, 578–79

INDEX

Burlington, Vt., XV, 226
Burlington (ship), XX, 4
Burnett, Sir William, XIX, 172, 221
Burnett, Mr., XVIII, 651
Burnham, Isaac, XV, 112, 121
Burnham, Maj. Thomas, XV, 113
Burns, Anthony, XVII, 238
Burns, James Glencairn, XVII, 128
Burns, Robert, XVII, 14, 27, 44, 128; XVIII, 308, 495
Burns, William Nicol, XVII, 128
Burns, William (seaman), XIX, 260
Burnside, Gen. Ambrose Everett, XVIII, 526
Burrett, Abby Pike, XVI, 619
Burrett, William, XVI, 619
Burroughs, Caroline, XVI, 350
Burroughs, Charles, XVI, 611, 618, 683
Burrows, Capt. E. R., XX, 162
Burton, Rev. Warren, XV, 531–33, 540, 554
Busco, Solomon (seaman), XIX, 281
Butcher, John J., XX, 33
Butler, Gen. Benjamin, XVIII, 442
Butler, Charles, XVII, 78; correspondence of, XVII, 80
Butler, Luther, XVI, 313
Butler, Samuel, XVII, 52
Butman, Francis C., XVII, 151
Buttman, Col., XV, 689
Buttrick, Joshua, XVI, 542
Byron, George Gordon, Lord, XV, 406; XVII, 140, 389; XVIII, 149, 294; *Childe Harold's Pilgrimage*, XV, 437–38
Bywater, T., XVIII, 86

Cade, Jack, XVI, 263; XVII, 491
Caernarvon, Wales, XIX, 202
Calcutta, India, XVIII, 532
Caldwell, James (seaman), XIX, 376
Calhoun (ship), XX, 168
California, XV, 383, 560; XVI, 267, 293; XVII, 267, 315, 571; XIX, 140, 187, 214

Calvert, George Henry, XV, 478; *Scenes and Thoughts in Europe*, XVI, 159
Cambridge, Mass., XV, 45, 68, 201, 229, 253, 255, 267, 398, 481, 486, 502, 554, 656, 673; XVI, 84, 85, 164, 183, 220, 225, 236, 239, 248, 283, 313; XVIII, 164, 325, 462, 540, 582, 601; Craigie House, XV, 45
Cambridge University, England, XV, 537; XVI, 602; XVII, 25, 46, 49, 60, 67, 75, 174, 210, 218, 263; XVIII, 268, 276, 285, 287, 289, 292
Camden, Me., XVIII, 663
Cameron, Simon, XVIII, 442, 496
Campagna, Italian, XVIII, 257
Campbell, James, correspondence of, XVI, 679
Campbell, John, Earl of Loudoun, XV, 570
Campbell, Peter (alias James Courtney Collins; seaman), XX, 92–93, 94, 132–35
Campbell, Gen. Robert Blair, letters to, XVII, 286, 535; XIX, 243, 252, 260; references to, XVII, 512; XVIII, 348; XIX, 76, 153
Campbell, Thomas, XV, 177, 631; *The Pleasures of Hope*, XV, 178; *Specimens of the British Poets*, XV, 631
Campbell, William J., letter to, XIX, 291
Campbell, Mrs. ("Mrs. Dromedary"), XVI, 124, 137
Campbell (seaman), XX, 16
Canada, XV, 198, 214, 224, 226; XVI, 491; XVII, 46, 63, 140, 191, 218, 335; XVIII, 106, 355, 511; XIX, 109
Canada (ship), XVII, 116; XVIII, 178, 213; XIX, 157
Canals, English, XIX, 199–200
Canning, Charles John, correspondence of, XIX, 90–91
Canova, Antonio, XVIII, 141

· 249 ·

INDEX

China, XVI, 14, 85; XVIII, 103
Choate, Rufus, XVI, 264, 275–76;
XVIII, 464; correspondence of,
XVI, 265
Chorley, Henry Fothergill, letters
to, XVIII, 238, 255; references
to, XV, 231; XVI, 476, 607–08;
XVII, 4, 5, 7, 9, 17, 22, 39, 40,
42, 44, 65, 68, 145, 502, 547;
XVIII, 52, 234; correspondence
of, XVIII, 240, 255; *Roccabella:
A Tale of a Woman's Life*, XVIII,
255
Christian Examiner, Boston, XV,
23, 80–81, 279, 389, 637
Christian Inquirer, New York,
XVII, 304, 342
Christy, James (seaman), XX,
132–35
Chronometric Expedition, U.S.,
XIX, 302–03
Chrysolite (ship), XIX, 178, 222
Church of England, XVII, 419;
XVIII, 354
Church Review, New Haven,
Conn., XVI, 387
Cicero, *De Officiis*, XVI, 561
Cilley, Jonathan, XV, 34–35, 37,
41, 51, 53, 66, 263, 264, 267,
272, 284; XVI, 277, 281; corre-
spondence of, XV, 34
Cincinnati, Ohio, XVI, 394; XVII,
54, 152, 505; XVIII, 145, 622;
XX, 32
Cintra (ship), XVII, 392, 410
City of Manchester (ship), XIX, 118
Civil War, U.S., XV, 36, 38, 67;
XVI, 38, 432, 658; XVII, 49;
XVIII, 8, 373, 379, 380–82,
387–88, 390, 394, 399–400, 412,
420–22, 426, 427–28, 434–46,
450, 468, 500–501, 516, 523,
526, 543–45, 584, 589–92, 621
Civita Vecchia, Italy, XVIII, 173
Clandeboye, Ireland, XVII, 140;
XVIII, 279
Clapp, Isaac, XVII, 568
Claremont, N.H., XIX, 245
Clarendon, Lord (George William
Frederick Villiers), XVII, 102,

185, 400; XIX, 19, 29–30, 66,
80–81, 90–91, 309, 359, 363,
380; XX, 56, 57, 92; correspon-
dence of, XVII, 395; XIX, 91,
114, 149, 227, 270, 361, 365;
XX, 110, 150
Clark, John T., XIX, 77
Clark, Capt. Joseph P., XX, 34–35
Clark, Lewis Gaylord, XV, 603
Clark, Peter, XV, 120
Clark, Stephen Merrill, XV, 141,
143
Clark, W. G., XVIII, 294
Clark & Hatch, Boston, XV, 471
Clarke, Anna, XVI, 354
Clarke, Rev. James Freeman, letter
to, XV, 637; references to, XV,
474; XVII, 263; XVIII, 7, 22,
529
Clarke, John Louis, XVII, 297
Clarke, Lillian Rebecca, XVIII,
528
Clarke, Rebecca Hull, XV, 25, 356,
383, 474
Clarke, Samuel C., XVIII, 6
Clarke, Sarah Anne, XV, 403, 473,
637; XVI, 58, 60, 235; XVII,
329, 542; XVIII, 7
Clarke, Sara Jane. *See* Greenwood,
Grace
Claughton, Birkenhead, Cheshire,
XVII, 397
Claussen, Capt. H. C. (Clauten),
XIX, 71–73, 265; correspon-
dence of, XIX, 73, 78
Clay, Henry, XVIII, 544
Clayton, John M., correspondence
of, XX, 69
Clayton-Bulwer Convention, XVII,
498
Cleaveland, John Payne, XV, 216
Cleaveland, Nehemiah, letter to,
XVII, 271; references to, XVI,
91, 593; XVII, 269; XVII, 271
Cleaveland, Susan Heard Dole
(Mrs. John Payne), XV, 216–17
Clements, George, XIX, 221; *Cle-
ments' Customs Guide*, XIX, 171,
221
Cleveland, Charles D., *Compen-*

INDEX

Cozzens, Frederick Swartout, letter to, XVIII, 454; *The Sparrowgrass Papers*, XVIII, 454
Crabbe, George, XVII, 381
Craig, John (seaman), XIX, 376
Craig, Margaret De Quincey (Mrs. Robert), XVII, 23, 247, 274; correspondence of, XVII, 19, 296
Craig, Robert, XVII, 248
Cram, George and Henry, XIX, 180, 222
Cram, Powell, & Co, Liverpool, XIX, 222
Crampton, John Fiennes Twisleton, XVII, 399, 445, 496, 499, 508, 541
Cranch, Christopher Pearse, XV, 512
Crashaw, Richard, "Wishes to His (Supposed) Mistress," XVIII, 466
Crawford, Abel, XV, 227
Crawford, Ethan Allen, XV, 227
Crawford, Louisa Ward (Mrs. Thomas), XV, 702
Crawford, Thomas, XV, 700; XVIII, 170
Crawford's Notch, N.H., XV, 226
Creany, William (seaman), XIX, 388
Crewe, Annabel Hungerford. *See* Milnes, Annabel Hungerford Crewe
Crewe Hall, Cheshire, XVII, 272
Crewe, Hungerford, Baron Crewe, XVII, 272
Crimean War, XVII, 25, 381, 444, 540; XIX, 20, 118, 120, 124–25, 126, 228, 259, 339–41, 342, 380
Critic: A Journal of British and Foreign Literature, London, XVI, 114; XVII, 36; XVIII, 59
Critic, New York, XVIII, 593
Crittenden, John Jordan, XIX, 66
Crittenden, Thomas Leonidas, XVI, 658–59; XVII, 106, 119, 204; XIX, 14, 26–27, 31, 44, 47, 65, 66, 67, 228; XX, 101; correspondence of, XIX, 27, 43, 86, 92, 347; XX, 38, 66, 69

Crocker, Frederick W., letter to, XV, 608
Cromek, R. H., *Remains of Nithdale and Galloway Song*, XV, 133
Cromwell, Oliver, XVII, 309; XVIII, 294, 509
Crosby Point, Liverpool, XX, 31
Croskey, Rodney, XIX, 30
Crosland, Camilla Dufour Toulmin, letter to, XVIII, 180; references to, XVI, 624–25; XVII, 31, 32, 134, 502; XVIII, 557; *English Tales and Sketches*, XVI, 625; *Landmarks of a Literary Life*, XVIII, 180; *Lydia: A Woman's Book*, XVI, 625
Crosland, Newton, XVII, 133
Cross, Henry, XV, 106
Cross, William, XV, 105
Crossman, Andrew I., letter to, XVIII, 328
Crowell, Capt. Higgins, XIX, 121, 127–28
Crowley, Michael (seaman), XIX, 318
Crowninshield, George, XV, 217
Crowninshield, Capt. John, XV, 11, 219
Crowninshield, Richard, XV, 209, 210, 219
Crowninshield, Sarah Hathorne (Mrs. John), XV, 11, 117, 126, 219
Cruikshank, George, XV, 532
Crusader (shipwreck), XX, 32–34
Cuba, XV, 25–30, 58, 686; XVI, 30, 188, 195, 203; XVII, 352, 531; XVIII, 20, 649
Cuba (ship), XX, 75
Cultivator (ship), XIX, 308–09, 310, 312, 332; XX, 7, 8, 11, 17, 18–19
Cumberland, Miss, XVII, 58
Cumberland, England, XVII, 341
Cumberland (ship), XVIII, 441, 445–46
Cummins, Maria Susannah, *The Lamplighter*, XVII, 304
Cunard, Samuel, XVII, 303, 313
Cunard Steamers, XVI, 685, 693;

• 256 •

INDEX

Demsey (seaman), XIX, 317
Denman, Richard, XVII, 523
Deptford, London, XVII, 573
De Quincey, Florence, XVII, 19, 23; correspondence of, XVII, 296
De Quincey, Margaret. *See* Craig, Margaret De Quincey
De Quincey, Thomas, letter to, XVII, 274; references to, XV, 87; XVI, 475, 486, 525–26, 534; XVII, 19, 23, 64, 65, 68, 115, 135, 198, 202, 274–75, 296, 434, 508; XIX, 11; *The Caesars*, XVII, 135; *Confessions of an English Opium-eater*, XVI, 475, 486; *Diary: 1803*, XVII, 202; *Klosterheim; or, The Masque*, XVII, 434; *Life and Manners*, XVI, 475, 486; *Memorials and Other Papers*, XVII, 508; *Writings*, XVI, 475; XVII, 508
Derbes, Alexandre, XVIII, 207
Derby, James Cephas, XVII, 435; XVIII, 444, 452; *Fifty Years Among Authors*, XVII, 14; XVIII, 453, 652–53
Derby, John, & Son, Salem, XV, 166
Derby, Mary, XVI, 235; *Crucifixion*, XVI, 235
Devens, Charles (1791–1876), XV, 355
Devens, Gen. Charles (1820–91), XV, 356
Devens, Mary Lithgow (Mrs. Charles), XV, 355
Devereux, George Humphrey, XVI, 271
Devereux, John, XVIII, 361
Devereux & Eager, Boston, XVIII, 517
Devonshire, England, XVII, 244, 501; XVIII, 200, 251
Devow, John (seaman), XX, 68
Devow, Mary, XX, 65
Dewey, Chester P., letter to, XVIII, 664
Dial, Boston, XV, 22, 513, 602, 637, 656–57, 673; XVI, 255, 298

Dicey, Edward James Stephen, XVIII, 444, 462, 583; correspondence of, XVIII, 584; *Six Months in the Federal States*, XVIII, 584
Dickens, Charles, XV, 74, 76, 77, 81, 84, 87, 406, 532, 608, 657; XVI, 159, 198, 396, 488, 534, 544, 551; XVII, 10, 30, 37, 136; XVIII, 178, 273, 286; XIX, 11; correspondence of, XV, 77; XVI, 396; *Oliver Twist*, XV, 532; *Sketches by Boz*, XV, 532; *Travelling Letters, Written on the Road*, XVI, 159
Digby, Sir Kenelm, XVII, 60
Dike, John (1783–1871), letter to, XVII, 171; references to, XV, 13, 20, 107, 120, 126, 129, 146, 155, 158, 161, 201, 203, 206, 209, 216, 218; XVI, 338, 339, 402–03, 409, 434, 498, 521, 526, 555, 563, 582, 597; XVII, 422; XVIII, 174, 222, 316; correspondence of, XV, 161
Dike, John Stephen (1807–91), letters to, XV, 201, 206, 216; references to, XV, 8, 13, 107, 146, 193–94, 214
Dike, Margaretta Woods (Mrs. John Stephen), XV, 206, 209, 218
Dike, Mary W., XV, 13, 107, 147
Dike, Nancy, XV, 210
Dike, Priscilla Manning (Mrs. John), XV, 13, 107, 111, 117, 143, 151, 153, 155, 201, 208–09, 218, 658; XVI, 118, 338, 403, 434, 521, 526, 582, 597; XVIII, 316
Dingley, Jacob, XV, 110
Dingley, Samuel, XV, 109
Dingley, Susan, XV, 110. *See also* Manning, Susan Dingley
Dinsmoor, Samuel, XV, 225
Disraeli, Isaac, XVIII, 204; *Miseries of Authors*, XVIII, 205; *Quarrels of Authors*, XVIII, 204
Dix, Sen. John Adams, correspondence of, XVII, 466
Dix, J. Augustus, XVII, 491, 513

erences to, XV, 533, 663; XVI, 55, 513; correspondence of, XV, 533
Dwight's Journal of Music, Boston, XVIII, 666
Dyce, Rev. Alexander, XVII, 492

Eagle (ship), XIX, 153
Eagleswood School, N.J., XVII, 259, 302
Earle, John, Jr. & Co., XVI, 408
East Boston, Mass., XIX, 90, 131
East Cambridge, Mass., XV, 411; XVIII, 528
Eastport, Me., XVII, 357
Eaton, Sarah B., XIX, 93–94
Eaton Hall, Cheshire, XVII, 242
Ebenezer (ship), XIX, 71–72, 265
Eckley, Sophia May Tuckerman, XVIII, 371
Edes, Rev. E. H., XV, 221
Edes, Lois Stone (Mrs. E. H.), XV, 211–12, 220
Edgeworth, Maria, XV, 134; XVIII, 466; "Waste Not, Want Not," XVIII, 466
Edgeworth, Richard Lovell, XV, 134; *Memoirs*, XV, 134
Edinburgh, Scotland, XVI, 296; XVII, 14, 19, 296, 485; XVIII, 75, 233, 299; XX, 157
Edinburgh Review, XV, 140; XVIII, 199
Edinburgh Ropery Company, Leith, Scotland, XIX, 174
Edmonds, Capt. John, letter to, XIX, 281
Edward the Black Prince, XVI, 192
Edward II, King of England, XVIII, 390
Edward III, King of England, XVI, 196
Edward VII, King of England, XVIII, 164
Edward O'Brian (ship), XIX, 345
Edwards, Arthur T., XVII, 491
Egerton, Francis, Earl of Ellesmere, XVII, 491; XVIII, 60

Egypt, XVI, 689
Eldridge, Capt., XIX, 95
Elegant Extracts, London, XVI, 626
Elgin, Lord. *See* Bruce, James
Eliot, George (pseud. of Mary Anne Evans), XVI, 608; XVII, 6; XVIII, 67, 223; *Adam Bede*, XVIII, 223
Eliot, Rev. John, XV, 535
Elizabeth, Queen of England, XV, 702; XVIII, 17
Ellen (ship), XIX, 269, 271
Ellenwood, C. H., XVIII, 50
Ellenwood, C. R., XVIII, 50
Ellenwood, T. B., XVIII, 50
Ellesmere, Cheshire, XIX, 202
Ellesmere, Lord. *See* Egerton, Francis
Ellicottville, N.Y., XVI, 494
Ellingwood, John Wallace, XV, 208
Ellingwood, Nancy Dike (Mrs. John), XV, 210
Elliott, Richard, XIX, 146
Ellis, Charles, XV, 563
Ellis, Sir Henry, XVII, 490
Ellis, Maria M. (Mrs. Charles), XV, 564
Ellsworth, Me., XVIII, 471
Ellwood Walter (ship), XIX, 358–59; XX, 92–93
Elsbery, Benjamin (Ellsbury, Ellsbery, Ellsberry; seaman), XIX, 249, 251
Elwes, Gervase, XVIII, 344
Ely, Richard S., XVII, 551, 561; XVIII, 19
Emerson, Charles Chauncey, XV, 32, 433, 442, 474
Emerson, Edward Waldo, correspondence of, XVIII, 407
Emerson, Ellen Tucker, XVIII, 325; correspondence of, XVIII, 407
Emerson, Lidian Jackson (Mrs. Ralph Waldo), XVI, 11; XVIII, 325
Emerson, Ralph Waldo
—letters to: XVI, 259, 379, 542; XVII, 540; XVIII, 107, 143

Emerson, Ralph Waldo (*continued*)
—references to: XV, 4, 20, 22, 25, 30, 32, 43, 45, 55, 56, 71, 87, 380, 382–83, 443, 474, 477, 478, 482, 506, 551, 626, 649, 659–62, 666–67, 670, 692; XVI, 3, 11, 14, 54, 55, 71, 85, 98, 99, 105, 117–18, 128, 183, 198, 248, 298, 299, 353, 398, 531, 562, 569, 576, 602, 616, 636, 692, 695; XVII, 11, 43, 46, 47, 49, 51, 53–55, 75, 77–79, 148, 180, 242, 263, 383, 474, 489, 490, 513, 518, 524, 525; XVIII, 10, 67, 69, 128, 308, 356, 407, 422, 458, 463, 492, 544, 575, 581, 585
—correspondence of: XV, 55, 56, 443, 513, 622, 661, 673; XVI, 11, 55, 99, 107, 117, 259, 379, 531, 542, 562, 578, 695; XVII, 78, 242, 491, 541, 576; XVIII, 332, 337, 357, 664
—journal of: XV, 45, 56, 506; XVI, 55, 99, 128
—works of: "Address to Kossuth," XVI, 542; "American Civilization," XVIII, 546; "American Nationality," XVIII, 423; "The American Scholar," XV, 43, 273; "Courage," XVIII, 464; *English Traits*, XVII, 540; XVIII, 52; "Fate," XVI, 578; *Nature*, XV, 30, 272, 273; "Ode Inscribed to W. H. Channing," XVII, 53, 54; "The Present Age," XV, 380; "Uriel," XVI, 62
Emerson, William, XV, 478; XVI, 117–18; correspondence of, XV, 661; XVI, 117
Emersonians, XV, 474
Emery, Capt. Amaziah, letter to, XX, 29
Emery, George F., XVII, 191–92, 214
Emery, Samuel H., letter to,

XVIII, 608; correspondence of, XVIII, 609
Emily (servant), XVII, 257
Emily St. Pierre (ship), XIX, 315
Emperor (ship), XX, 22–24
Empire State (ship), XX, 141
Encyclopedia Britannica, Edinburgh, XIX, 112, 186, 223
Endicott, Gov. John, XVI, 7
England
—climate of: XVII, 146, 237, 239–40, 243, 322, 364, 372, 408, 454, 455, 465, 485, 497, 504, 531, 558, 585
—comments about: XV, 5, 14, 15, 31, 36, 46, 52, 65, 77, 81, 84–86, 88, 260; XVI, 7, 122, 127, 216, 230, 242, 258–60, 379, 395, 424, 429, 434, 446, 459, 461, 471, 476, 511, 520, 534, 547, 551, 557, 562, 578, 602, 604, 608, 612, 623, 694; XVII, 24, 28, 46, 81, 124, 153, 219, 224, 245, 250, 266, 293, 311, 317, 319, 329, 340, 345, 350, 355, 357, 370, 388, 422, 426, 429, 540, 577; XVIII, 95–96, 105, 132, 139, 140, 151, 161, 177, 198, 200, 216, 227, 229, 246, 272, 274, 344, 354–55, 421, 422, 482, 500, 501, 543, 545
—literature and publishing in: XVII, 6, 7, 14, 163, 164, 256, 261, 272, 277
—NH's ancestors in: XVII, 8, 124, 317, 319
—NH writing in: XVII, 8, 9, 47, 67, 68, 79, 80
—travel and residence in and departure from: XVII, 103, 223, 304, 315, 325, 326, 328, 347, 358, 368, 378, 385, 409, 413, 422, 465, 500, 522, 552, 587; XVIII, 4, 14, 18, 23, 27, 32, 53, 56, 63, 80, 84, 85, 90, 99, 116, 121, 123, 124, 127, 136, 138, 173, 181, 201, 211, 213, 236–37, 248, 262, 287,

Hachette, Louis Christophe François, XVII, 536
Hackley, Charles William, letter to, XVI, 693; reference to, XVI, 675
Hackley, Susan Wheldon (Mrs. Charles William), XVI, 693
Hadley, Capt. S. D., letter to, XIX, 242
Hale, John Parker, XV, 223; XVI, 75, 594
Hale, Nathan, Jr., letters to, XV, 598, 608, 619; references to, XV, 644–45; XVI, 159
Hale, Sarah Josepha Buell, XVI, 42, 47; *The Good Housekeeper*, XVI, 44
Halifax, Nova Scotia, XVII, 23, 133, 228; XVIII, 305
Hall, Anna Maria (Mrs. Samuel Carter), letter to, XVIII, 287; references to, XVII, 16, 31, 464, 479, 523, 539, 554, 577, 578, 592; XVIII, 42–43, 178, 292, 469; XIX, 11; correspondence of, XVIII, 288
Hall, Cornelia. *See* Park, Cornelia Romana Hall (Mrs. Thomas B.)
Hall, Frances (Fanny), XVII, 578, 592; XVIII, 287
Hall, Col. Joseph, XV, 354, 400, 402, 406–07, 410, 423, 425, 435, 437, 441, 451, 453, 458, 469, 473, 475, 477, 482, 491, 498, 536, 616–17, 700; XVI, 29–30, 397, 559, 671; XVIII, 12, 662
Hall, Samuel Carter, XVII, 16, 31, 479, 539, 578, 592; XVIII, 42–43, 178, 287, 469; XIX, 11
Halleck, Fitz-Greene, XV, 551
Hallet, Frank, XVIII, 112
Hallett, B. F., XIX, 141; correspondence of, XIX, 141
Hallowell, Me., XVIII, 471
Hallyman, Thomas (seaman), XIX, 113
Ham, Ben, XV, 111, 115
Ham, Mrs. Ben, XV, 115
Hamilton, Alexander, XV, 233
Hamilton, Gail (pseud. of Mary

Abigail Dodge), XVIII, 579, 587, 644; correspondence of, XVIII, 580, 587; *Country Living and Country Thinking*, XVIII, 581
Hamilton, Mass., XVI, 313
Hamilton (ship), XVI, 190
Hamlin, Hannibal, XVIII, 43
Hammett, Alexander, letter to, XIX, 93–94
Hammond, Edmund, correspondence of, XIX, 227; XX, 150
Hammond, James Lemprière, XVIII, 276, 293
Hammond, Thomas (seaman), XIX, 258
Hampton (shipwreck), XIX, 369–70
Hampton Roads, Va., XVIII, 442
Handel, George Frederick, XV, 119
Hansard's Parliamentary Debates, London, XVIII, 187; XX, 79, 81
Hansom, John (seaman), XIX, 376–78; XX, 9
Hantress, Mrs., XVII, 397
Harbinger, New York, XVI, 157; XVII, 55
Harding, Chester, XV, 32
Harding, Capt., XIX, 318
Harkin, Charles (seaman), XX, 160–61
Harlequin, XVIII, 230
Harnden & Co., Liverpool, XIX, 140
Harper & Bros., New York, XV, 258; XVI, 26
Harper's Magazine, New York, XVII, 13, 14, 502; XVIII, 633
Harper's Ferry, Va., XVIII, 437
Harraden, Stephen, XVI, 160
Harris, Addie A., letter to, XVIII, 552; reference to, XVIII, 542
Harris, Jeremiah or John G., XV, 283
Harris, Thaddeus Mason, XV, 631
Harrison, Joseph (1810–74), XVIII, 652
Harrison, Joseph, XX, 134
Harrison, Thomas & Co., Liverpool, XIX, 144

Harrison, William Henry, XV, 501; XVI, 160, 282

Hart, A., & Co., Philadelphia, XVII, 415

Hartford, Conn., XV, 47, 63, 238; XVI, 437; XVII, 76; Female Seminary, XVIII, 516; Retreat, XVIII, 103, 516

Hartley, William M. B., XVIII, 132; XIX, 16, 17

Harvard, Mass., XVI, 45

Harvard University, XV, 24, 44, 61, 63, 76, 77, 82, 161, 203, 280, 289, 301, 481, 546, 622, 651, 655, 656, 702; XVI, 17, 31, 48, 71, 164, 174, 209, 221, 250, 388, 614; XVII, 11, 53, 211, 234, 251, 305, 341, 519, 523, 576, 580; XVIII, 337, 351, 357, 529, 541, 548; Observatory, XIX, 302; Smith Professorship of Modern Languages and Belles-Lettres, XV, 44; XVII, 251

Harvard University Press, XVI, 209

Haskell, Elizabeth, XV, 129

Haskell, John W., XV, 129

Hastings, Sussex, XVII, 183, 466

Hatch, F. H., XX, 178

Hathaway, William (seaman), XX, 99

Hathorne, Daniel (1731–96, "Bold Hathorne"), XV, 10, 11, 36; XVIII, 524

Hathorne, Capt. Daniel (1768–1805), XV, 11

Hathorne, Elizabeth (ca. 1614–ca. 1676), XVII, 124

Hathorne, Elizabeth Clarke Manning (1780–1849)
—letters to: XV, 117, 120, 124, 126, 130, 131, 135, 138, 143, 146, 148, 150, 153, 157, 163, 164, 170, 171, 226
—references to: XV, 8, 10–20, 24, 105, 107, 111, 113, 115, 119, 122, 123, 125, 128, 131, 156–57, 167–69, 173, 175, 177–79, 182–83, 185–86, 190, 191, 193, 194, 196, 220, 228, 232, 238, 240, 255, 256, 269, 275, 302, 325, 373, 428, 471, 510, 555, 562, 611, 627, 628–29, 630–31, 639, 660, 668, 675, 690–92, 695–96, 701; XVI, 7–8, 15, 20, 30–31, 33, 57, 58, 61, 62, 66, 67, 72, 117, 124, 126, 129–32, 173–74, 213, 227, 228, 237, 293, 339; XVII, 171
—correspondence of: XV, 105–06, 118, 125, 137, 140, 163; XVI, 131

Hathorne, Elizabeth Manning. See Hawthorne, Elizabeth Manning

Hathorne, Eunice, XV, 11, 126, 144, 155

Hathorne, Judith. See Archer, Judith Hathorne (Mrs. George)

Hathorne, Capt. Nathaniel (1775–1808), XV, 11, 16, 111; XVI, 77, 79, 400

Hathorne, Nathaniel (of Pennsylvania), XVI, 81

Hathorne, Rachel (1757–1823). See Forrester, Rachel Hathorne (Mrs. Simon)

Hathorne, Rachel Phelps (1734–1813), XV, 11

Hathorne, Ruth, XV, 11, 126, 144, 155; XVI, 77

Hathorne, William (ca. 1607–81), XVII, 124, 519; XVIII, 344

Hatton, John Liptrot, XVII, 30

Havana, Cuba, XVIII, 649

Havre, France, XVIII, 177

Hawaii, XVII, 288

Haworth, Euphrasia Fanny, letter to, XVII, 483

Haworth Parsonage, Yorkshire, XVII, 31

Hawthorne, Elizabeth Manning (1802–83)
—letters to: XV, 131, 134, 159, 174, 184, 187, 191, 193, 194, 230, 234, 241, 242, 243, 244, 245, 247, 256; XVI, 402, 597, 668; XVII, 413, 446; XVIII, 311, 316, 395, 459, 528

Hawthorne, Nathaniel (*continued*)
General opinions of:
—alcohol and tobacco: 156, 205,
210, 219, 290, 340–42, 379,
381, 429, 467, 474; XVIII,
379, 445, 461, 514, 576–77,
650
—American Indians: XV, 570,
656; XVII, 80, 279, 352;
XVIII, 520
—ancestors: XVII, 124, 153,
317, 319, 355, 519; XVIII,
344, 524, 531–32
—blacks, slavery, and abolition:
XV, 25–26, 75–76, 97, 432,
456, 573, 626, 638, 664–65;
XVI, 25–26, 75–76, 97, 432,
456, 608, 626, 638; XVII, 125,
230, 238, 245, 345, 414, 559;
XVIII, 8, 13, 19, 89, 117, 227,
381, 385, 420, 515, 590,
592–93, 595. *See also* Abolitionists, Fugitive Slave Law
—chastity: XV, 679; XVI, 144,
235; XVII, 190, 202; XVIII,
223
—children: XV, 466; XVI, 15,
19–21, 22–25, 29–31, 33–34,
37, 42–44, 52, 54, 56–57,
68–69, 71, 173–74. *See also*
Hawthorne children
—college, anticipation of: XV,
117–18, 132, 134, 136–37, 138
—consulship in Liverpool: XVI,
600, 605–06, 647, 671, 679,
684–85, 689, 690, 697; XIX,
3–5, 6, 10, 19–20, 34–35,
39–41; XX, 143–49
—death: XV, 109, 368, 472;
XVI, 26, 392, 476; XVII, 297,
302, 304, 333, 410
—duels: XV, 34, 262–63, 264
—East wind: XV, 298–301, 336,
339, 412, 416, 431–32,
464–65, 470, 472, 476, 485,
534, 536, 557; XVI, 124;
XVIII, 570
—friendship: XV, 157, 160, 163,
187, 262, 278, 291; XVI, 141,
225, 344–46, 493, 498, 607,

621, 643, 670, 684, 690–91;
XVII, 123, 187, 189, 207–08,
212, 214, 226, 229, 253, 280,
295, 298, 303, 330–31, 351,
437–38, 504; XVIII, 133, 152,
359, 553, 586, 589, 599,
652
—insanity: XV, 202, 467; XVI,
606; XVII, 566, 570; XVIII,
66, 69, 71, 74, 99, 102, 324,
350, 515
—love: XV, 115, 312, 326, 332,
338, 340, 372, 492, 687; XVII,
436, 463
—marriage: XV, 160, 189,
206–07, 218–19, 270, 279,
329, 334, 347, 372, 378, 385,
452, 629–30, 637, 639, 671;
XVI, 25, 71, 238; XVII, 298,
330, 433, 457–58, 464
—nature: XV, 318, 366, 445,
475, 526, 575; XVI, 23. *See
also* Religion
—pets: Beelzebub (cat), XV,
230, 245, 325, 690; Leo (dog,
Una's "lion"), XV, 56; XVI,
34, 44, 47, 50–51; XVII, 264;
Pigwiggen (cat; also named
"Megara" and "Moloch"), XV,
639, 659–60, 668, 674; Watch
(dog), XV, 128, 129, 137, 138
—poverty: XVII, 154, 327, 520,
528–29; XVIII, 135, 165, 177,
553, 613
—suicide: XV, 201, 207, 467
—women: XV, 212, 345–46,
352, 358, 513, 577, 679; XVI,
25, 47, 70, 87, 213, 273, 375,
532; XVII, 176, 388, 438, 457;
XVIII, 53, 209, 456
On literature and the arts:
—allegory: XVI, 321, 324, 509;
XVII, 201; XVII, 334
—artists, destitution of: XV,
139, 248, 688; XVI, 23, 487;
XVII, 166, 477
—epic: XV, 688
—inspiration: XV, 114, 385,
465, 547, 579, 605; XVI, 302,
338; XVII, 340

Hawthorne, Nathaniel (*continued*)
On literature and the arts:
—poetry: 372, 402, 414, 426;
XVIII, 232, 557
—reading: XV, 114, 132, 134,
152, 153, 160, 175, 252, 395,
405, 454, 470, 473, 538, 566,
667, 671; XVI, 13, 89, 106,
241, 361–62, 460, 476, 486;
XVII, 279, 359, 510; XVIII,
134, 204, 229
—reviews by: XV, 237; XVI, 1,
154, 158–59, 205, 207, 215,
515; XVII, 161, 309; XVIII,
259
—reviews of: XV, 230, 249,
254–55, 257, 279, 599, 602–
03; XVI, 5–7, 9, 27, 86, 113,
161, 168, 327, 361–62, 387,
421–22, 435, 452, 459, 475,
488–89, 537, 598, 607–08,
621; XVII, 123, 152, 198,
427; XVIII, 51–52, 59, 61,
134–35, 199, 223, 237–39,
247, 259, 267, 271–73, 288,
296, 321, 334, 599–600, 603,
612–13
—romance: XVI, 344, 371, 386,
406, 427, 436, 445, 605; XVII,
309; XVIII, 24, 256, 262
—satire: XVI, 270; XVIII, 561
—sculpture: XV, 441–42, 473,
507, 557, 576, 647, 700; XVI,
361; XVIII, 140–41, 143–44,
157, 226, 230, 276, 386, 468,
563
—theater and acting: XV, 120,
122, 136, 146, 202; XVI, 277;
XVII, 166, 178, 184, 464
—women writers: XV, 31; XVI,
624; XVII, 161, 177, 201, 304,
307–08, 456–57; XVIII, 53,
64, 202, 579
Personality of
—descriptions by himself: XV,
9, 32, 36, 44–45, 49–50,
57–58, 66, 89, 117–18, 119,
124, 132, 136–37, 138–39,
160, 174, 184, 187, 194, 202,
213–14, 218, 220, 224, 226,

251–53, 259, 279, 312–13,
373, 401, 437–38, 445–46,
462, 472–73, 494–96, 526–29,
550, 566, 572–73, 575–76,
582, 599, 605–06; XVI, 420,
604, 663; XVII, 380–81,
485–86; XVIII, 97, 152, 178,
303, 447
—descriptions by others: XV, 7,
16, 21, 29–30, 37, 48–49,
51–52, 60–61, 69, 70–71,
73–75, 79–80, 82–84, 88, 113,
115, 118, 124–25, 156, 194,
250, 263, 267, 277, 283–84,
292, 311, 335, 399, 478, 546,
555–56, 583, 601; XVI,
60–61, 183, 192–93, 420, 631;
XVII, 9, 18, 20, 26, 39–40,
41–42, 44, 46–47, 62–63, 67,
69, 71–72, 73, 74–75, 78–79,
104, 106, 131, 176, 180–81,
189, 195, 206, 220, 294, 302,
316, 320, 356, 377, 381, 427,
458, 473, 490, 502, 543, 565,
586; XVIII, 89–91, 152, 580
—depressions: XV, 184–85,
236–37, 262, 278–79, 316,
391–92, 420, 458, 504–05,
563–64; XVI, 105, 266, 312;
XVII, 402, 433–34, 436, 440,
444, 448, 463–64, 471, 479–
80; XVIII, 156, 225, 394, 577,
582, 620, 626, 630, 632, 641
—dreams: XV, 138, 317–18,
334, 344, 351–52, 357–58,
421–22, 427, 461, 504,
511–12, 566, 584, 589–90,
634, 674–75, 678; XVI, 29,
126, 228–29; XVIII, 77
—homesickness: XV, 112, 117,
181; XVII, 123, 224, 315, 379,
392–93, 406
—illnesses: XV, 105, 164, 224,
431, 441, 534, 538; XVI, 34,
163, 320, 324, 520, 632; XVII,
431, 433–34, 436, 440, 444,
448, 463–64, 471, 479–80,
485, 518; XVIII, 138, 163,
166, 333, 427, 468, 508,
575–76, 613–14, 623, 625–26,

INDEX

19, 61, 388, 409, 466, 478;
XVIII, 58, 77, 122, 134–35,
191, 198, 199, 223, 240, 521,
620; XIX, 5; "Howe's Mas-
querade," XV, 314, 524; "The
Inland Port," XV, 227; "The
Itinerant Storyteller" (see
"The Storyteller"); "Jonathan
Cilley," XV, 34, 264, 267,
272; XVI, 277, 281; XVIII,
591; *Journal of an African
Cruiser* (NH, editor; *see*
Bridge, Horatio); "Lady Elea-
nor's Mantle," XV, 280; "Leamington Spa," XVIII, 471,
486, 493, 533; *Liberty Tree*,
XV, 503, 528, 547, 570, 573,
610; "Lichfield and Utto-
xeter," XVIII, 567, 569, 572;
Life of Franklin Pierce, XV, 36,
175–76; XVI, 545, 550–51,
557, 559–61, 566, 583–92,
595, 597, 601, 604–09, 611,
617; XVII, 4, 19, 73, 189;
XVIII, 591; "The Lily's
Quest," XV, 282; XVIII, 628;
"Little Annie's Ramble," XV,
49, 52, 71; XVI, 6; "Little
Daffydowndilly," XV, 698;
XVI, 502; "A London Sub-
urb," XVIII, 508, 514, 523,
533, 558; "Lost Notebook,"
XV, 23, 28, 30, 62, 64; XVII,
502; "Main-street," XV, 23;
XVI, 267, 409; "The Man of
Adamant," XV, 572–73, 600;
The Marble Faun, XV, 32–33,
46–47, 75, 84–85, 254; XVI,
200, 551; XVII, 3, 38, 40, 55,
62, 65, 66, 74, 145; XVIII, 22,
143, 151–55, 160–62, 164,
175, 181, 182, 189–239, 242,
245, 247, 248, 250–53,
256–60, 262, 263, 266, 267,
271–73, 276, 277, 287, 288,
296, 300, 314, 334, 352, 377,
518, 522, 541, 592, 601, 632;
"The May-Pole of Merry
Mount," XV, 200, 231; XVI,
7; "The Minister's Black

Veil," XV, 231; "Monsieur du
Miroir," XV, 214, 572, 600;
Mosses from an Old Manse, XV,
48, 54, 69, 71, 76, 227, 250,
403, 451, 460, 482, 574, 601,
607, 613, 642, 657, 662, 673,
676, 683, 702; XVI, 18, 24,
62, 88, 111, 118, 139, 142,
146, 148, 151, 154, 155, 158,
162, 165, 167–70, 172, 178,
188, 194, 195, 230, 242,
251–52, 305, 307, 351, 355,
363, 382, 396, 550, 653; XVII,
7, 15, 54, 55, 74, 105, 106,
201, 202, 225, 227, 228, 265,
425; XVIII, 366, 371, 467,
521, 612, 637; "My Kinsman,
Major Molineux" ("My Uncle
Molineux"), XV, 199, 222,
571, 600; XVI, 501; XVIII,
627; "My Visit to Niagara,"
XV, 227; *Nathaniel Haw-
thorne's Tales* (piracy), XVI,
455; "Near Oxford," XVIII,
379; "The New Adam and
Eve," XV, 574, 683, 685; XVI,
86; "New England Historical
Sketches," XV, 389; "A Night
Scene," XV, 227; "Northern
Volunteers. From a Journal,"
XVIII, 438, 444, 462; "The
Notch of the White Moun-
tains," XV, 227; "The Old
Apple-Dealer," XV, 656; XVI,
151; "Old Esther Dudley,"
XV, 280, 314; "The Old Maid
in the Winding-Sheet" (see
"The White Old Maid");
"The Old Manse," XV, 7, 76,
89, 403, 451, 676; XVI, 24,
88, 94, 105, 122, 127, 136,
152, 155, 159, 167; XVIII,
467; "Old Ticonderoga," XV,
227; XVI, 434, 455;
"Old-Time Legends," XVI,
301; XVII, 20; "An Ontario
Steamboat," XV, 227; "Our
Evening Party among the
Mountains," XV, 227; XVII,
228; *Our Old Home*, XV, 36;

• 281 •

Hawthorne, Sophia Amelia Peabody (*continued*)

—references to: 601, 652, 655; XIX, 4, 7, 11, 42, 149, 380

—correspondence of: XV, 6, 8–10, 18, 26, 29, 30, 31, 62, 76, 86, 88, 268, 274, 275, 284, 292, 301, 302, 315, 327, 359, 365, 383, 396, 474, 482, 546, 549, 560, 577, 585, 622, 626–27, 631–32, 639–41, 642, 645, 648, 649, 660, 668, 669, 673, 676, 680, 683, 689–90, 692, 694, 702, 703; XVI, 8, 16, 18, 27, 28, 31–32, 40, 64, 66, 71, 74, 75, 77, 81, 85, 90, 98–99, 101, 111, 113–14, 118, 119, 125, 131, 138, 144–46, 151, 157, 162, 165–66, 201–02, 213, 216, 232, 234, 247, 253–54, 260, 261, 267, 271, 274, 295, 299, 310, 313, 330, 354, 378, 388, 401, 438, 442, 455, 463, 471, 480, 485, 491, 509, 512, 543, 578, 585, 594, 642, 680, 693; XVII, 4, 46, 57–58, 59–60, 83, 102, 106, 126, 136, 144, 149, 153, 162, 176, 217, 238, 240, 242, 259, 290, 302, 309, 319–20, 329, 331, 341, 365, 369, 371, 377, 383, 399–400, 403, 440, 505, 517, 523, 525, 527, 542, 547, 557, 578, 586; XVIII, 4–5, 7, 9, 28, 40, 52, 64–65, 116, 120, 152–53, 162, 180, 185, 194, 197, 207, 223, 224, 233, 249, 263, 297, 309, 318, 319, 325, 361, 394, 397–98, 400–01, 404, 407, 411, 429, 436, 439, 442, 444, 464, 469, 481, 488, 493, 501–02, 509, 514, 530, 532, 550–51, 559, 570, 571, 576, 581, 582, 584, 588, 596, 613–14, 629, 634, 641, 642, 646, 649; XIX, 11, 18, 160, 227–28

—journals of: Cuban Journal, XV, 26–28; 1842 diary, XV, 637; 1843–44 journal, XV, 29, 702; XVI, 18; 1850–51 journal, XVI, 390, 391, 401, 407, 413, 434; 1852 diary, XVI, 599–600; XIX, 4; 1861 Pocket Diary, XVIII, 345, 366, 379, 384, 386, 389, 407, 411, 425; 1862 Pocket Diary, XVIII, 431, 433, 436, 450, 455, 457, 458, 462, 464, 467, 481, 484, 491, 495, 499, 505, 507, 509, 530, 572, 593

—works of: "Bronson Alcott Talking to the Children at His School" (drawing), XV, 32; "Endymion" (sculptured relief), XVI, 6, 12, 13; "Isola" (painting), XV, 403, 404–05, 414, 415, 527; Medallion of Charles Emerson, XV, 433, 441–42; Medallion of George Francis Peabody, XV, 443; "Menaggio" (painting), XV, 401–02, 403, 404–05, 415, 427, 527; *Notes in England and Italy*, XVII, 72; "The Puritan and the Gentle Boy" (drawing), XV, 32, 297, 314; "St. George and Una" (drawing), XVI, 16

—addressed as "Phoebe": XV, 699, 701; XVI, 29, 37, 39, 42, 47, 67, 68, 70, 72, 124, 125, 133, 134, 137, 201, 212, 224, 228–29, 238, 468, 469, 470, 472, 490, 593

Hawthorne, Una

—letters to: XVI, 237, 529, 596; XVII, 281, 460; XVIII, 279, 282, 293, 306, 309, 312, 396, 436, 437

—references to: XV, 25, 30, 32, 33, 56, 83, 134, 702; XVI, 5, 12, 13, 15, 19–25, 27, 29–31, 33–35, 37–39, 42–44, 47, 48, 52, 54, 56–58, 60–62, 65–69, 71–75, 79, 80, 84, 85, 87, 90, 91, 98, 109, 110, 112, 115–17, 120, 125, 129, 130, 132–34, 137, 142, 148, 156, 157, 171–74, 188, 190, 192–94,

INDEX

Hesiod, XV, 365

Hewitt, Mary E., *The Memorial*, XVI, 359–60, 376, 387

Heywood, Abel Barrett, XVI, 51

Heywood, Anna Maria Jones (Mrs. John Pemberton), letters to, XVII, 175, 441, 476; XVIII, 122; references to, XVII, 50, 56, 59–63, 67, 74, 75, 174, 197, 262, 273; XVIII, 59, 133, 193, 600; correspondence of, XVII, 174

Heywood, Arthur, XVII, 50, 52

Heywood, Benjamin, XVII, 52

Heywood, James, XVII, 49; XVIII, 268

Heywood, John Pemberton, XVII, 50, 56, 59–61, 63, 74, 75, 262, 273; XVIII, 356

Heywood, Nathaniel, XVII, 60, 61

Heywood, Richard, XVII, 52

Heywood, Arthur, Sons & Co., XVII, 50; XVIII, 356

Heywood family, XVII, 51–53

Hibbard, Col. Ellery Albee, XVIII, 656

Hibernia (ship), XVI, 31

Hicks, Augustus (seaman), XIX, 243

Higgins, John, letter to, XIX, 256; reference to, XIX, 84; correspondence of, XIX, 22

Highlands, Scotland, XVII, 485

Hildreth, Caroline Gould Negus (Mrs. Richard), XVI, 53

Hildreth, Richard, XVI, 55; XVIII, 199

Hilen, Andrew, XV, 4; XVI, 85

Hill, Barney S., XVIII, 471, 474, 476–79, 481, 487

Hill, Charles L., XV, 500

Hill, Charlotte, XVIII, 476, 479, 487

Hill, Dudley and Mrs., XV, 211, 214

Hill, Capt. George S., letter to, XIX, 106

Hill, Increase S., XV, 500; XVI, 181

Hill, Isaac, XV, 214

Hillard, George Stillman
—letters to: XV, 550, 641; XVI, 11, 22, 35, 41, 63, 119, 263, 273, 277, 279, 309; XVII, 154; XVIII, 184
—references to: XV, 62, 75–86, 89, 268, 358, 365, 383, 388, 393, 403, 412, 419, 450, 474, 476, 481, 525, 551, 581, 602, 608, 623, 641, 643, 664, 696, 699, 700, 702; XVI, 29, 67, 73, 96, 98, 164, 182, 183, 216, 258, 265, 271, 275–76, 285, 384, 386, 396, 398, 500, 562, 564; XVII, 69, 124, 130, 190; XVIII, 155, 179, 222, 272, 345, 522, 588; XIX, 31, 51
—correspondence of: XV, 525; XVI, 24, 274, 310
—works of: "The Comparison of Ancient and Modern Literature," XV, 76; *The Franklin Fifth Reader*, XV, 84; *Poetical Works of Edmund Spenser*, XV, 474; "Selections from the Papers of an Idler," XV, 77; *Selections from the Writings of Henry R. Cleveland, with a Memoir*, XV, 641; *Six Months in Italy*, XV, 81, 85; XVI, 216; XVII, 130; XVIII, 185; "The Relation of the Poet to His Age," XV, 700; XVI, 11

Hillard, John, XV, 81, 450, 481

Hillard, Susan Tracy Howe (Mrs. George), XV, 76, 365, 414, 476, 522, 527, 606, 641, 643, 696, 703; XVI, 11, 24, 63, 216, 264

Hillard infant, XV, 76; XVI, 24

Hillsborough, N.H., XV, 35, 223; XVI, 562; XX, 9

Hingham, Mass., XVI, 85

Historic Society of Lancashire and Cheshire. *See* Lancashire

History of the Great Western Sanitary Fair, XVIII, 621–22

Hitchcock, Gen. Ethan Allen, XVIII, 590; correspondence of, XVIII, 644

Hitchcock, Capt., XIX, 331

Hitchen, Thomas (seaman), XX, 166

Hoar, Ebenezer Rockwood, XVI, 119, 142, 145, 350; XVIII, 302

Hoar, Elizabeth Sherman, XV, 432, 442, 661; XVI, 13, 119, 350

Hoar, Samuel (1788–1856), XV, 433; XVI, 3, 4

Hodges, Mary, XV, 202

Hoffman, Charles Fenno, XV, 52

Hoffman, Francis Suydam, letter to, XVIII, 654

Hog Island, Me., XVIII, 483

Hogg, James, XV, 132; *Winter Evening Tales Collected among the Cottagers in the South of Scotland*, XV, 132

Holbrook, Amory, letter to, XVI, 178

Holbrook, Marion Marshall (Mrs. J. G.), XVI, 230, 356

Holbrook, Samuel F., XVII, 447–49, 472

Holcom, William J. (seaman), XX, 102

Holden, George P., XV, 60, 65; correspondence of, XVI, 631; XVII, 37

Holden's Dollar Magazine, New York, XVI, 404, 420, 422, 444; XVII, 53; XVIII, 273

Holland, Charles, letters to, XVII, 127, 132, 384; XVIII, 298

Holland, Elizabeth Gaskell (Mrs. Charles), XVII, 127, 132

Holliston, Mass., XVI, 615; Congregational Church, XVI, 615

Holman, R. W., XV, 425

Holme & Slater, Messrs., Liverpool, XX, 162

Holmes, John S., XVI, 250

Holmes, Oliver Wendell (1809–94), XV, 77, 87, 229; XVI, 356, 384, 398, 451, 500, 562, 564; XVII, 30; XVIII, 223, 241, 308, 445, 509, 511, 580, 621–22, 656; correspondence of, XVI, 399, 451, 500; "Never or Now: An Appeal," XVIII, 446; *Poet at the Breakfast Table*, XVIII, 377

Holmes, Oliver Wendell, Jr. (1841–1935), XVIII, 422

Holt, Elizabeth Bright (Mrs. George), XVII, 58, 59, 75

Holt, George (1790–1861), XIX, 225

Holt, George, J.P., XVII, 59, 75

Holt, George, & Co., XIX, 208, 225

Holyhead, Wales, XIX, 215

Home, John, *Douglas*, XV, 147

Homeopathy, XV, 606; XVI, 31, 48, 49, 156, 166, 174, 301, 349, 578; XVII, 383, 393, 455, 532; XVIII, 175, 233, 439, 460, 484, 550

Homer, XV, 365, 543, 567; XVII, 77, 78; *Iliad*, XVIII, 383, 571

Homes of American Authors, XVI, 530, 567–69, 572, 573

The Home Journal, New York, XVI, 328

Honolulu, XVI, 639, 685

Hood, George, correspondence of, XVI, 148

Hood, Thomas, *Poems*, XVI, 159

Hooker, James Clinton, XVIII, 230

Hooper, Anna Maria, XV, 304

Hooper, Anne Sturgis (Mrs. Samuel), XV, 304, 463; XVI, 8, 14, 310, 350; XVIII, 395

Hooper, Ellen Sturgis, XVI, 14

Hooper, Samuel, XV, 292, 295, 461, 463; XVIII, 395

Hooper, Mr., XVI, 240

Hopkins, Thomas, *On the Atmospheric Conditions Which Produce Rain, Wind, Storms, and the Fluctuations of the Barometer*, XIX, 198–99, 225

Hopkinson, Francis ("Peter Grievous"), XVI, 420; *A Pretty Story*, XVI, 423

Horace, *Epistles*, XV, 128

Horizon (ship), XX, 160–61

Horn Pond, Woburn, Mass., XVI, 124

Horner, Capt. William Henderson, XIX, 268

Horsburgh, James, *The India Directory*, XIX, 197, 224

James, George Payne Rainsford (*continued*) *Life of Edward the Black Prince*, XVI, 451
James, Henry, Sr., XVII, 383; correspondence of, XVIII, 357
James, Henry, Jr., XV, 22, 60, 85; XVII, 6, 7, 11, 13, 24, 44, 51, 70–72, 74; XVIII, 193; correspondence of, XVII, 44, 51; *Bostonians*, XV, 22; *Hawthorne*, XV, 60, 85; XVII, 7, 70–72, 74; "Mr. and Mrs. James T. Fields," XVII, 11, 13; *Portrait of a Lady*, XVIII, 297
James, William, XVIII, 561
James Brown (ship), XIX, 95
James Cheston (ship), XIX, 272–75, 276, 277, 292–93, 300–01, 324–25, 344
James L. Bogart (ship), XVIII, 11; XIX, 34; XX, 111, 132–35, 230
James Watt (ship), XIX, 280
Jameson, Hugh, XV, 283
Jameson, Thomas (seaman), XIX, 304, 384
Jameson, William, letters to, XIX, 374; XX, 8
Jane (servant), XV, 120
Jane H. Glidden (ship), XIX, 299
Japan, XVII, 470
Japan (ship), XIX, 288; XX, 224
Japp, Alexander Hay (H. A. Page), XVII, 68, 72–74
Jarvis, Mary C., XVIII, 635
Jay, John, letter to, XVI, 296; references to, XVI, 313; XVIII, 187; correspondence of, XVI, 296–97, 313
Jean-Paul. *See* Richter, Jean-Paul Friedrich
Jefferson, Thomas, XV, 234, 238, 245, 247; correspondence of, XVII, 290
Jeffrey, Francis, XV, 140
Jenkins, James (seaman), XIX, 389
Jennings, Mrs., XVII, 19
Jephson, Henry, XVII, 358
Jephson, Miss, correspondence of, XVII, 19

Jerdan, William, XVII, 31, 149, 151; *Autobiography*, XVII, 149
Jerrold, Douglas William, XVII, 472, 514, 584; correspondence of, XVII, 473
Jersey City, N.J., XVI, 592
Jewett, Miss L., letter to, XVI, 314
Jewett, John P. & Co., Boston, XVII, 305
Jewsbury, Geraldine, XVII, 523
John and Albert (ship), XIX, 113–14, 115–16, 121–22, 123, 127–29, 150, 152
John Bright (shipwreck), XX, 20–21, 226
"John Bull," XVII, 9, 108, 184, 218, 266, 312, 380, 388, 402, 444, 496, 499; XVIII, 71, 177, 266, 271, 515
John Knox (ship), XVII, 357
Johns Hopkins University, Baltimore, XVI, 614; XVII, 536
Johnson, Cave, XVI, 103
Johnson, Eastman, XVI, 183, 206
Johnson, Capt. Edward John, *Practical Illustration of the Necessity for Ascertaining the Deviations of the Compass*, XIX, 197, 224
Johnson, Capt. Henry, XIX, 298
Johnson, Henry Norris (seaman), letters to, XIX, 373; XX, 7; references to, XIX, 308–09, 310, 312, 332, 360–61, 374; XX, 8, 11, 17, 18–19, 50, 70; correspondence of, XX, 7
Johnson, John F. (seaman), XIX, 362–63, 366, 367
Johnson, Samuel, XV, 493; XVII, 502; XVIII, 351; "Prologue at the Opening of Drury Lane Theatre," XVII, 150
Jones, Mrs. Benjamin, XVII, 174
Jones, Elizabeth Heywood (Mrs. Hugh), XVII, 50
Jones, Hugh, XVII, 50
Jones, Jeremiah (seaman), XX, 133
Jones, John Paul, XV, 52; XX, 61
Jones, John S. (seaman), XIX, 362, 366, 367
Jones, J. S., XVII, 535

INDEX

Mackintosh, Mary Appleton (Mrs.
Robert), XVIII, 280, 282
Mackintosh, Robert James, XVIII,
279, 281, 282
Maclean, Maris & Co, Liverpool,
XIX, 358
Macmillan, Alexander, XVIII,
228
Macmillan's Magazine, London,
XVIII, 228, 584
Macready, William Charles, XV,
81
MacWhorter, Rev. Alexander,
XVII, 76–77; XVIII, 516
Madan, Cristobal, XVI, 189
Madan, Mary O'Sullivan (Mrs.
Cristobal, formerly Mrs. Samuel
Langtree), XVI, 188, 195; XVII,
482
Madeira, XV, 57; XVI, 75, 82;
XVII, 433, 439, 442, 444, 446,
448, 449, 453, 455, 464, 472,
489, 497, 506, 539
Madison, Dolley, XVI, 183
Madrid, Spain, XVIII, 40
Madrid (ship), XVII, 387, 392
Magenta, Italy, Battle of, XVIII,
170
Magician (ship), XX, 95
Magnetism, XV, 588–90, 593, 634;
XVI, 224, 581
Maherey, James (seaman), XX,
134–35
Main, H. P., letter to, XVIII,
405
Maine, XV, 24, 34, 38, 42, 76,
105–73 *passim*, 213, 254, 406,
407; XVI, 2, 188, 232, 346, 559,
590; XVII, 72, 321; XVIII, 143,
444, 459, 469, 501, 526
Maine Law, XVI, 549, 563, 583
Maine Stage Coach Co., Portland,
XV, 178
Makin, Samuel (or William E.; sea-
man), XIX, 289–90, 299
Malaga, Spain, XV, 466
Malden, Mass., XV, 492
Malony, Capt. Daniel, XIX, 294–
97
Malta, XVII, 376; XIX, 124–25

Malton, Yorkshire, XVIII, 182
Malvern, Worcestershire, XVII,
368; XVIII, 224, 249
Manassas, Va., XVIII, 394, 437,
438, 443
Manchester Arts Exhibition,
XVIII, 65, 77, 95
Manchester, England, XV, 65;
XVI, 680; XVII, 30, 32, 35, 49,
52, 53, 118–19, 148, 159, 188,
209, 231, 326, 356, 493; XVIII,
59, 64–65, 74, 77, 83, 93, 95, 96;
XIX, 74; Albion Hotel, XVII,
493; Manchester New College,
XVII, 55, 176. *See also* Consu-
lates, U.S.
Manchester, Mass., XVI, 403, 480;
XVIII, 393, 395, 404; Kettle
Cove, XVI, 403, 585; XVIII,
395, 404, 459
Mangosteen (ship), XIX, 268
Manhattan (ship), XIX, 254
Mann, Ambrose Dudley, XVII,
204, 292
Mann, Benjamin Pickman, XV, 27;
XVI, 229, 237, 543; XVIII, 194
Mann, George Combe, XV, 27;
XVI, 135, 237, 449, 490, 543;
XVIII, 194
Mann, Horace (1796–1859)
—letters to: XVI, 284, 287, 289,
291
—references to: XV, 21, 25–27,
66, 293, 383, 686; XVI, 3, 4,
6, 130, 157, 247, 268, 275,
349, 449, 462, 490, 507, 508,
543; XVII, 13, 402, 423;
XVIII, 83, 194, 665
—correspondence of: XV, 26;
XVI, 290; XVII, 13
Mann, Horace, Jr. (1844–68), XV,
27; XVI, 20, 134, 227, 230, 236,
237, 247, 349, 354, 449, 490,
543; XVIII, 194, 312, 476; correspondence of, XVIII, 653
Mann, Lydia, XVI, 8
Mann, Mary Peabody (Mrs. Horace)
—letters to: XVI, 3, 275; XVII,
479

· 301 ·

—references to: XIX, 307; XX, 70

—correspondence of: XIX, 386; XX, 70, 74

McCulloch, John Ramsay, *Descriptive and Statistical Account of the British Empire*, XIX, 220, 226; *Dictionary Practical, Theoretical, and Historical, of Commerce and Commercial Navigation*, XIX, 167, 168, 170–71, 175, 206, 208, 209, 217, 220–21

McDonald, G. (seaman), XIX, 388

McDonald, Michael (seaman), XX, 170, 171–72, 174, 175

McElroy, F. G., letter to, XVIII, 367

McGuire, J. C., letter to, XVI, 367

McIntyre, Capt. Duncan, XIX, 269–70

McKay, Daniel (seaman), XX, 126, 128

McKay, Donald, XIX, 80, 130–31, 138, 140–41, 184, 187, 288

McKay, Lauchlan, XIX, 90, 130–31, 138, 140

McKeen, John, XV, 159, 163, 169, 177, 193

McKeen, Rev. Joseph (1757–1807), XV, 161

McKeen, Joseph (1787–1865), XV, 169

McKeon, John

—letters to: XIX, 367, 376–77, 388–89; XX, 9, 18, 64, 117, 164, 168, 174, 175

—references to: XIX, 375, 387; XX, 17, 60, 62, 154, 156, 167, 172, 231

McKnight, Samuel P. (Knight; seaman), XIX, 362–63, XX, 227

McLaughlin, George, letter to, XVIII, 621

McMichael, Morton, XVI, 18

McNeil, John, XV, 283, 360, 450

McRitchie, Alexander (seaman), XIX, 369–70; XX, 86

Mead, Rev. Asa, XV, 178, 189

Means, Abigail Atherton Kent (Mrs. Robert), XVI, 680

Means, Robert, Jr., XVI, 680

Medford, Mass., XV, 383

Medici family, XVII, 48, 49

Medill, William, XX, 185–86

Mediterranean Sea, XV, 38, 466; XVI, 685; XVII, 408

Meincke, Andrew F., XIX, 381

Melbourne, Australia, XVII, 58; XIX, 79, 131, 141, 147

Melly, George, XVII, 50, 59, 75, 551, 561

Melly, Sarah Elizabeth Bright (Mrs. George), XVII, 58–59, 75, 561

Melville, Allan, XVI, 639; XVII, 573

Melville, Elizabeth Shaw (Mrs. Herman), XVI, 412, 413, 639

Melville, Herman

—letter to: XVI, 412

—references to: XV, 18, 46, 55, 68, 71–74, 422, 597; XVI, 230, 348, 355, 357, 361, 362, 374, 399, 404, 421, 425, 455, 473, 508, 564, 608, 639, 669; XVII, 405, 473; XVIII, 23, 621; XIX, 39

—correspondence of: XVI, 363, 399, 413, 423, 455, 509, 565, 608

—works of: "Benito Cereno," XVIII, 285; *Confidence Man*, XVIII, 52; "Hawthorne and His Mosses," XV, 71; XVI, 361; *Mardi*, XV, 72; XVI, 362, 426; *Moby Dick*, XV, 72–74, 422; XVI, 508; XIX, 316; *Omoo*, XV, 72; *Pierre*, XV, 72, 74; XVI, 509; *Redburn*, XV, 72; XVI, 362; XIX, 39; *Typee*, XV, 71, 72; XVI, 153, 158; *White Jacket*, XV, 72; XVI, 362; XIX, 39

Melville, Malcolm, XVI, 500

Melville, Robert, XVI, 432

Menaggio, Italy, XV, 403, 529

Mendelssohn, Felix, XVII, 30, 145

Mercantile Marine of America, XVIII, 11, 13–14, 18–19, 73–74, 167, 186–87

Mercersburg, Pa., XVII, 211

Meredith, William Morris, correspondence of, XVI, 265, 276, 282, 285, 290

Meridith, Owen, XVII, 502

Merivale, Charles, XVIII, 600

Merivale, Herman, "The Corrector of Shakspeare," XVII, 492

Merrill, John (seaman), XIX, 322

Merrimack (ship), XVIII, 440–41

Mersey River, England, XVII, 115, 120, 123, 127, 149, 394, 397, 417

Messmore, D., letter to, XIX, 331

Methuen, Mass., XVII, 403

Mexican War, XV, 35; XVI, 258, 283, 560, 562, 585, 608, 658, 685; XVII, 54, 121; XVIII, 250

Mexico, XV, 241; XVI, 560

M'Glashan, James, XVI, 552

Miami University, Oxford, Ohio, XVIII, 302

Michael Angelo (Ticknor & Fields employee), XVIII, 557

Michelangelo [Buonarroti], XV, 478

Michaels, Capt. J., XX, 4

Michigan, XVI, 562; XVII, 403, 405; XVIII, 75

Middlesex County, Mass., XV, 409

Middlesex *Freeman*, Concord, XVI, 546

Milan, Italy, XVIII, 170

Miles, T., Jr., XVI, 505

Mill, John Stuart, XV, 436; XVII, 23

Miller, Charles S., XVIII, 547

Miller, Col. Ephraim, letters to, XVII, 156, 184, 268; references to, XVI, 163, 253, 254, 278, 281, 284, 290–92, 364, 366, 393, 409, 498, 563, 629, 641, 642, 645, 657, 679, 687, 688; XVII, 138, 161, 219, 379, 532; XVIII, 44; XIX, 126

Miller, Gen. James, letters to, XVI, 179, 184, 186, 203, 219, 222, 223, 246; references to, XVI, 160, 164, 253, 322, 688

Miller, John, XVII, 23, 216, 416,

419; XVIII, 250; XIX, 255; XX, 83, 188, 224

Miller, Kingsbury N. (seaman), XX, 126, 128

Miller, William, XV, 681; Millerites, XV, 680, 683

Miller, William Rickarby, XVI, 530–31

Millet, Daniel, Jr., XVI, 232

Millet, Nathan, XVI, 214, 294, 341, 681

Mills, James, XVI, 285

Milman, Henry Hunt, *Fazio*, XVII, 184

Milnes, Annabel Hungerford Crewe (Mrs. Richard Monckton), XVII, 273; correspondence of, XVII, 273

Milnes, Richard Monckton (later Lord Houghton), letters to, XVII, 272, 277, 279; XVIII, 186; references to, XV, 45; XVI, 460; XVII, 38, 51, 52, 61, 64, 70, 75, 79, 261, 519, 523; XVIII, 235, 280, 285; XIX, 38; XX, 111; correspondence of, XVII, 38, 61–62, 273, 280; XVIII, 423–24; "In Memoriam. Henry Bright," XVII, 52; *Poetical Works of John Keats, with a Memoir*, XVII, 280

Milton, John, XV, 54, 231, 365, 470, 667, 671; *Paradise Lost*, XV, 231, 471, 671; XVI, 62, 471; XVIII, 429, 466; *Poetical Works*, XV, 471; *Prose Works*, XV, 471

Milton, Mass., XV, 548, 597

Minnesota, XV, 27; XVI, 217

Minot, Josiah, letters to, XIX, 304–05, 306, 326, 327–28; reference to, XIX, 264

Mirror. See *New-York Mirror*

Mississippi, XVII, 125, 535; XVIII, 593

Missouri, XVIII, 420

Missroon, John S., XVIII, 553

Mitchell, Donald Grant ("Ik Marvel"), letters to, XVIII, 449, 631; reference to, XVI, 679; correspondence of, XVII, 142; XVIII, 632–33; *My Farm of Edge-*

New York City (*continued*)
—streets of: Broadway, XVI,
676; XVIII, 453; Park Place,
XVI, 676; XVIII, 453; Wall
Street, XV, 448; Washington
Place, XVII, 354; Waverley
Place, XVI, 676; West Twenty-
second Street, XVI, 676
New York (state), XV, 49, 50, 57,
58, 68, 73, 75, 78, 225, 274,
613, 617, 680, 683, 686, 688,
690; XVI, 347, 356, 421, 510,
606; XVII, 76, 289, 318, 395,
482, 508, 512, 544, 572, 585;
XVIII, 37
New York Supreme Court, XVIII,
64
New York *Enquirer*, XIX, 255
New York *Evening Post*, XVI, 507,
689; XVII, 539; XVIII, 64, 593
New York *Herald*, XV, 680; XVI,
637; XVII, 486; XVIII, 389,
429
New York *Mirror*, XV, 228, 285,
657
New York *Morning News*, XVI, 83
New York *Observer*, XV, 192
New York *Sun*, XV, 655
New York *Times*, XVIII, 593; XIX,
120, 266, 275, 368, 378, 388;
XX, 60, 64
New York *Tribune*, XV, 40; XVI,
236, 379, 608; XVII, 486; XVIII,
103, 273, 464; XIX, 368; XX, 9
New York *World*, XV, 657
New-Yorker, XV, 22, 273, 282, 286,
297
Newburyport, Mass., XV, 17, 107,
127, 142, 146, 191, 202, 212,
221, 606; XVI, 57; First Reli-
gious Society (Congregational),
XV, 607
Newby Bridge, Lancashire, XVII,
365
Newcastle-upon-Tyne, Northum-
berland, XVII, 30
Newcomb, Charles King, XV, 670
Newfoundland, Canada, XVII, 265
Newhall, Daniel, XV, 558
Newhall, Mary Bailey, XV, 32, 558

Newlands, Capt. Alexander, XIX,
140–41
Newman, Cardinal John Henry,
XVII, 584
Newman, Peter (seaman), XIX,
244
Newman, Samuel Phillips, XV,
155, 164, 167
Newman, Mrs. Samuel Phillips,
XV, 164, 167
Newport, R.I., XVI, 612, 614
Newport News, Va., XVIII, 441
Newton, Mass., XVI, 538
Niagara (ship), XVI, 685, 693, 697,
700; XVII, 25, 102, 110, 146,
191, 233, 263; XVIII, 73
Niagara Falls, N.Y., XV, 224, 227
Nicaragua, XVI, 662; XVII, 498
Nichols, Rev. Arthur Bell, XVII,
31
Nightingale, Florence, XVII, 523
Nightingale, Frances Parthenope,
XVII, 523
Nightingale, Frances Smith, XVII,
523
Nile River, Africa, XVI, 424, 425,
569
Nineteenth Century, London, XV,
632; XVII, 62
Nitier, Joseph, XX, 225
Noble, Capt., XIX, 197
Noble, Thomas (seaman), XX, 166
Norfolk, Va., XV, 467; XVII, 473;
XVIII, 442
Norie, John William, *A Complete
Epitome of Practical Navigation*,
XIX, 196, 224; *The New Sea-
man's Guide*, XIX, 196, 224
Norridgewock, Me., XV, 254
Norris, Frank, *The Octopus*, XVII,
49
Norris Green, West Derby, Lan-
cashire, XVII, 56, 57, 59, 61,
62, 176, 362, 441; XVIII, 122
North, J. Bartram, letter to, XVI,
657; references to, XVII, 200;
XVIII, 535, 555
North, Margaret Bridge (Mrs. Wil-
liam A. S.), XVI, 191
North, William A. S., XVI, 191

Rome, Italy (*continued*)
—travel to and residence in: XVII,167, 242, 320, 329, 331, 532, 542; XVIII, 38, 84, 96, 127, 133, 137, 141–43, 147, 152–53, 155, 160, 165, 169, 173, 176, 185, 190, 207, 216, 231, 240, 270, 282, 285, 371, 562, 601, 637
—places: Capitol Sculpture Gallery, XVIII, 276; Catacombs, XVIII, 240; Palace of the Caesars, XVIII, 139; Sistine Chapel, Vatican, XVIII, 139; Vatican Sculpture Gallery, XVIII, 277
Ropes, Hannah, XV, 202
Rosa, Salvator, XV, 32
Roscius (ship), XIX, 95
Roscoe, William, XVII, 48, 49, 53
Roslyn, N.Y., XVI, 327
Ross, C. E. (seaman), XX, 55–56, 57, 60
Rossetti, Dante Gabriel, XVII, 30
Rothschild family, XVII, 361
Rotterdam, Netherlands, XIX, 291
Routledge, George, XVII, 202, 359, 524, 526; XVIII, 347
Routledge, George, & Co., London, XVI, 539, 550; XVII, 202, 541
Rousseau, Jean-Jacques, XV, 134; *La Nouvelle Eloise*, XV, 134
Rowe, Joseph (seaman), XIX, 283
Rowena (ship), XX, 162–63
Rowlinson, John, XIX, 356
Roxbury, Mass., XV, 260, 537; XVI, 142, 497
Royal Horticultural Society, London, XIX, 212–13
Royal Literary Fund, London, XVII, 477; XVIII, 280
Royal Mail Steam Packet Company, London, XVII, 305
Royle, John Forbes, XIX, 212–13, 225
Rugby School, Rugby, Warwickshire, XVII, 59, 66, 75
Ruggles, George B., XIX, 93–94
Ruggles, John, XV, 273
Runcorn, Cheshire, XIX, 202

Russell, Amelia, XV, 597
Russell, Ida, XV, 597
Russell, John B., XV, 248
Russell, Jonathan, XV, 597
Russell, J. Rutherford, XVII, 393
Russell, Lydia Smith (Mrs. Jonathan), XV, 597
Ruskin, John, XVIII, 228, 596; *Modern Painters*, XVIII, 281
Russia, XVI, 608; XVII, 245, 266, 321, 444, 449, 540, 561; XVIII, 496–97; XIX, 211; XX, 130
Russworm, John Brown, XVI, 91, 638
Ryan, Charles (seaman), XIX, 309, 310, 312, 332; XX, 18
Rye Beach, N.H., XVIII, 393, 580

Saco, Me., XVI, 131
St. Albans, Hertfordshire, XVII, 79
St. Petersburg, Russia, XVII, 264; XVIII, 496
Salem, Mass.
—references to: XVII, 152, 305, 321; XVIII, 141, 154–55, 301, 360, 377
—history of: XVII, 124
—comments about: XV, 19, 23, 66, 110, 119, 149, 150, 153, 155, 225–26, 276, 518, 521, 522, 596; XVI, 157, 329, 332, 338, 340, 346, 365, 369, 385, 397, 433, 435, 445, 457, 487, 496, 628; XVII, 5, 7, 49, 108, 122, 223, 329, 339, 409; XVIII, 140, 174, 311, 312, 399, 468, 524, 528, 555
—politics or religion in: XV, 19, 36, 37, 61, 63–65, 137, 216, 217, 407, 411, 488, 658; XVI, 65, 102, 131, 148, 161, 214, 253, 254, 263–64, 279–81, 284, 287, 289–90, 293, 295, 322, 329, 335, 340–42, 365, 416, 599, 621, 629, 665, 667, 682, 689; XVII, 238, 343; XVIII, 326
—NH writing in, XV, 44, 494,

271, 278, 279, 288, 312, 448;
XVI, 271
Silsbee, Nathaniel (1773–1850),
XV, 263, 279
Silsbee, Nathaniel, Jr. (1804–81),
XVI, 271, 329
Silsbee & Case, Boston, XVIII, 428
Simms, William Gilmore, XV, 72;
XVI, 114, 159; *Views and Reviews
in American History, Literature,
and Fiction*, XVI, 159
Simpson, A. W., XX, 162
Simpson, Capt. James, XX,
176–78; correspondence of, XX,
178
Simpson, Capt., XIX, 243
Sinclair, Catherine, XVII, 523
Singer, S. W., XVII, 492
Sir Harry Smith (ship), XIX, 253
Skinner, Benjamin H., XVII, 402
Slade, Elizabeth Bromfield (later
Mrs. Henry Schmidt), XV, 557
Slade, Ellen, XV, 543, 558
Small, Samuel, XV, 256
Smalley, Capt. W. W., letter to,
XIX, 311
Smith, Albert Richard, XVII, 467,
474, 502
Smith, Augustus, A., XV, 66
Smith, Daniel (seaman), XVII,
344; XIX, 30, 294–96
Smith, Enos, XVI, 298
Smith, George, XVIII, 181, 193,
221, 228, 281, 293, 419, 587
Smith, Gideon Northrop, XVI, 298
Smith, James, XV, 501, 502
Smith, John, XVI, 316, 320
Smith, John (seaman), XX, 94–95
Smith, John (another seaman), XX,
160–61
Smith, John Peter George, XVII,
136
Smith, Sydney, XV, 140
Smith, Thomas M., letters to, XX,
40, 67; references to, XIX, 386;
XX, 68–69; correspondence of,
XIX, 386, 393; XX, 40–41,
68–69
Smith, William Henry, letter to,
XVIII, 60; references to, XVII,

491, 546, 548, 556; *Bacon and
Shakespeare. An Inquiry . . .*,
XVIII, 60; *Was Lord Bacon the
Author of Shakespeare's Plays? A
Letter to Lord Ellesmere*, XVII,
546, 548, 556; XVIII, 10
Smith, Dr. (of Hanover), XV, 106
Smith, Mrs., XVIII, 512
Smith, Elder, & Co.
—letters to: XVIII, 208, 215,
220, 224, 234, 235, 242, 250,
252, 295
—references to: XVII, 72, 561;
XVIII, 191, 200, 204, 206,
211, 213, 216, 222, 226, 228,
230, 232, 245, 247, 249, 251,
253, 262, 266, 281, 287, 293,
371, 418, 469, 519, 579, 603
Smith & Sons, London, XIX, 212
Smithells Hall, Lancashire, XVII,
61
Smithsonian Institution, Washing-
ton, XVI, 85; XVII, 478; XVIII,
447, 638; XIX, 6, 74
Smollett, Tobias, XV, 406; *The Ad-
ventures of Ferdinand Count
Fathom*, XV, 114; *Roderick Ran-
dom*, XV, 114
Smyrna, Turkey, XIX, 346
Snow, Caleb Hopkins, *History of
Boston*, XV, 570
Snyder, Philip, letter to, XVIII,
490; *Winter Scenes on the Nile*,
XVIII, 490
Socrates, XV, 45
Soden, Samuel S., XV, 644
Somers family, XVIII, 532
Somerville, Sir William Meredyth,
XVII, 523
Somerville, Mass., XVI, 213
Soule, Pierre, XIX, 20
South (U.S.), XVII, 56, 294;
XVIII, 342, 355, 381, 387, 390,
394, 421, 424, 425, 437, 458,
462, 464, 591
South America, XV, 10, 52; XVI,
661
South America (ship), XIX, 335
South Carolina, XVII, 344, 513;
XVIII, 14, 20, 356; XX, 164

587; *Hours in a Library*, XVIII, 585
Stephenson, Rev. W., letter to, XVII, 317
Steubenville, Ohio, XV, 203, 209
Stevens, Charles (or Theodore; seaman), XX, 55–56, 57, 59–60, 62, 64, 228
Stevens, Henry, letter to, XVII, 477
Stewart, John, XVII, 429; XX, 15, 56, 115, 152
Stewartstown, Ireland, XIX, 289, 299
Stirling, William (later Sir William Stirling-Maxwell), XVIII, 284; *The Cloister Life of the Emperor Charles V*, XVIII, 284
Stirling, Scotland, XVIII, 75
Stirling (ship), XVI, 223
Stockbridge, Mass., XV, 46, 448, 601; XVI, 299, 356, 383, 417, 426, 450, 451; XVIII, 499; Housatonic Bank, XVI, 383, 417; Monument Mountain, XVI, 359; Oxbow Farm, XVI, 432; St. Paul's Church, XVI, 437
Stockton, John Potter, XVIII, 156
Stoddard, Elizabeth Drew Barstow (Mrs. Richard Henry), letter to, XVIII, 531; references to, XVI, 663; XVIII, 524, 528; *The Morgesons*, XVIII, 524, 528, 531; *Two Men: A Novel*, XVIII, 531
Stoddard, Richard Henry, letters to, XVI, 648; XVIII, 524; references to, XV, 10, 254; XVI, 381, 624, 663, 676; XVIII, 532; XIX, 5, 13; correspondence of, XVI, 625; *The King's Bell*, XVIII, 525; "Nathaniel Hawthorne," XVI, 381, 663; *Poems*, XVI, 625
Stoddard, Wilson, XVIII, 525
Stoke College, Suffolk, England, XVIII, 345
Stoke-on-Trent, Staffordshire, XVII, 59
Stokes, Henry Sewell, XVII, 367
Stokes, Whitley, XVII, 367

Stone, Eliza Atkins (Mrs. Jacob), XV, 214
Stone, Jacob, Jr., XV, 211, 212
Stone, Lois, XV, 214
Stone, Minnie, XVIII, 282
Stornaway (ship), XIX, 178, 222
Storrow, Sarah Irving, XVIII, 620
Story, Emelyn Eldredge (Mrs. William Wetmore), letters to, XVIII, 154, 168; references to, XVI, 396; XVIII, 193
Story, Joseph, XVIII, 155
Story, William Wetmore, letters to, XV, 608; XVI, 395; references to, XVII, 22; XVIII, 154, 193, 226, 230; correspondence of, XV, 608; XVI, 396; XVIII, 228; *Cleopatra*, XVIII, 228
Stowe, Calvin E., letter to, XVIII, 334
Stowe, Harriet Beecher, letter to, XVIII, 515; references to, XVII, 76; XVIII, 199, 334, 511; correspondence of, XVIII, 516; *Uncle Tom's Cabin*, XVI, 608; XVII, 6
Strahan, Alexander, XVII, 72
Strain, John (seaman), XIX, 95–96
Strange, Franklin (seaman), XX, 49
Stratford-on-Avon, Warwickshire, XVII, 78–80, 83, 85, 358, 517, 548, 563, 570; XVIII, 31, 67, 69, 71, 74, 99, 103, 350, 507
Stroudwater, Me., XV, 110, 111, 115
Stuart, Charles, "the Young Pretender," XV, 52
Stubbs, Edward, XIX, 385, 386; XX, 183
Stucket, John (seaman), XIX, 153
Sturgis, Anne. See Hooper, Mrs. Samuel
Sturgis, Caroline (later Mrs. William A. Tappan), letter to, XVI, 481; references to, XVI, 14, 98, 110, 238, 299, 313, 343, 347, 349, 350, 353, 425, 471–73, 492
Sturgis, Elizabeth Marston Davis (Mrs. William), XVI, 13, 98
Sturgis, Ellen, XVI, 14

382, 383, 385, 387, 390, 403,
406, 434, 447, 448, 492, 495,
498, 500, 501, 503, 511, 513,
518, 540, 546, 550, 562, 589,
597, 601, 625, 694; XVII, 10,
12, 15, 18, 19, 21, 64, 74,
106, 108, 120, 131, 132, 135,
143, 146–47, 156, 171, 189,
197, 199, 259, 262, 265, 271,
365, 389, 403, 423, 427, 449,
473, 508, 576; XVIII, 21,
54–55, 120, 241, 273, 285,
302, 322, 361, 366, 371, 373,
419, 491, 493, 510, 516, 580,
599, 607, 627, 632
—correspondence of: XVII, 473
Tieck, Ludwig, XVI, 7
Tiffany, William A., letter to, XIX, 257
Tigress (ship), XIX, 348, 349, 355, 356–57, 365
Tigris (ship), XVI, 203
Tilden, Samuel J., XVI, 123; XVII, 375; XVIII, 426
Tilley, J., correspondence of, XIX, 81
Tillou, Francis R., XVII, 334
Timmins, Samuel, letters to, XVIII, 114, 296; *History of Warwickshire*, XVIII, 114
Tippecanoe, Ind., Battle of, XVII, 586
Token, Boston, XV, 44, 49, 51, 200, 205, 214, 222, 230, 232, 237, 238, 245, 247, 249, 315, 550, 574, 600; XVI, 174, 501; XVII, 4
Tom Thumb, XVIII, 112
Topsfield, Mass., XV, 23
Torquay, Devonshire, XVII, 244
Toucey, Isaac, *House Committee Appointed to Investigate . . . the Death of the Hon. Jonathan Cilley*, XV, 273
Towle, George Makepeace, letter to, XVI, 672; *Young Folks' Heroes of History*, XVI, 672
Towson, John Thomas, XIX, 195, 196, 201, 223–24, 229; XX, 53–54; correspondence of, XX,

110; *Tables to Facilitate the Practice of Great Circle Sailing*, XIX, 195, 196, 224
Toxteth, Liverpool, XVII, 176
Tozzer, Capt. William, XVI, 246
Tracy, Rev. Thomas, XV, 376; XVI, 90
Train, Charles Russell, XVIII, 439
Train, Enoch, XVII, 191, 223
Train, Enoch, & Co., Boston, XVII, 390
Train, George Francis, XVII, 102; XVIII, 469
Transcendentalism, XV, 20, 22, 29, 45, 74, 268, 506, 527, 637, 656; XVI, 54, 55, 485, 621; XVII, 54, 525
Transcendentalist Club, Boston, XV, 506; XVI, 55
Treadwell, John, XV, 201
Treadwell, John W., XV, 201
Treasury Department, U.S., XV, 498; XVI, 81, 282, 657, 667, 697; XVII, 190, 192, 200, 210; XVIII, 118, 127, 372–73
Trenton Falls, N.Y., XV, 78, 641
Trinity College, Cambridge, XVII, 49, 60, 75, 174, 263; XVIII, 268, 276, 286, 293, 584, 587
Trinity College, Hartford, Conn., XV, 63; XVI, 437
Trollope, Anthony, XVIII, 228, 275, 294; *Autobiography*, XVIII, 231; *Framley Parsonage*, XVIII, 193, 231
Troy, N.Y., XVI, 303, 318, 321; XIX, 279
Trübner, Nicholas, XVII, 161, 237, 240, 297, 387
Tucker, Joshua Thomas, letter to, XVI, 615
Tucker, Nathaniel Beverley, XVIII, 9, 98, 111, 116, 118–19, 132, 372; XIX, 16–17, 42, 48–49, 51; XX, 101, 151, 173, 181; correspondence of, XIX, 48
Tuckerman, Frederick Goddard, letters to, XVIII, 370, 374; correspondence of, XVIII, 371, 375; *Poems*, XVIII, 370, 374

Yearbook of Facts in Science and Art, London, XIX, 172, 221

York, England, XVII, 555; XVIII, 75, 182

Yorkshire, England, XVII, 31, 40, 42, 272, 558, 561; XVIII, 50, 53

Yorktown, Va., XVIII, 451

Young, Alexander, XVIII, 199

"Young America," XV, 54, 57–58; XVII, 142, 402; XIX, 153

"Young American's Library," Wiley & Putnam, New York, XVI, 154

"Young Men of Boston," letter to, XV, 608

The Young People's Book, Philadelphia, XVI, 18

Zerega, Capt., XX, 164, 167

Zingari (ship), XIX, 69